Backstage
You Can Have

My Own Story

Betty Hutton

With Carl Bruno and Michael Mayer

Backstage You Can Have: My Own Story

Published by
The Betty Hutton Estate
P.O. Box 3124
Palm Springs, California 92263
www.BettyHuttonEstate@dc.rr.com

Printed in the United States of America.

ISBN 978-0-578-03209-2

First Edition, July 2009

Book design: Michael H. Mayer

Acknowledgments

This book would not be possible without the courage and determination of one woman, Miss Betty Hutton. Her story is an inspiration to us, because it is a story about the power of the human spirit. We dedicate this book to her memory, with hope that she may continue to live long in the hearts and minds of old and new fans alike throughout the world. We thank our families for their unending support throughout the process of compiling this book from the mountain of notes and pages Betty left to us: Mr. and Mrs. George Arcaro, Ms. Trish Mayer; for listening to page after page on the phone for hours on end, and Mr. Kerry Mayer. To our newly adopted sons, David and Eric, who already know most of Betty's songs by heart; your daddies love you both more than you will ever know. Thank you to Judy Coppage and Dawn Bellett, for helping to proofread the text and finding our unintentional mistakes. Appreciation goes out to Mrs. Judy Rector and Mr. Ben Carbonetto, Betty's life-long friends. You both made all the difference in her continued happiness. A special thank you to Mr. A.C. Lyles, whose support and guidance throughout the years saved Betty on more than one occasion. Recognition to the memories of Father Peter Maguire and Gene Arnaiz, Jr., without whose trust in God and loving guidance, Betty would surely have perished decades before her time. Thanks to Betty's care-givers; particularly, Charlene and Velma. We could never have endured without your assistance. To Betty's daughters and their families, we hope this book serves as affirmation of your mother's love for all of you, despite her sometimes difficult means of expressing it. Not to be forgotten are Betty's fans. She did it all for you!

Preface

In the early 1970s, Betty Hutton began writing a book about her life entitled, *Backstage You Can Have*. The idea for the name derives from the fact that Betty felt so rewarded while performing in front of an audience, it never ceased to be a huge disappointment for her when the curtain came down, and she was left all alone in the dark. Backstage was never a place she wanted to remain.

Betty had her reservations about churning up bad memories from her past and putting them down on paper, but she did it, nonetheless. She had a story to tell, and a burning desire to let her public know the background and sequence of events that led to her downfall. She felt she owed it to her fans, but it was for her a sometimes painful process. In the end, Betty never managed to finish her story, but then how could she have? Every single day that she lived beyond where she left off was a new and developing story. She never knew where the day might take her. To finish her story would have meant that it was over, and Betty's story was never over.

In the end, we finished Betty's book for her. She talked often about the two of us tying together the loose ends after she was gone. Along with the actual pages of the book she wrote, she left us countless handwritten letters and notations which we painstakingly edited. In the five years prior to her death, we made over two-hundred and fifty hours of recordings in which Betty casually talked about her life and career. Putting everything together was a sometimes monumental task, but also a labor of love.

The woman wasn't a recluse by any stretch of the imagination. Instead, she saw herself as a hostage of her own fame. Betty never wavered once during her life, or in this her autobiography, from the belief that her audience was everything to her. On the rare occasion she went out in public, she never wanted to disappoint. She realized better than anyone, that her fans still saw her as *Bessie Dale* or as *Trudy Kockenlocker*. When someone met her for the very first time, she felt she had a duty to "become" Betty Hutton for their benefit. She would do her best, and although it was never discussed, without doubt it saddened her to know she couldn't live up to what her fans found irresistible about the young and vibrant characters she had portrayed years before; those they had grown so fond of up there on the big screen.

After everything that happened in her life, Betty had a burning desire to be just Betty. She wanted to feel Betty, the person, and Betty, the movie star, were two separate entities, but that distinction was clear to only those people who were the closest to her. To everyone else, she was one and the same, Betty Hutton, the movie star.

Toward the end of her life, she found contentment in recounting happy stories from her past to the two people who cared for her until the very end, Carl Bruno and Mike Mayer. She never initiated the conversations. About all that was necessary to get her started was to ask her one simple question, such as, "Did you really carry Eddie

Bracken up that huge flight of stairs?", and she was off to the races. One thing led to another, and two hours after telling us how *Dwight D. Eisenhower* had taken her to an extremely important luncheon in Washington which eventually led to a little known peace treaty with *Liechtenstein* , she would say, "Carl, what time is it? You know I don't like missing my Oprah show on TV at 3:00."

It is with great joy that we bring you this book. It is in keeping with the spirit of the Betty Hutton everyone knew and loved on the big screen, and Betty Hutton the private individual we took in as our very own. It is our desire to keep her memory alive, and at the same time have the woman understood once and for all. It would be a tragic loss if no one were ever to listen to the story she has written. At times, she was a victim of her own undoing. Hers was a life full of unpredictability, but in the end, it is a conquest of the human spirit. Betty was truly a survivor.

When asked how much longer she was going to keep knocking herself out, she responded to the press, "I'm going to be a second Sophie Tucker. When I get too old for the camera, I'll hit the night-club circuit. Spice up the lyrics a bit and I'm good to go for another thirty years."

That you did, Betty. That you did.

Carl M. Bruno
Executor, The Betty Hutton Estate
And
Michael H. Mayer

Introduction

There is never ample time to drink in the love you feel from an audience at the end of a performance. Inevitably, the show must end, and it always ends abruptly. Backstage, I stand rooted in place, and stare in silence as the massive stage curtain begins to fall. It appears out of nowhere, as if magically descending right out of heaven. Understandably, there will be more nights exactly like this, but for right now; I must accept the unavoidable end to this one. After everyone has left, peace and quiet are finally restored to the theater. This is the time turmoil begins to creep back into my soul.

The dream world I lived in, what I fought so hard for is no longer a dream. It is a reality, and it has happened to me. I have made it. The fear should be gone. All the loneliness and hunger should be over. From here on out, my world should be filled with only beauty from the soft pink and blue stage lights as they stream down upon me. They should envelop and surround me forever, but they don't. They can't.

I make my way around the corner of the curtain, and gaze down at all of the vacated seats. I have a burning need to reach out to the audience, to reassure myself they were indeed real. I bend over to touch the theater seats and find they are still warm. A program bearing my likeness has been thrust to the floor. My once captive audience is now gone and all is silent, only warm seats remain to validate their existence. The love that poured from my heart into the heart of everyone who sat out there in the dark has been extinguished, just like the dazzling stage lights. It was the only gift I had to give. The applause has stopped, and now I am left alone and lost in the empty darkness of the theater. This marks the return of an inside terror; a fear only God in all his infinite mercy can help me to contain.

I don't want this entire book to be about my fears. I would really like to show you some of the happiness I experienced; some of the love I had in my life. Yet, how can I tell you about love, when the only love ever shown to me was love wrought with pain? Painful love came to me at an early age. By the time I could differentiate between painful love and happy contented love, it was too late. Unfortunately, it was the same painful love I received that I eventually imparted to others. There was much happiness that came my way; I was just too blind to recognize it for what it was. From an early age, I became conditioned to believe applause from an audience was a true and sustainable love for me. Entertaining an audience is what I was born to do. I should never have strayed beyond that concept of love as I saw it; I would only hurt everyone in my path.

I have been unable to tell my story in its entirety until now. For years, I have struggled with the ability to organize my thoughts and feelings on paper. Even now, the words that flow onto these pages emerge as painful memories from some dark place within me. As I attempt to write them down, I first speak them to myself. I choke on every single word as they rise up in my throat. My fear of rejection has always been so powerful, I feel helpless in front of this stupid sheet of paper. I am very angry about that. Feeling helpless is not a feeling I like, but it is definitely a fact of my life. So I make myself sit down and write, this is all I have to offer you now, and I owe all of you so very much. Writing this book is the least I can do in an attempt to answer a few of the many questions you have been asking for so many years, and to help you to understand.

My career is long over. These days I rarely see anyone, except for the few who people who remain close in my life; the ones I depend upon. On the rare occasion I stray from this pattern, and the moment I confide in anyone else my unhappiness, or let them feel my pain, they run. Who the hell wants to be around a troubled Betty Hutton? Everyone wants to see the Betty Hutton who gave them so much pleasure up there on the silver screen all those many years ago. That Betty, I assure you, is long gone. She is empty, forgotten, and out of style. The image I had built up around myself has come back to haunt me. I can't live up to that image. There is no way out. So in my own little way, I stand very still and continue to go quietly mad. Thank God for those people around me who don't require me to be anything more than simply Betty. Only with their help, through my trust in God, and the ripening of years have I been able to forgive and forget.

In order to complete the monumental task of writing this book, I need a large chunk of confidence to descend and plant itself right on my shoulders. I only hope to hell my book doesn't end up sounding as confused as I am. That is my *current fear* as I write this. Fear has always been a part of everything I have done. Fear can keep you from making choices. When you do make choices, fear can cause you to make really bad ones. I guess I could say now without reservation, fear turned me into my own worst enemy. You see, fear caused me to alienate myself from the people and the things that I loved most in this world. I have tried all my life to conquer my fears. Conquering them is all important to me now. It only makes sense, because of who Betty Hutton was; people have always turned to me for insight. If I fail, it means the advice I have given so freely to others will have been empty and meaningless.

The more I write, the more confident I become. Comfort with putting my feelings down on paper is brand new to me, it's almost addicting. Like everything else in my life, I'm becoming compulsive about it. This time, I hope the compulsion works toward some sort of constructive end. This is almost like psychoanalysis, only with me as the analyst. My gut feeling is I'm finally on the right road. As these words flow from my heart for your eyes to see, I hope it will give you some insight into the life and soul of a frightened girl. A girl called *me*.

Betty Hutton

Part 1

My Own Story
The Rise from Poverty to Stardom

Betty Hutton

Betty Hutton

Chapter One

It can't possibly get much colder than Michigan in February. Only after the final frenzied holiday festivities slowly fade to memory does the real burden and monotony of winter grab hold in the Midwest. Everywhere, people settle into a solemn, numb existence; in all probability as a countermeasure against the brutal cold that will last for more months than anyone cares to admit.

On February 26, 1921, I broke the solemnity of another Battle Creek winter night by screaming my way from Mabel Mae Thornburg in the bedroom of our modest grey frame house at No.12 Stone Avenue. It had been five hours of painful hell for my dear mother. At 1:30 in the morning, Dr. James Elliott's car momentarily resisted starting in objection to the cold, before finally laboring away from the curbing in front of our house, and off into the night.

My birth was uneventful. I did not appear as anything special to anyone. On the contrary, I was quite plain looking, with my suspicious expression and random wisp of blonde hair. However, one thing did set me apart; it was the noise I could make. My mother said I came out screaming and kicking, as if to awaken everyone in Battle Creek, Michigan from their winter induced slumber. It's funny - the screaming was just the beginning of the screaming I was to do all my life. Several years would pass before I came to the realization; the underprivileged life I had just been born into would treat me as coldly as that winter Michigan day in 1921.

I detected early on, my mother was not keen on the idea of another child. If mama could have only foreseen this scrawny baby girl would one day become a famous Hollywood movie star, maybe it would have made a difference. Even so, mama wouldn't have given a damn about that anyway. You see, nothing of much good had ever happened in my mother's life. As far as she saw it, nothing good was probably supposed to happen. Mama already had my two-year-old sister, Marion, at home. All my arrival represented was more diapers to wash and more work to occupy her already full days. God only knows, but at her young age, mama probably felt her station in life had already been pretty much decided. At the very least, she must have felt trapped in a dead end existence. I know she desired a bit more from life, but it seemed an unlikely possibility.

A railroad brakeman by the name of Percy Thornburg married my mother when she was just sixteen. I don't think he took well to the name Percy, since everyone called him Jack. He enjoyed the new uninhibited spirit of the *Roaring Twenties*, but that rarely if ever included his wife. It was quite obvious that old Jack had the wanderlust. His restlessness was kept in check, at least for awhile, by traveling away from home with the railroad for days at a time. The bad part is, when Jack was out riding the tracks, mama was left home to fend for herself. During his short stays at home, Jack seldom ever talked to his wife; ignoring her both physically and emotionally. Mama suddenly found herself in a loveless marriage, with two small babies, and unable to enjoy what should have been the best years of her young life.

All women have the desire to be loved, and mama was no exception. So it comes as no great surprise, as a direct result of her husband's habitual absence, she eventually surrendered her affections to someone who made her feel wanted and needed. In due course, she confided in me most of the details surrounding this wonderful "other man" and their tender affair. When telling me the story, she managed to skirt around the fact that all this romance resulted in one sure thing - her pregnancy with me.

Their brief affair was over before it had started. When mama realized she was pregnant with me, she broke off the relationship with him. Mama was from poverty, and this man came from money; both from opposite ends of the social spectrum. She knew their indiscretion could have destroyed the life and career of this distinguished composer and conductor forever. Such shameful behavior just wasn't acceptable in those days. To make matters worse, it was typically the woman who was held responsible in such situations. So, mama bore all the guilt for what had happened. I don't believe that he ever knew of my existence. I sometimes wonder how my life would have been different had he known. However, just like my mother, her secret was taken with her to the grave.

Even though nobody ever really said so, I always felt Jack Thornburg wasn't my real father. I didn't learn the truth until after my mother's tragic death in a fire at her Hollywood apartment on New Year's Eve in 1961. While going through a box containing old clippings mama had saved about my career, one particular envelope discolored with time caught my attention. I recognized my mother's handwriting on the front; it said: *Betty's Father.* I could barely breathe as I removed the tattered newspaper clipping from the envelope. Hurt shot through me like fire, but only momentarily. Almost in the same instant, I nearly burst at the seams with pride. I understood now why my mother had kept this information a secret from me. My father was a well-known man. It must have killed her to hold this secret in her heart for so many years. As I stared at his photo, I thought of an old saying; *Talent is born, not made.* Thank God my *real* father had given me his musical gift. I sure as hell would need it during the nightmares ahead.

More importantly, I finally had a true father - and a very celebrated one at that. He will remain nameless. If mama wanted his identity to remain a secret then, well I do now. There is no need to know. No one could benefit from the knowledge of this information today anyway.

My mother was a very vivacious and beautiful woman. Ultimately, her life was something of a tragedy. She needed more than love; she needed acceptance. Thankfully, this is something she would eventually get to experience vicariously through her daughter's success. A natural performer; she could do it all. Mama could sing, dance, and play the piano and ukulele - all by ear. I truly believe, possibly a generation later, my mother could have become a great star in her own right. Somehow it just wasn't meant to be, and I fear she lived with the feeling she was stuck forever nowhere, being nobody.

Born Mabel Mae Lum in Nebraska, she seemed as unloved as any child ever could be. Her own mother died right after her ninth birthday. Her drunken father's only happiness came from beating her into insensibility. On one such occasion, she quickly and quietly grabbed her little brother, Frankie, and headed out into the cold winter night. They ran as far as they could through deep snow until they dropped from sheer exhaustion. Mama told me the story countless times; how she never looked back and never once shed a single tear. Holding her brother tightly, she whispered to him, "Don't fret Frankie. I'll find a job and a place for us to stay. I promise."

There were no child labor laws in the early 1900's, except for in the prosperous New England mills. Children were often subject to long hours at what basically amounted to slave labor elsewhere. With equal parts of diligence and luck that cold evening, Mama chanced upon a sign in the front window of a big house which read: *Child Wanted, 9 or over for housework.* She cautiously approached the imposing front door and rang the bell. A woman opened the door, and in a surprised tone asked, "What on earth are you two children doing out in this weather?"

"Excuse me ma'am, I'm here for the job. I'm a strong girl and I'm hard working. I hope it's alright if my brother stays on too? He doesn't eat much food, and I'll watch after him."

Mama had landed her first paying job at the ripe age of nine. The missus showed her around the large house. Young Mabel was informed of her duties, which turned out light compared with what she had become accustomed. After her first round of chores, she and Frankie were shown to a sparsely furnished sleeping room on the upper floor. "Frankie," she said, "it's a tiny room, but it will keep us warm and safe."

The next morning, she spotted a pair of roller skates in the front entry hall. Her eyes lit up as she asked the man of the house, "Are these for me?" His wife interrupted before he could even answer. "Yes Mabel Mae, but these are not for fun. When the weather permits, they are to get you to school and back home in ten minutes flat. If you are unable, you will be punished. Do you understand, child?" Obediently mama whispered, "Yes ma'am."

Mama worked hard and did as she was told; the entire time plotting her next plan of action. While cradling Frankie in her arms one evening, this extremely maternal older sister said, "Frankie, we have an Aunt Jessie and Uncle Ray in Battle Creek, Michigan. I know that's a long way from Nebraska, so we gotta save every penny I earn until we have enough money to pay for our train tickets to Battle Creek. I know it may take some time, but you just wait and see, it's gonna happen."

For three long years, she counted and saved every penny until the day finally came. When the timing was right, mama and Frankie made a beeline for the train station. She approached the ticket window, and with all the confidence in the world, said to the man behind the counter, "Two tickets to Battle Creek, Michigan please." God only knows how a mere child managed to plan and execute such a feat.

Once aboard the train and safely headed out of the station, mama engagingly asked the conductor, "My uncle Ray Walker is a famous railroad conductor from Battle Creek. Do you happen to know him, sir?"

Indeed the conductor did know mama's Uncle Ray. For the remainder of the trip, while mama recounted her well rehearsed story for all to hear, the train's attendants pampered their two special young passengers. After arriving in Battle Creek, the kind conductor led the children over to where a group of uniformed men were gathered. He slapped a huge man on the shoulder. "Ray," he said, "look what I got for you." Uncle Ray turned and inquired with a look of amazement, "Mabel?" Before mama could say a word, he swept them both off the ground and up into his huge safe arms.

The Walkers accepted my mother and her little brother, Frankie, into their home as if they were their very own. Mama stayed with them until she reached the marrying age of sixteen. She had developed a mind like a whip, although schooling had not been part of her living arrangements while staying with the Walkers. It was considered by many, at the time, more important for girls to learn their way around a kitchen, rather than spending valuable time with formal studies. The emphasis typically focused upon marriage for young women. Sixteen was the time for a girl to find a husband, set up a household of her own, and start having babies.

Mama really had no desire to be married. She wanted desperately to take a good bite out of life. However, when Aunt Jessie unexpectedly announced that she had found the perfect man for her, with love and respect for the only real parental figures she had known, mama reluctantly gave in. Uncle Ray and Aunt Jessie wanted someone who could protect and provide for her by having a good steady job. The man they arranged to marry mama was Jack Thornburg. He worked with Uncle Ray on the railroad.

At sixteen, mama went ahead and married a perfect stranger. She had done what she thought was expected of her, but she certainly didn't love him. Shortly thereafter, Marion came into the picture. Two years later I arrived. Mama slowly settled into a life of screaming children, diapers, and long stretches at home alone.

One day, something quite unexpected happened. A few short weeks after mama brought me home from the hospital, Jack Thornburg walked out of our lives. He just up and left for good. Not even a goodbye. I believe he took one look at me and must have decided that I just wasn't his. The timing of his leaving seemed too much of a coincidence. Not until 1936 did we receive any news, and then it came as the first and last time we heard anything about Jack Thornburg. It seems old Jack took his own life while at the *Sawtelle Veterans' Hospital* in West Los Angeles.

My mother now had two little girls to support on her own. Instead of being frightened by the prospect, she felt relief. For the first time as an adult, she could have a life of her own. It was time for her to make the decisions, and to deal with things on her own terms. In that very spirit, mama announced to Aunt Jessie that she would like to take Marion and me to Lansing. There she hoped to get a job at the Oldsmobile car plant. In a way, I believed mama wanted to leave Battle Creek as a means to put a bad chapter in her life behind her once and for all. Aunt Jessie agreed the change would do her good. She and Uncle Ray offered to drive us to Lansing, and helped mama to get settled. God bless them both, I will always remember them for being the most caring people in the world.

With her blonde hair and good figure, mama presented herself very well. She sure didn't seem to have any trouble being hired by Oldsmobile. With a steady job, we moved into the upstairs unit of a yellow house outfitted with few creature comforts, but it was all ours. I remember, even at the early age of four, we had to share the downstairs bathroom with the family who lived below us. I find it ironic; today a shiny brass plaque is attached to the front of that very house, which states, "Betty Hutton lived here." The irony is in the fact that we were thrown out of Lansing by the time I had turned six. It was because mama had started to bootleg. Little did any of us realize, one day I would be invited to return to Lansing to premier one of my movies at the request of those who ran the city. My return was a triumphant one, I might add.

Mama had little difficulty meeting people, due to her great personality. She made two special friends who worked with her at the plant. I came to know them as Aunt Ida and Aunt Merna. They were to become a very important part of our lives. Anything was possible when these three single gals got together. It was the *Roaring Twenties,* and they could burn up the town dancing to such tunes as the *Black Bottom.* Mama had a natural ability to play the ukulele and dance. If you add to that her natural wild streak; she had plenty of guys around her at all times.

On account of their resourcefulness, mama and the girls also started looking like they had dressed right from the pages of some fashion magazine. These gals surely couldn't afford to pay retail prices for designer labels. However, with a small amount of money saved from working at the plant, the three women opened up a small resale business selling used fashions unloaded by the well-to-do society dames from Detroit. The majority of the clothing taken in was practically new, having been worn only once or twice. From that time on, mama and her pals always had fine things to wear. It made me proud that dressing well had a way of making mama feel better about her life and position.

Naturally intuitive at business, my mother could have been quite successful had it not been for her unfortunate booze habit *and* her bad taste in picking men. Both vices were her downfall. At our young age, my sister Marion and I were powerless in our ability to help her. All we could do was stand idly aside and wait for mama's next bad choice relating to boozing or men to rip into our lives.

Booze was everywhere, even though a 1919 act of Congress outlawed alcohol for everything except medicinal uses. One way around it was having an illness that only alcohol could help. Drug stores made fortunes selling the stuff. Mama carried her own flask wherever she went. The only real crime from all of this was in getting caught.

The other thing that happened as a consequence of the *National Prohibition Act* was that alcohol went underground, so bootleg joints and speakeasies began popping up all over the place. Mama began to bootleg booze out of our kitchen. Out of bad comes some good, because that's when I first started to perform. Marion and I enjoyed singing and dancing for mama's inebriated "clients" and friends. She would lift me up on the kitchen table which I used as my stage. While she played the ukulele, I would belt out a tune for everyone to enjoy.

Mama would grab some guy's derby and place it on my head. I'd start singing, *"Black bottom, she's gottum..."* or other contemporary song; all the while slapping my skinny thighs. Mama taught me most every popular song around at the time.

While I was performing, somebody would pass the hat. After making the rounds, it came back filled with shiny nickels and dimes. More than the money, I ate up the excitement of the moment and the reaction from the crowd. After I came to the realization how hooked I was on being in front of an audience, it was really the applause I waited for. Just like my mother, it was acceptance that I craved. I'm sure I didn't know it then, but it was the beginning of the only real love I would ever know.

As young as I was, I felt terribly lonely when my performance was over. I have always preferred staying on stage, singing my heart out in front of bright lights and a cheering crowd. When it's all over and the curtain has descended, you are left alone behind it in the dark. For that reason, I've always said, *"Backstage you can have."*

It's funny how fickle an audience can be. One minute you have their undivided attention as the recipient of all their adoration and applause. The next minute it's over. Suddenly, you are forgotten, and your once attentive audience is back at whatever they were doing before the show started. They callously forget that moments before you were up there singing your heart out and working like hell to establish that special connection with them. Backstage gets very lonely, and I know from experience; lonely is an awful place. The various times throughout my career when I viewed entertaining as a thankless job were always the most disheartening for me. Performing is really all I had.

I think my mother was enjoying the happiest year in her young life. It seemed to me as if she was trying hard to grab and run with all the happiness she had missed out on for so long. The booze flowed freely, and handsome young men came and went. Mama was so busy with her new freedom, she essentially lost track of me and Marion. I was a somewhat frail child, and I always required more of mama's attention than she had time to give.

With so many guys and so much booze, mama failed to notice my paleness in the middle of one of her lively parties one evening. Everyone was having too much fun to notice. On my stage, I danced around and around. Suddenly, I collapsed like a sack of potatoes right in the middle of the table.

As I started to come around, mama had me grasped close to her bosom. With tears streaming down her cheeks, she cried, "Betty, Betty." I felt a hand on my forehead, and then a voice cried out, "My God, she's burning up!" As the room spun around and around, I heard Aunt Merna blurting out orders. "All of you, get out of here. Don't panic, Mabel. I'll run for the doctor."

I was riding on cloud nine; so happy that my mother cared enough to cuddle me in her arms with such love. In my delirium, I began to apologize. "Oh, mommy, I'm so sorry. I've gone and spoiled your party, and just when we were enjoying ourselves so much."

"Hush, my baby, you're gonna be all right." I looked straight into her eyes and remember how frightened she was. Strangely enough, at that moment I felt like I needed to comfort her. She quickly took my temperature. After checking the thermometer, she grabbed me closer to her and said in a voice filled with panic, "Baby, baby, hang on tight." She began to sing me the lullaby she hadn't sung in a very long time. *"I have a dear little dolly. She has eyes of blue ..."*

Despite my fever and mama's panic, the whole scene gave me an overwhelming sense of joy. I almost wanted to die if it meant my mother could love me that much. Aunt Merna came tearing in with the doctor. After scanning the joint, he suddenly became very agitated. All he seemed to focus upon was the fact the living room was littered with smashed out cigarette butts and plenty of half-empty booze bottles. In all the excitement, there had been no real time to tidy up. Cigarette smoke still hung heavy in the air.

"You people... Why is it so damned cold in here? Get out of the way and let me take a look at the kid." His tone terrified me. I clung to mama even tighter. If you ask me, it seemed like this guy resented poor people. This rich doctor couldn't possibly relate to the depth of my mama as a human being and parent, simply because of our poverty. The doctor only saw what he wanted to see. He chose to take his aversion to us and our situation out on mama.

The doctor turned to my mother, and with a true look of disdain, said, "She's got black pneumonia. I can't help you. She'll probably be dead within an hour." He could have cared less that she was holding on to me for dear life.

Mama begged him to take me to a hospital. He glared at her as though he were both judge and executioner. Finally, he responded coldly. "It's of little use. You see, you've waited too long." With that, he turned abruptly around and walked out, leaving mama to decide my fate.

She stared at me with her unbelieving eyes, as tears rolled down her soft face. She screamed at Merna, "God damn him! She's not gonna die, not my baby."

The two women started moving about the room in all directions. "Merna, hurry, hurry! Oh, it's all my fault. We've got to get her over to Ida's house. She's the only one who has any heat. If we don't break this fever soon, my baby's not gonna make it." Mama's tone of voice worried me for the first time. "Wrap her up good and tight. We don't want that wind getting at her."

"Calm down, Mabel. Don't give out on me now. We'll get her over to Ida's house." I must have looked like a mummy all wrapped up the way I was. They both knew they were taking a terrible risk rushing me out into the winter night air. Pneumonia almost always killed people back then, particularly the very young and the very old. There was no such thing as antibiotics. What they really needed to do was bring my temperature down as quickly as possible by whatever means necessary. Taking me out into the cold was chancy at best. I think Mama and Merna ran all the way.

Arriving at Aunt Ida's house, my mother started barking orders immediately. "Ida, quick! Grab all the blankets and towels you have in the house and start boiling water in big pots. After that, soak the blankets in water as hot as your hands can stand. Merna, you take some of the wet towels outside and let 'um get good and cold."

Merna yelled at my mother. "What the hell are you going to do, Mabel?" Mama responded this time with relative calm, "Just listen, please, and do exactly as I tell you." Through all of the chaos and fear, she knew exactly what to do. It was an old remedy, and this time she had no alternative but to make sure it worked. My temperature was reading 106. "My God, if this fever doesn't break, we're gonna lose her. Quick, Merna, first put the hot blanket on her, then lay your body across her to hold in the heat; five minutes only. Ida, then you grab a cold one and do the same thing."

This went on for almost an hour. I had no idea my life was in peril. I was busy relishing the attention from all sides. I guess they finally had done just about all they were capable of doing when the frantic activity started to calm. Still, all eyes in the room were on me. Suddenly, I shouted out, "Mama, mama, I'm hot. I'm hot." My mother cried out, "Merna, Ida, look at her, she's soaking wet. The fever's broken. My baby's gonna live!"

With my fever finally down, everyone seemed to be laughing and crying at the same time. Mama started giving me sips of a drink into which she had smashed an aspirin in a shot of bootleg booze with lemon. It tasted awful! I kept crying and kissing her, and telling her how happy I was to be able to breathe again. All she could say was, "Hush, I don't want you to talk."

Less than an hour later, I was sitting up. I was still very weak, but laughing and kissing everyone as if nothing had ever happened. I was once again back among the living. It was as if a miracle had happened. Mama had done what she intended; my life had been spared.

A short while later I was starving. "Please mama, make me something to eat. I feel much better, but I'm hungry." Hunger is a sure sign that a child is on the mend. Mama knew this, and it made her smile from ear to ear.

"Well, I'll be damned. One minute you're almost dead. Now you want breakfast in bed? The next thing I know you'll be up singing the *Black Bottom* again." After inhaling my food, mama hugged me and said, "Well, with all this energy, we need to stick a broom up her ass so she can dance and sweep up the room at the same time." This type of slum humor was pretty typical for people with whom we shared our daily lives. It was our mechanism for coping with our station in life. Everyone laughed hysterically; it was a laugh of relief all around. Joy once again returned to all of the faces in Ida's kitchen who had witnessed my return from the dead that late winter evening.

My mother's wonderful sense of humor always carried us through our darkest moments. Mama didn't believe in giving up. I am exactly the same – I get it from her. To be sure, no one could tell mama something was impossible if and when her kids were involved. When push came to shove, her love for us transcended everything else. The three of us had each other, and not much else. For that reason, and that reason alone, we stuck together like glue.

Despite our close family bond, it was troubling when I came to the realization; Marion was the one who usually got most of the attention. There is no question in my mind; my sister got noticed because she was the most beautiful child who ever lived. From the day I could walk and talk, her beauty had become a thorn in my side. Comments like, "Isn't it a shame that Betty doesn't look more like Marion", intensified my desperate feelings of insecurity. Because of it, I would do anything necessary for mother to notice me. I would stand on my head, do cartwheels, or jump and holler at the top of my lungs – anything to take the attention away from my pretty and more refined sister, Marion. Little wonder, the only time I felt *really* good about myself was when mama let me sing and dance out of our bootleg kitchen. My jealousy of Marion haunted me for many years. On top of all else, I had the fear that someday someone would take mama away from me forever.

My thoughts about losing mama were not based entirely upon my fears; they had a ring of reality to them when mother began sending Marion and me to stay with strangers. We knew full well, mama's social associations centered mainly upon her bootleg joint and the type of people who were accustomed to hanging there. She dated plenty good looking men, and would send us to stay elsewhere when she wanted to entertain her gentlemen friends at home. It wasn't any secret they stayed overnight. Because of it, I instantly hated every single one of those men.

Mama never knew any of the bad things that happened when she made me stay elsewhere overnight. On several occasions, I was left in the care of a lady named Mrs. Beacham. She was a lovely woman, with a very kind husband. Unfortunately, they had a Greek boarder who was not so nice.

When I stayed overnight, Mrs. Beacham would always come to tuck me in and say goodnight. On one particular evening, no sooner had she turned out the lights and left the room, I felt a body climb into the bed beside me. For some reason, it didn't frighten me at first. Maybe I was used to mama climbing in next to me for a few minutes to say goodnight, sometimes when I was already half asleep. In any case, I was suddenly gripped with a paralyzing fear when this person began to whisper close to my ear in a heavy foreign dialect, "Put your hands here like so, for to warm me". I leapt from the bed, but was having trouble navigating my way out of the darkened room. Fortunately, Mrs. Beacham picked that exact moment to rush back in. In my panic, I had more than likely let out a bloodcurdling scream. Whatever the case, it had signaled my need for help. She grabbed me up in her arms, all the while yelling obscenities at my naked male intruder.

I'd been saved from another near disaster. It seemed clear to me, someone or something was watching over me. I knew nothing about God, but I did feel as if I had a special *something* on my side. Mama never knew about the bad Greek. I made Mrs. Beacham promise never to mention it. It was always my number one priority to try and protect mama; she had enough on her plate.

I never blamed my mother for anything bad that happened during our childhood. Considering the way mama was raised, I know she did the very best she could with what she had. When children are involved, the mistakes a parent can make are immeasurable. Nevertheless, it is also amazing to me the depths of despair people can sink to and still emerge whole on the other side.

I hope with all my heart that my own three children whom I have lost, and who will be reading this for the first time, may begin to understand and pardon their own mother's faults and weaknesses. I wanted desperately to protect you. I thought if you knew the truth about my sordid background, you would be ashamed of me.

I wanted all of you to have everything growing up that I never had. In order to do that, it required long hours at work to earn the type of money that would afford us the good life. It always seemed to me if I didn't have money, nobody would want or love me. I know it was a mistake, and I admit to being inadequate as a mother. The pressures of attempting to keep everyone in my life happy overwhelmed and eventually destroyed me. Pills were the only way I knew to cope. I really would have preferred to stay home with you. I desperately desired a simpler life. It became a vicious circle.

I only hope one day you will be able to forgive me, and that we can be united once again under one roof. If that is never meant to be, I want all of you to know one thing; my biggest fault was in loving you all too much.

With my mother, Mabel, in Battle Creek, Michigan, 1922.
Photo: Betty's private collection, The Betty Hutton Estate

At age three, Battle Creek, 1924.
Photo: Betty's private collection, The Betty Hutton Estate

The three of us, Marion (right), 1926.
Photo: Betty's private collection, The Betty Hutton Estate

Chapter Two

One day, quite out of nowhere, mama decided we should spend the summer at Park Lake in Bath, Michigan. Park Lake was a popular destination for vacation folks, particularly from throughout the Lansing area. Here families could swim, take boat rides, and loll away the warm summer afternoons. Other than a well needed change of scenery, the intention was for a place to go that might in some way benefit my less than perfect health.

"How are you going to swing that, Mabel? There just isn't enough money in the kitty," Aunt Merna said quite logically.

Mama wasn't in the habit of putting logic before one of her hot new ideas. "Wait a minute. I've got it! We all can sing and dance, right? Well, of course we can. Now, since that lousy Calvin Coolidge still won't allow any liquor to be sold, why not go and rent us a cottage on the lake where we can open up a *blind pig*?"

A blind pig is just another name for a small-scale bootleg joint usually operated out of someone's house.

Whoever happened to be running it would charge customers to see an attraction and provide a "complimentary" alcoholic beverage; all in an attempt to get around the law. A speakeasy, on the other hand, was usually a higher class establishment which offered food, live bands, and floor shows. Both blind pigs and speakeasies were springing all over the place in the 1920s.

Ida piped in, "I just don't know, Mabel."

Mama shrugged. "Don't be silly. It's damned near foolproof. They're not going to bother with three honest gals like us. Besides, it won't be anything major like one of those big joints in Chicago or Detroit."

The three of them had a hearty laugh following mama's somewhat oversimplified string of reasoning.

"But Mabel, we could be barkin' up the wrong tree here. What if we get busted by the cops? You know, we could all end up in jail."

"Don't worry. It'll just be smalltime stuff. Anyway, we'll only sell to friends and locals. So, how about it, gals? Do we all agree it's a deal?" The other two finally agreed, but rather reluctantly. When my mother set her mind to something, her two friends in crime most often found her ideas hard to resist.

A blind pig usually made beer, known as home brew. You couldn't be arrested simply for having it. The only way to get in trouble was by selling it, since sales were positively illegal. Naturally, most blind pigs weren't set up for family consumption, but rather as a cash business. The big money wasn't in home brew anyway - it was in the *alky* (uncut alcohol) which wasn't allowed by law on the premises under any circumstances. You were committing a federal offense if you were caught with alky in any amount and faced a ten-year sentence in a federal penitentiary. Due to the bootlegging going on in major cities like Chicago and New York on such a grand scale, there was a real push by government prosecutors to bust the small kitchen operations to set an example throughout the country. The 1920s were truly a crazy and exciting time to be alive in America.

Our move to Park Lake got closer as the weeks passed. Day by day, everyone became more excited at the thought of going. My sister was happy to be out of school for the summer, and dreamed of spending countless days on the beach. Since Marion had already started to notice boys, her expectations for the summer ahead were way more ambitious than mine. I was anxious to start school for the first time in September, but for the summer, I would be content just to be in new surroundings and to see mama happy.

Summer finally arrived. One glorious day, we all piled into our enormous Hudson for the ride to Bath. If I had known in advance what was going to happen while we lived at Park Lake, I wouldn't have been so excited about spending the summer there. But for now, and coming from the city, my sister and I were momentarily speechless when we saw the beautiful blue lake water for the very first time.

We pulled up the drive and stopped in front of the cottage mama and my aunts had rented for the season. It was adorable; all in cream-colored clapboard siding with dark green trim. Marion and I ran ahead of the others, eager to see what was on the inside of our new home.

The living room was a big long room with four bedrooms off to the right. None of the bedrooms had any doors. Instead, checkered curtains looking very much as if they had been tablecloths in a former life, hung in their place. These were strung up on wooden rods from the top of the door jams and reached almost down to the floor. At first glance, this arrangement didn't appear to allow for much privacy, but it did make the room appear warm and cozy. The absence of bedroom doors didn't bother me much at first notice, but it would later in the summer.

Off to the left was the kitchen. A cast iron cooking stove stood out like a sore thumb, in contrast to the rest of the modest room, because of its gleaming white enamel doors and ornate chrome handles. A small screened-in porch overlooking the lake connected off the kitchen. The biggest thrill of all was waiting for us down at the pier; our own private rowboat. It looked as if it had seen better days well in advance of our arrival, even though it did sport a relatively fresh coat of red and white paint. Despite the years of wear and tear, it sat there patiently waiting for someone to hop in and shove off for the open waters.

The lake and rowboat weren't the only new additions to our surroundings. A two-seater outhouse with a crescent moon carved out of the tall squeaky door sat off in the side yard under some towering trees. It immediately caught my interest, since I had never before seen such a contraption. That was, of course, until I went inside. The holes in the seat board looked way too large to safely accommodate a small child's bottom. From the very first day, I feared falling straight through and continuing down beyond all the muck until reaching China. Needless to say, I spent as little time inside the outhouse as necessary.

A rope swing hung from a large old tree in front of our cottage at Park Lake. This swing became the first toy that I ever really remember playing with. I'd swing from it like crazy. I never broke any bones, much to my mother's amazement, but I did take a couple of good spills that left me with scabby knees and elbows for most of the summer.

We no sooner arrived when some of the neighboring kids appeared. They had heard that some city kids were moving in, and they came over to check us out. They were mostly farm kids, so I felt like a big shot coming from the city. A few of the kids began nagging Marion and me into taking them out on the lake in our rowboat. Neither one of us had ever rowed one before, so we were totally unfamiliar with how the thing was maneuvered. Even so, that didn't stop me! I had plenty old-fashioned tomboy spirit, making it no big deal to be the first volunteer to row. After about an hour out on the lake, my little hands began to hurt like hell. I just kept on rowing. I didn't dare let those farm kids know this was my first time in a rowboat. As it turned out, I'm glad that I quickly learned to manage that boat. Before too long, I'd be putting my rowing skills to good use for mama and her new business.

We enjoyed swimming in the lake with the other kids. We would usually meet up late morning and linger around a particular pier near our cottage for hours on end. One afternoon, a bunch of us got playing pretty rough. Some boy shoved me so hard that I went flying off the pier, landing further than normal out into the lake. As I fell, a nail that protruded from a piling in the water snagged my left cheek, right near my eye. Mama patched me up the best she knew how. The other kids took to calling me *Bad-eye Bodie* for the remainder of the summer; a name for which I showed little fondness.

Right from the start, mama's blind pig became an almost immediate success. She spent time planning her strategy well before we ever left Lansing. Once we were at the lake, she made the rounds from door to door, quickly making friends and gaining the trust of neighboring folks. After a bit of small talk, mama would casually get around to explaining that it was her aim to provide her new friends with a place where they could come to have a good time. All she asked, if they showed the slightest interest, was their silent cooperation. Looking back, I am absolutely dumbfounded that everybody so easily went right along with mama's proposal. Every detail of her plan seemed to progress smoothly without a single hitch.

Even the owner of a small grocery store down the road agreed to be our signal if the cops or Feds were snooping around the area. His signal gave us just enough time to load the partially filled large cans of alky into our boat. In the event of a raid, as planned, Marion and I would row like hell out to the middle of the lake and dump them. Air trapped in the tops of the cans allowed them to float just below the surface of the water. After we'd completed our important mission, we'd take our time rowing back to the pier, tie up the boat, and come back into the house to show off our innocent little faces. The Feds would often be swarming all over the place, but all they ever found was mama entertaining friends with home brew from a large old wooden keg. Any money from cash sales was always stashed out of habit, just in the event we were ever raided.

Believe me, we had the best time playing cops and robbers with mama's booze. Of course, it wouldn't have been any picnic if they'd caught mama selling the hard stuff. In spite of everything, we were just kids, oblivious to the dangers involved with mama's new business. My mother took some really careless risks during these times. If she'd stopped for a moment to think about the consequences, I doubt she would have continued. The result could have been disastrous for us as a family. Mama might well have received a stiff prison sentence, and worse yet for Marion and me, we could have been taken away from her for good.

The cops were tough bastards, especially the Feds. Mama always complained, "Those damn coppers hate seeing decent folks make a living." The definition of decent in the 1920s was subject to many interpretations. It just depended on who you were, and who you were talking to. It didn't matter. I loved mama no matter how many laws she broke.

After the Feds had raided and left, everyone broke into a rousing laughter of relief. My sister and I were quickly dispatched back to the middle of the lake to retrieve the floating cans of booze. Sometimes they were difficult to spot. Any sun or moonlight hitting them as we approached made them shine like jewels and assisted in our recovery.

On the rare occasion when the cops showed up too close to our house for us to have time to use the boat, all of the alky went into the car. One of mama's admirers had given her a 1925, 7-Passenger Hudson Sedan. These cars resembled models far more expensive, but really weren't. It was so large that it reminded me of a big old touring boat that I had seen often on the lake. Only ours had big brake and clutch pedals. My legs were too short to reach them, so mama had one of her friends make two wooden boxes that we attached to the pedals as risers. Mama taught me how to make the car go forward and reverse. So, on those rare occasions when the cops came too close for us to make it to the lake, it was my job to stash the car with the alky loaded in the back seat. I'd turn over the engine, shove the clutch in with all of my might, and slap the lever into gear. I could barely see over the windshield, even while sitting on several thick pillows piled atop an orange crate. My instructions were simple, just drive straight forward into the woods and wait it out until the coast was clear.

After the raid, everyone would gather outside the cottage and watch with glee as I stuck my little head out of the huge car window in order to navigate backing up to the house. With that maneuver complete, they'd all band together and drag the booze back into the house where the party would resume as if nothing had ever happened.

I had been having a ball one evening, up until the time my mother got drunk. She'd been drinking a lot more since our joint had become such an overnight success. In an attempt to get her to release the drink from her hand, if only for a few short minutes, I shouted out, "Come on mom, let's sing."

I had just started into one of my numbers when someone asked, "Where the hell does the kid get all her energy?" Slurring her words, mama used her usual response, which always sounded like a broken record.

"Why she's a chip off the old block. She's just like a fart in a skillet."

Everyone roared with laughter, except for Marion and me. I always knew and dreaded what came next. The more they drank, the looser everyone got. Men began groping women's breasts, and bodies began plopping down on top of their partners wherever there was room. The couches, chairs, and even the floor were fair game; wherever two bodies could safely land. No one ever once seemed to take notice that there were kids in the house. I knew it should have been mama who monitored the action. Since she never said a word about it to anyone, I suppose they just assumed it was alright to do what they wanted in front of Marion and me.

Without doors, the bedrooms became nightly public playgrounds. It was not easy as a five year old to have to listen repeatedly to the chorus of moans and groans and other words of pleasure and delight that flowed easily from room to room. I swore that some day, some way, I would rescue my mother from this horrid scene.

As the crowd started to thin, I wanted nothing more than to go to bed. Suddenly, I spotted mama heading toward our bedroom with some strange man. I ran as fast as I could to block them from going through the door. Crying and screaming, I grabbed at her in desperation. "Please, mommy, don't go in there. Mommy, please." I don't think I had *ever* witnessed her so drunk.

She brushed me aside with the sweep of her hand. "Oh, come on honey, he's just being a little friendly. You go on outside." She slurred, "Why don't you go down the road and play with some of your friends. You have such nice little friends." There were no nice little friends down the road at midnight, but she was so far gone that the time of day was inconsequential. Apparently, she just wanted me out of her way.

I stood in the doorway with tears flowing down my face as I watched the man help mama take off her dress. By the time he removed her bra, I had witnessed about all I could tolerate. I began screaming at the top of my lungs until every last person in the cottage had fled. I guess they were frightened away with worries that someone might call the authorities.

Mother grabbed me by my arm and yelled, "What in the hell do you think you are doing, girl?"

I stood up to her. "I don't want those kinds of people in our house, mama. What you were doing looked ugly and sick, and letting that man take off your clothes... I just know he was going to hurt you."

Instead of slapping my face, mama picked me up into her arms and carried me back into our bedroom. I started to sob uncontrollably. "Sorry, baby. Some day you will understand that I'm not a married lady. Sometimes men and women do what you saw us doing, just for fun."

I just stared at her hard and asked, "Why does it *always* have to be when you get so drunk?"

Now I had pushed her too far. She slapped me so hard I thought a few of my teeth might dislodge and fly down my throat. Suddenly, mama appeared sober for the first time that evening. We just stared at each other in silence. She had never slapped me in my entire life.

As she reached out and pulled me close to her, she said, "Baby, please forgive me. *I promise you I'll never do that again.*" It was a promise I would hear repeatedly for the next twenty years, when men and booze were involved. I don't think mama was capable of not drinking. My mother was an alcoholic. To make matters worse, terms like treatable illness or chronic disorder weren't available then to soften the impact of what my mother was. Ritzy rehab centers with meditation fountains in the middle of cozy courtyards where you could sit and ponder sobriety over a leisurely calorie controlled lunch didn't exist then.

Oh, no. Plain and simple, decent people in the 1920s had only one name for my mother. "She was a damn drunk!"

The weeks of summer continued to fly by. Mama, out of a combination of shame and sorrow for what she had done, was on her best behavior. Despite her need to repent, a certain detachment developed between the two of us following the bedroom blowout. Mama was unable to grasp that my disapproval of her actions was only a natural result of my deep love and devotion to her. With that deep love, I vowed a commitment to save her from her herself. Her alcoholism could well have destroyed all of our lives. If I had not been a born fighter, I might have given up long before my star took off. Instead, I found a new determination. I made it my goal to become famous. With fame comes fortune, and with lots of money I would be able to lift us out of poverty. Once out of poverty, mama wouldn't have to sell booze any more, and naturally she would stop drinking. It's ironic that when I finally did make it big, mama still didn't quit; she just switched from beer to good Scotch. Now we could afford the best.

During this time, I dedicated myself to learning how to sing like a pro. Every night became as important to me as New Year's Eve. I sang and danced my heart out for the folks in mama's bootleg joint. At the same time, a change deep within me started to take hold. I began to welcome applause and acceptance from the audience as a replacement for the personal love I wasn't receiving. *Applause and acceptance equaled love.* It sure was better than booze and men.

During prohibition, ballrooms sprung up all over the country. Around 1920, the *Park Lake Dance Hall* was built. It drew big name bands from all over the area. Every time mama had a date, she took me along. I loved it because she always allowed me the first dance.

One special evening, a popular mid-western bandleader by the name of *Ted Weems* came to town with his big band orchestra. They were featuring a good looking young singer named, *Perry Como*. I remember standing down front, swooning over this swell looking fella. How could I ever have known, a few years down the road, Perry and I would become personal friends? On top of that, he would become Godfather to one of my sister, Marion's, sons. It's a fitting tribute to our friendship that one of my many successful songs, *I Love You a Bushel and a Peck*, was sung by us as a duet.

We all jumped into our big touring car and left the ballroom that evening in a wonderful mood. With every window down, we sang songs all the way back to the cottage. I recall that night so clearly because summer was slowly coming to an end. Those hot days of August had been replaced by mild, almost cool, evenings. Marion was waiting for us at home. She had just returned from Battle Creek where she had spent a week visiting Aunt Jessie and Uncle Ray before the start of school. Everyone enjoyed a nightcap before mama said good night to her date. Things seemed to be settling into a calmer routine. Mama had cut back on both the booze and the boys. I liked thinking that I had a little something to do with her change in behavior. If that were true, it would have been a real feather in my cap, but unfortunately, that wasn't the case. Mama was just taking a break of sorts.

Mama figured we should stay on at the lake since everything seemed to be going along so well. I think she was merely too afraid to upset the applecart. Mama enrolled Marion and me in the local school. I was excited to ride on a school bus; it would be a brand new experience for us both. Going to school would also give us the chance to meet a whole new bunch of kids; those who lived in the surrounding rural communities. I felt that I was going to love going to school there.

The bus ride was all I had hoped for, and more! Unlike our car that floated along like a boat, the bus bounced up and down over the rough country roads. All the kids fought to sit in the very back where it bounced the most. When we reached school, Marion and I said goodbye to each other before being directed to our respective classrooms. To my utter amazement, I had a *man* teacher. I had always thought only women taught school. He introduced himself to the class by writing his name on the blackboard; Mr. Elton Kane. Boy, was he good looking.

A few short weeks after classes started, a student talent show was announced. It was organized as a means to involve the children, along with their parents and the teachers, in the school. My Mr. Kane was in command of the show. He asked for a show of hands from the children who were interested in participating. I was eager to help by volunteering to sing a song. I asked if my mother could accompany me on the ukulele. Mr. Kane said he saw no problem with mama helping out. After all, part of the objective of the show was to involve parents in the school.

When the bus dropped us off at home late that afternoon, I ran as fast as my feet could carry me into the house. "Oh, Mama, I'm so excited. We're gonna be in a show."

"Ok, not so fast. Betty, do you always have to slam the screen door like that? Now, slow down and tell me what this is all about."

"At school, I'm gonna sing, and Mister Kane said you could play for me. I can't believe you and me get to perform together on the stage."

"Who is Mr. Kane?"

"He's my teacher, mama. I already told you, remember?"

"You have a man teacher? Baby, hand me those three potatoes... over there on the table."

"Yes, and wait until you meet him. Oh mama, he's not like any man I've ever met. He treats me like a young lady."

"Well, honey, you are a young lady."

"Gee, mama. I wish you could get to know a real gentleman like Mr. Kane, instead of all those drunks that come around here..."

She stopped her slicing and cut me short with a wave of her knife. "Betty, don't you get smart. This is a business I run here, and I make our money from those men who you don't like. Just how do you suppose we afford to live in this nice place? That money pays our bills and puts food on our table. So you mind your mouth, young lady."

"Well I know Mr. Kane's not the type to go to a blind pig, that's for sure. And when you meet him, *please* mama, don't tell him you run a bootleg joint."

The night of the show, I was a nervous wreck trying to make sure everything was perfect before we left home. That way, I knew for sure we would be the hit of the show.

"Hurry up, mama. I don't want to be late. Don't forget to bring your *uke*."

"It's right here, for God's sake, calm down, Betty. We'll be wonderful!"

Before we walked out on stage, Mr. Kane came over to meet my mother. I'm sure I wasn't mistaken - he looked at her in a way I had never seen anyone look at mama before. It was like he could see right inside and know everything about her that there was to know.

After all the formalities and announcements, the show was ready to begin. Mother and I were scheduled as the first act up. I had been planning all along to sing *The Sweetheart of Sigma Chi*. I was so determined to make good, that suddenly the only lyrics that came to my head were the ones mama had taught me, the dirty ones I sang for the men at our blind pig.

The girl of my dreams has dyed her hair.
She's dyed it a fiery red.
She drinks, she smokes,

She tells dirty jokes.
Why, there's not a brain in her head.
She drinks White Mule –
Makes the world go 'round.
She can drink more than you or I.
But the girl of my dreams
Is a cigarette fiend.
She's the sweetheart
Of six other guys.

After I had finished singing, I came to realize my mistake from the nervous laughter in the room. Mama shot me a real stern look. My face immediately turned cherry red. Mister Kane approached me slowly. Bending down to look at me squarely in the eye, he said, "Well, those are not *exactly* the lyrics I expected from a sweet young lady." Mama jumped in before I could think of a word to say. "Oh, Mr. Kane, I'm so very sorry. You see, the truth is, I run a blind pig. I'm afraid I've been teaching Betty a few songs that she shouldn't be singing in school. However, Betty here, she just loves to get the laughs." Mama began to giggle as a means to ease her discomfort. "Fact is, Mr. Kane, there's really no way in hell that I could have stopped her once she started." I could see Mr. Kane was mildly amused by what mama was saying, if not instantly charmed by her honesty. He wasn't mad at all. If he was, he sure didn't show it.

After the show, mama invited Mister Kane back home with us for a cup of coffee. "Although I run a blind pig, Mr. Kane, which incidentally I wasn't supposed to tell you, I do have some nights off. Lucky you, tonight just happens to be one of them." With that comment, I was sure mama's chance with Mr. Kane had been spoiled for good. However, to my amazement, he graciously accepted her invitation. He said he would follow us home in his car.

While we sat around having coffee and sandwiches, I noticed that Mr. Kane was trying not to, but he kept staring at my mother. I believe that he became hooked by her natural charm. Oh, how I hoped that for once in her life she could win over a real gentleman like Mr. Kane. Mama was notorious for her bad taste when it came to men. Her time for a new beginning was way overdue. I remember thinking; here is one guy I wouldn't mind staying overnight.

Just before Marion and I headed off to bed, Mr. Kane started a fatherly sounding conversation with us. In a soft-spoken voice he inquired, "Before you climb into bed, would you like me to listen as you both say your prayers?"

Both of us sat there with blank expressions on our faces. Neither of us really knew what a prayer was, or how to say one. It must have been our expressions that exposed our lack of understanding, because Mr. Kane suddenly turned back into a teacher. He showed us how to kneel and asked us to follow him in reciting the *Lord's Prayer*. When we finished, I glanced over at mama; tears flowed gently down her cheeks. We were absorbed in a beautiful moment of silence I hoped might last for ever. I truly believe that to be the exact moment when *God first entered my heart*. A feeling of warmth and contentment seemed to surround me; a feeling so beautiful, I was sure I would never again be the same.

I knew for sure Mr. Kane was no accident. He was actually more like an answer to a dream. This man was intelligent and gentle. Moreover, he didn't drink. He was attracted to my mother, and it was obvious that he cared for both Marion and me. It was clear to me these two adults made the perfect couple. From the very start, they seemed to get along famously.

I truly thought the problems in our lives were now gone for good. When Mr. Kane moved in with us, my mother stopped drinking and started behaving like the perfect lady. I prayed that one day soon he would be asking for her hand in marriage.

One morning, as we were rushing out to catch the school bus, Mr. Kane flew out of the cottage door behind us. He was running late, and never realized the bus had not already picked Marion and me up. When he saw the bus, he turned pale white. We boarded a silent bus of confused looking kids. Nobody said a word during the ride; the bus remained perfectly silent.

When we reached school, I grabbed Marion for support. We went to our classrooms, but were told to report to the principal's office. The word had obviously already reached him. I saw in the principal's eyes what I can only describe as a look of total disgust. I quickly raised all my defenses. No matter how frightened I was, I had already decided to defend my mother.

"Just because my mother runs a blind pig and a nice man like Mr. Kane falls in love with her, you can't wait to throw us out. You don't scare me. Mama has had to deal with people like you before." I held nothing back.

With a fist clenched and raised above his head, as if he was about to cast out demons, he roared, "Betty and Marion Thornburg, get your things and leave this school immediately!"

"What are you gonna do about Mister Kane?" I barked.

"That problem has already been addressed, young miss. You can rest assured the school board will see to it that he is transferred out of our school district."

"Does Mr. Kane know what you're doing to us?"

"Mr. Kane already knows you for the lowbrow creatures that you really are. *Now*, get out!"

Principals kept a sort of miniature whip in those days, the kind used to control race horses. It was for a show of authority. He reached behind his chair and grabbed it from a hook on the wall. You never saw two tearful little girls flee anywhere so fast. We ran from his office and out the front doors. We practically ran the five miles home. We were both devastated by the humiliation and embarrassment of the event.

Mama saw us running toward the cottage through the screen door. She said absolutely nothing to either of us. There really was nothing to say, nothing she could do. Sadly, we were never again to see the man I hoped would marry my mother. My dreams of having a complete family with a stabilizing male influence were over. I knew this marked a very dark day in our lives. There would be no more happiness for us in this house ever again.

After a time, mama cuddled Marion and I close to her. With the saddest look I ever remember seeing in her eyes, she said, "Girls, remember this. Behind each dark cloud, there is a darker one."

Mama went about her normal duties of preparing our dinner. As I watched her, I thought; if we all just acted normal, everything would be fine. Before we ate, she walked over to the bar and apologetically announced, "I'm going to have a few drinks, you know, just to settle my nerves."

Although I wanted to believe that acting normal would make everything fine, a feeling deep inside told me that something even more terrible was going to happen - and it did.

Me and my sister, Marion (standing), 1924.
Photo: Betty's private collection, The Betty Hutton Estate

Chapter Three

It's amazing how a door eventually closes, putting an end to even the worst imaginable event. After several weeks of lying low at home, the hurt I experienced after the awful incident of being run out of school began to fade. With that put behind us, my hope was for a new door to swing open and give us all a fresh start.

Somehow mama knew different. "Every dark cloud seems to be followed by an even darker one" became her constant reminder to us. So it came as no real surprise when our front door opened one evening and in entered a brand new nightmare by the name of Gilbert Adams. The very sight of this slippery figure of a man made my flesh crawl.

By now, I had more than my share of experience in sizing these guys up. The kind of men mama brought home to her bed always came from the same twisted and broken mold. It was not difficult for me to dislike them all. I particularly detested this Gilbert Adams fella from the very moment I laid eyes upon him. He had no sooner entered our blind pig when I noticed his beady eyes already transfixed on my budding adolescent sister, Marion. Already half in the bag, mama failed to notice where his attentions had turned. I couldn't help but wonder if this sort of low-life had some special power, whereby mama became instantly hypnotized the very second she looked into their eyes.

I was beginning to get the impression that my mother's lust for men came before anything she felt for me or Marion. It had gotten to the point where her apparent total lack of self control was having a terrible effect on us as a family. Her routine of one more drink and one more man had become all too predictable at home. So, on the night Gilbert Adams walked into our lives, I knew we were staring trouble directly in the face all over again.

At the peak of the evening's festivities, mama did something out of the ordinary. She turned to her paying customers and with an abrupt command ordered, "Last call! I'm tired and we're closing up." Mama made one deliberate exception. She pulled Gilbert aside and in a suggestive voice whispered, "You stay." I was quite shocked mama would go to this extreme. By closing up early, we faced the loss of an entire night's worth of booze receipts. At that point, I don't think she really cared.

Slurring her words, mama commanded, "You two girls, off to bed." Immediately, the tiny voices of anger and disgust inside my young head went on full alert. Instead of going to bed, I positioned myself on the nearby sofa to lay in wait to rescue mama. With one hand on her hip and the other stretched out as if she were begging for a drink, she implored, "Come on, big boy. Wanna learn how to say your prayers?" Both were so inebriated, they had difficulty navigating to the bedroom door.

In their drunken condition, moments of silence were followed by tremendous bursts of noise and laughter. The longer I listened, the more agitated I became. The moans and groans seemed to be reaching a feverish pitch. Upon hearing the bedsprings screech like never before, mama screamed out, "Oh yes. That's it! Do it! It's happening. It's happening."

The random noises swiftly subsided, followed by one thunderous slap. My mind raced, until suddenly I lost it. I ran and grabbed a butcher knife from the kitchen drawer and ran back into mama's bedroom. "Mama, mama...are you alright?" I stopped cold, my back up against the cold bare wall.

Gilbert's face turned ugly and distorted when he saw me. "Hi ya, kid. Here to watch the show?" I lunged toward him, butcher knife raised high above my head. I got close enough to the bed to recognize by her blank expression that mama had passed out. I had seen it all too often in the past. Gilbert began to laugh at the sight of little me with the large raised knife. "She's all right, kid. Just a bit too much booze and a little too much of big old Gil..."

I backed away slowly, too stunned to say anything. Gilbert's laughter reverberated in my head. I not only hated him, but for the first time in my life, *I hated my own mother.* I dropped the knife on the counter and ran out through the back kitchen door. Outside, I threw up violently. I had been sickened by not only what I had seen, but also by the depraved way we were living. I saw no escape from this life for any of us.

Just then, with such disparity in my heart; when I figured all was just about lost, something miraculous happened. A warm feeling began to flush over me as my lips instinctively began to recite *The Lord's Prayer*, just as my teacher Mr. Kane had taught to us. A cleansing wave of hope emanating from my mind washed over my body. I really didn't know this man called *The Lord*, but I sure was ready to seek him out. I was all of six years of age, and ready to welcome God into my heart.

The next morning, probably due to her massive hangover, mama said nothing regarding the escapades of the night before. We were never really sure if mama actually remembered what happened the day after one of her big drunks. On this particular morning, Gilbert slithered arrogantly about the house, as if he owned it. If mama wasn't aware of what had happened the previous night, I thought a good strong cup of coffee and his mere presence in our house might jar her memory. I was sure that as soon as mama's hangover went away, so would Gilbert. That's usually how it went when mama allowed one of her men to stay overnight. Marion and I loathed him and we both wanted him gone soon, and gone for good.

When it came to mama's feelings about Gilbert, this time, things were going to be a lot different. Instead of his departure after breakfast, mama went ahead and invited the jerk to not only stay, but to move in. Nobody cared for him much. It seemed not even most of the drunks, whose habit it was to depend upon my mother to supply them with their booze, liked him. Many of them stopped coming around. As a result, business began to go sour. I don't think Gilbert was the complete cause for our drop in business, as folks had already started to shy away from us ever since the fiasco at school that ended with Mr. Kane's transfer out of the district.

It didn't take long for mama to decide that we would be better off moving back to Lansing. It was the only logical choice with our business going down the drain. We also needed to be in school, and knew damned sure the local school wouldn't be inviting us back into classes any time soon. Mama already had plans on opening a bigger and better blind pig once we got settled in Lansing.

Picking up and leaving Park Lake and our cozy cottage for good was difficult. I knew I would miss the small town atmosphere and the beauty of the lake. In addition, most of our so-called friends had turned against me and Marion. Still, we were saying good bye to a casual freedom which we all had grown to enjoy. I would miss our cottage most of all; a place we finally got to call home. As a family, it had offered us the greatest amount of normalcy that I'd seen or would see for a long time to come. The decision had been made. Immediately, we began packing for the move back to the city.

Back in Lansing, mother leased a house in her name alone. She had sole control of the purse strings. Good old Gilbert didn't have a red cent to his name. Business began to pick up after mama hired on a man by the name of Mac to help out. Mac treated us well, and I liked him a lot. It felt good to have a man in our lives who, for a change, wasn't sharing mama's bed. She had used whatever sense was left in her head by hiring Mac to take care of the real chores, as half of her day was usually spent in bed with Gilbert. It no longer mattered to mama what Marion or I thought. Gilbert wasn't the bread winner, but, in all other respects, he dominated mama's life. With a constant flow of men normally in and out of her life, I had never seen one man manage to stick around as long as Gilbert.

Mama had to have noticed that I barely spoke to her anymore. Since Gilbert joined our happy little household, the relationship between mama and me became very strained. I knew darned well that she wasn't making any special attempts to accommodate me. Then one morning over breakfast, and quite out of the blue, she just up and said, "I'm taking you to a motion picture today, Betty." I'd heard talk about motion pictures, but I'd never been to one. I guess mama decided to take me as a sort of peace offering. My excitement over going sent old Gilbert into a real fit. He'd been particularly antagonistic toward me since the night I came close to planting that big knife in his chest. Despite his protests, mama said, "No, I'm taking Betty and that's final."

We went to the Bijou, where I saw my first motion picture, *Ramona*, starring Dolores Del Rio. Even though it was a silent picture, mama tilted her head toward me and read the subtitles in a soft, patient voice. I could feel her warm breath on my cheek. I was in seventh heaven. As I sat watching the actors up on the big screen, an indescribable thrill came over me. I suddenly had the feeling this was a night that would change the course of my life. I knew right then and there how to save the three of us from the nightmare life we had been living.

As we walked home from the theater in the dark, I looked up at mother and said, "Mama, I know what I'm going to be. I am going to be a big Hollywood movie star." I knew that someday people would be watching me up on that big screen; I would be famous. More importantly for the three of us, I would be able to buy us out of the life we were living. Mama laughed. "Honey, go on and dream away if it makes you happy."

Business at our blind pig in Lansing really started to take off. I continued singing every night as usual. With all the practice, my style continued to improve. Mama even paid more attention to my singing by bragging to her customers how mature my singing voice had become. When she had a few drinks under her belt, it changed to asking the crowd, "Have you all heard the news? My daughter is going to be a star." Everyone laughed, and I laughed with them. No matter what they thought, I knew that someday I'd have the last laugh. I *would* become a star. For now, concentrating on my singing helped me to focus on something other than Gilbert; the son of a bitch.

I kept hoping mama might take me to see another movie. She finally agreed when she found out *Al Jolson* had made the first picture to also have sound. We stood in a long line for an entire hour just to reach the box office to see a matinee performance of *The Jazz Singer*. We were only just entering the theater when I froze. The wonderful sound of Jolson singing, *Climb Upon My Knee, Sonny Boy* bounced off the screen, out of the theater, and into the lobby. I could barely wait to get inside and claim my seat.

I will always remember Al Jolson as the greatest performer to ever have lived. He mesmerized me with his talent and style. It was impossible for mama to extract me from my chair. I made her sit through the film five times before I relinquished my seat. After leaving, we walked home in complete silence. Mama never understood the depth of my emotions that evening. More than ever, I became convinced that one day I would be a big star, singing and dancing my way into the hearts of people all over the world. I never once doubted my abilities or convictions. I stopped wasting my dreams of stardom on mama. In turn, she stopped making jokes about me and my ambitions with all the drunks at the blind pig.

I slowly began turning to that man, *The Lord*. I knew he would help me to achieve my lofty aspirations. Whenever I thought of *Him*, a warm sensation shrouded my body, and my eyes automatically filled with tears. Singing and dancing were good, but alone they could not maintain that warm, fuzzy feeling within. I began to confide in him more than just about my lofty aspirations. *He* helped me to make it through all the bad things that were happening at home. These were my own private feelings, and I never dared to share them with anyone except *Him*.

Nothing extraordinarily bad had happened since retuning to Lansing. With mama's dark cloud warnings always hovering a short distance above our heads, we were anticipating the arrival of doom on our doorstep any day. One night after all the customers were gone, Marion, and I cooked up a new batch of home brew. We were preparing for bed when mama announced our supply of alky also needed replenishing. She decided to send Gilbert in the car for a fresh new batch.

Less than an hour later, and without any kind of warning, we heard a big commotion out in front of the house. Mama looked out the side window just as Mac motioned to her from outside to open up so he could speak. "Mabel, be fast! Grab the kids and get out the back door. Run like hell. I'll stall 'um by saying the alky is in the garage. Hurry now. Get them kids out of here."

It took an instant to process what was happening. Marion and I were in footed pajamas, all ready for bed. Luckily, we heard what Mac had told mama. Marion and I were already on full alert and ready to act. Mama ran in, white as a sheet. She grabbed us, and we grabbed our coats as we headed out of the room. We heard Mac from the front of the house directing the cops in the direction of the garage. Seconds later, good old Gilbert drove up with at least fifty cans of alky in the car, oblivious to the sting already in progress. Before he could get out of the car, the Feds surrounded him from all directions. Both men were taken into custody.

We'd never been caught before, so the seriousness of this raid didn't immediately register with me. Mama yanked me away from the window where I was peeking through a slit in the curtain. "Come on girls, we need to go *now*!" We headed out the back door. The three of us ran aimlessly down the back alley. Thank God for our pajamas with feet; otherwise we would have been barefoot to the cold autumn night.

"Mama, mama," I loudly sobbed, "what are we going to do?" She dropped my hand, knelt down and said, "Betty, for God's sake, what are *we* going to do? I can't take you girls with me. I made arrangements with the postman long time ago that if anything like this ever happened, they would take you in until I could come back for you."

"But, why can't we go with you?" I found it hard to believe my mother could just walk off without us.

"Because Betty, if they caught me, they would certainly put me in jail. If they caught me with you and Marion, they would put me in jail and take you two away from me forever. So go, go now to the postman's house. Marion, take her hand and mind your sister."

What a laugh this all was. Could it be possible, after all the booze and the boys, my mother finally grasped the idea that what she had been doing managed to put us in harm's way? Never before had I met such a dismal situation head-on. I knew that I had always given mama a difficult time, but that aside, mother and I had never been separated from each other before. What was to happen?

Mama headed in the opposite direction down the alley. I stood and watched as her figure became smaller and smaller, and finally disappeared into the night. She never turned around once to look back. I did as I had been told by mama and took Marion's hand. Together we trudged off toward the postman's house. We arrived cold and scared.

The postman was a pleasant man who referred to his wife as *mother*. A mother who looked like her, I doubt any child could truly love. "Mother," he said, "these are the two girls I've been telling you about."

As she lumbered toward us, I noticed an ugly wart on her chin. "Oh, so it's the bootlegger's brood." I knew right away that my sister and I had stumbled through the gates of hell. I stood trembling before this witch. I looked over to notice Marion had remained as cool as a cucumber. Only then did I realize, my sister had sampled too much of our new batch of home brew before the Feds showed up. I had been aware for quite some time; Marion was already drinking by the age of nine. Still, Marion's charm, something my sister could turn on and off at will, was an immediate attraction. The postman's wife fell all over her with affection. Naturally, the postman's wife took an immediate dislike to unattractive little me.

No kind voices were there to soothe my agonies that night. *The Mother* had four children of her own. Their needs would surely take precedence over mine. To make matters worse, the postman's wife had suspicions that her husband and my mama had more going on than friendship. She was dead wrong. Her husband was a good man, and merely felt sorry for us girls being caught up in adult situations over which we had absolutely no control.

Since mama wasn't around, the bitch took her frustrations out on me. I was always the easy target, since I wore my heart on my sleeve. Everybody always knew how Betty felt, because I always showed it. Marion was older and wiser. She had learned to disguise what she was really feeling. Despite my jealousy of her, I adored my sister. I'm not sure if she ever felt the same about me. Once into our teens, we were never close. As adults we were still sisters, but never on the same page.

For dinner, the postman's wife would make creamed carrots; something I have always loathed. I think she came up with creamed carrots several times a week, just to see me squirm. No matter how hard I tried to swallow them, my stomach involuntarily began to retch, and out came the damned carrots, cream and all.

This woman's greatest delight came in yanking me by my hair away from the table. For failing to finish my carrots, I was sentenced to twenty-four hours of lockup in a closet with an old army blanket pinned to me as a diaper. The claustrophobia that I developed from this cruel and unusual confinement has stayed with me for my entire life. The postman begged his wife to leave me alone. "The child is blameless for anything her mother might be responsible for," he'd plead. Her only response was a haughty little laugh. The more she looked at my little face distorted with hurt, the more enraged she became. I really do think the fear I exhibited egged her on in some very strange and sadistic way.

I prayed the prayer my teacher Mr. Kane had taught me and added a few words of my own, "Please Dear God, before I die, please send my mama for me." My prayers unfortunately went unanswered. The brutal torment continued for the remainder of my detention in the home of that ruthless woman.

She began bringing newspapers home and would read the headlines with great satisfaction to Marion and me: *Local Police on the Lookout for Blond Woman with Two Children, Six and Eight - Wanted for Bootlegging.* This depraved woman would warn, "I've a good notion to call the cops and turn you in. I bet they would pay me handsomely for that information." She always directed her animosity toward me, because she knew I would fall to my knees and beg her not to do it. For the rest of the day, she would revel in her victory over me.

The postman had always been a nice man; nevertheless, it had been a cowardly act on his part to have allowed his wretched wife to treat us so badly. In any case, the cruel punishment continued for several more months. Sadly, we were so young and had no way of knowing mama had forked over a large sum of money to this couple to take care of us. Had we known, we might have been able to use that information as ammunition in some way against her.

Suddenly, one day, just like Christmas, mama walked right through the front door. When it finally registered in my own little head this was reality, I rushed into her arms. She squeezed me tightly as tears flowed freely from both our eyes. I had become so gaunt, she almost didn't recognize me. "Betty, my God, what has happened to you? What have you been doing to my baby?"

"Mama, Mama! I thought you had forgotten all about us and would never come back. I have missed you so. Please, don't ever leave me again. I would rather die than be without you."

Mama pursued her questioning of the witch with persistence, "I asked you a question, what have you done to my baby?"

Marion approached mama at that moment bearing little sentiment. "We've been fine, mama, and I'm happy to see you, too." Maybe it was because she hadn't been treated as severely as I had during mama's absence. Then again, Marion didn't wear her heart on her sleeve as I did. It angered me that Marion was concealing the truth concerning our stay here in hell. Likewise, I'm not sure why I decided to rat out this awful woman now. Typically I wanted to shield mama from any unnecessary hurt; my principal goal always to protect her at any cost. This time, however, I was mad as hell and decided to spill the beans. "She forced me to eat creamed carrots and when I threw them up; I had to wear an army blanket for a diaper and got locked in the closet for a whole day!"

The witch shot back defensively, "Well, Betty was bad. She wouldn't eat, and that just couldn't go unpunished. Children need to learn there are consequences for unacceptable behavior."

Mama rose from her kneeling position between Marion and me. I'm sure she intentionally advanced toward the postman's wife quickly to be intimidating. The witch backed up and only stopped when her back hit the icebox. When their eyes finally met, mama deliberately raised a threatening hand and fired off, "You filthy son of a bitch, how dare you do this to my child!" As we were nearing the door, and surely not to be outdone by mama's hostile remark, the postman's wife yelled, "You dirty bootlegging whore, I hope they get you good."

As we opened the door to leave, the postman walked into the kitchen from an adjacent room. We had no idea he had been home. His head was bowed down to avoid eye contact with anyone. There he stood in pathetic silence. Mama had already said her mind.

We turned and walked out the door. We made our way down the driveway toward the cab that mama had waiting for us out on the street. Not until the doors were finally slammed shut, and we were driving away, did the sound of the wife flinging obscenities at her husband from inside the house fade away. Mama made no comments about what had just happened. All she said it that we were on our way to the county line to meet up with Gilbert and Mac directly.

I later learned that we were being expelled from Lansing for good. It was my mother they had *really* wanted to bust. Gil and Mac had been cut loose from the county jail on a technicality. The cops escorted them to the county line with a stern warning; *"If we ever find either of you, or Mabel Thornburg back in Lansing, we'll put you away - even if we have to plant the booze on you."*

Under the law, Gil and Mac could have been detained only if the house where the booze was found had been in their names. Since the lease on the house was solely in mama's name, they had to be released. Needless to say, the authorities were furious that they'd been unable to nab mama. I have to praise Gilbert and Mac, after everything that happened; they were never disloyal to mama. Once away from Lansing, Gilbert knew just where to contact mama. He told her to pick us up, and we would all meet up in the next county. From there, it had already been decided that Detroit would be our destination and new home.

On the way to our rendezvous, I was petrified of being spotted by cops and mama being hauled away. Shortly after passing over the county line, Gilbert finally came into view waiting for us behind the wheel of mama's big touring car. With both of her hands reaching skyward, my mother shouted out, *"Hallelujah! We were lost and now we are found, I was blind and now I can see..."*

I had no clue what she was taking about, but if we were out of harm's way, it must have been a good thing. Everyone exchanged hugs and kisses to celebrate our new-found freedom. I was just so happy to have mama back. Even seeing Gil again came as a breath of fresh air after spending all that time around the postman's hideous wife. As we sailed down the road in our big boat, I had to thank *Him* for helping us to evade another dark cloud in our lives. Only God knew what surprises were in store for us when we reached Detroit.

Chapter Four

The Detroit of 1929 was one huge impoverished nightmare of a city. At the height of the bootleg era, this place was sure to afford nothing but misery for a single mother with two small children and no money. Crime was in abundance everywhere, as a direct result of the escalating poverty. Consequently, we really had no clue what was in store for us when Gilbert and Mac dropped us off in front of the beat-up old tenement house which was to be our new home. As both men drove off in mama's car, despite my masquerade of goodwill toward Gil for extracting us from harm's way earlier in the day, I now thanked God he was gone. His presence had been a destructive force in our lives; I hoped we'd never see him again.

As we stood out front, my eyes quickly darted back and forth in an attempt to take in everything this visual banquet had to offer. Half-dressed women, hanging precariously from their windows, exchanged angry sounding banter with men out on the street. Disheveled men wandered suspiciously in and out of the building, but paid no attention to the children loitering aimlessly on the steps and in doorways as they stepped over them. It looked like a mad house. In my mind, it was difficult to imagine anything resembling this anywhere.

I looked up at my mother's face to see if I could read what she was thinking. As she stared at the building, the color was draining from her face.

"Mama," I asked, "Who are those women? What are they doing?"

My mother sat us down on the curb next to our few belongings. Her lower lip quivered as she started in. "Marion, Betty, we are broke. Those six months that Gilbert and Mac were in jail cost me every dime we had. There will be no one here to look after us now, so we are gonna have to stick awfully close together if we hope to make it here in Detroit."

"But we have you, mama," I protested.

"You'll always have me baby, but Gilbert and Mac are gone. One good thing, the police won't be pestering us here. Even so, listen to me, and listen good. Those women there, they're what you call whores. You both stay away from them, and they won't cause us any trouble, understand?"

In my confusion I interrupted, "But, the postman's wife called you a whore, mama, and we still talk to you."

Mama, who only moments before had looked as if she might die, threw her head back and squealed with laughter. The blood rushed back to her face. I was pleased; I had been able to make her laugh. Marion and I both started in, too; mama's laugh was that infectious.

The laughter permitted all of us to relax for the first time since we had been abandoned in front of this nut house. "Oh, mama, it's so good to see you laugh again. But, could you please tell me, what did I say that you found so funny?"

She giggled. "Well, you see, honey, these women get paid for having men in their beds. That's how they make a living. It's kind of like a business."

"But, mama," I protested. "I still don't get it. You let all kinds of men sleep in your bed, and we got into nothing but trouble." My exposure to sex was on par with that of an adult, nevertheless, my understanding of sex left much to be desired. At my young age, I did understand one thing, after having been exposed to it so casually and so often, sex was just an everyday occurrence. So it came as a shock to be informed a whore gets paid for what mama did regularly free of charge.

I peeked down my shirt at my own flat chest, and then glanced quickly over at my sister's nicely developing one. "Hey Marion, you could make a ton of money in that business with what you got!" I dodged out of the way just in time to miss a good swift kick from Marion, heading straight for my shin.

Mama bent down to pick up our two bags. "Hey, cut it out, you two. How about we go on in and give ourselves a tour of this fancy resort hotel?"

We navigated our way up to the second floor via staircases littered with trash, start to finish. The hallway to our apartment reeked of urine, dirty diapers, and some unpleasant smell which mama guessed to be food related, but she wasn't exactly sure. We were all nauseated at the combination of odors. The three us stood in front of our apartment door, but not one of us could commit to opening it. Mama finally turned to us and spoke in an apologetic voice. "If we can all put up with this for a few weeks, I'm sure I can snag some sort of job at the Chrysler plant. We'll be all right then, but we all have to be real strong right now. Got it?"

My Aunt Merna had moved to Detroit in advance of our arrival. She already had an apartment in our building, and now promised to help mama find work. We were nearing a depression, and times were truly tough. The 1929 stock market crash would soon put a padlock on the American economy, making things even worse for thousands who already had very little.

Our apartment was worse than any of us had even suspected. Bugs of varying varieties scurried across floors, along cabinets, and over counter tops. The place looked pretty retched as we wandered around. We immediately invented a game to see who could be the first to spot at least one redeeming feature in the apartment. Unfortunately, none of us felt like playing any games. Nervously, mama began rummaging through her purse. She pulled out her wallet, and after opening it abruptly revealed, "We have seven dollars to our names, and somehow we need to come up with money to pay the rent due in one week's time. But, all that aside, I want you to remember what I am about to say. We may be poor, but by God, we are going to be clean. Now, here's two dollars. I want the two of you to go out and buy everything we'll need to clean this place up."

"Mom," Marion proposed, "Don't you think it would be better if we just went ahead and burned the place down?"

Mama chuckled. "Why would you want to go ahead and destroy a lovely place like this? Go on now, go get the cleaning supplies. Just remember one thing when I'm making us soup. If there's a teeny tiny bug in it, I don't want to hear any complaints. Just look closely, if it's not doing the backstroke, go ahead and *eat it*! In this place, there are always going to be bugs. It would be best for us to pretend we are camping out." Thank God for mama's sense of humor. It always meant that she was back to thinking straight. When those dark clouds advanced, she often times came up with something to make us all laugh.

With Marion and me gone on our errand, mama took the opportunity to meet the hooker across the hall. Beanie was her name, and she and I were to become partners in crime. She told me about her first meeting with mama several months later. It had not been a social visit at all, but rather an attempt by mama to round up as much food from neighbors as possible to feed us that first evening. Beanie had invited mama in after she knocked on her door and introduced herself as Mabel. My mother walked in her apartment, sat right down, and instantly started to cry. Beanie jumped in, "You're the new dame with the two kids that just moved across the way, huh?" Mama bobbed her head in acknowledgment. "So what the hell are you crying about, honey?"

Mama spewed her entire story as Beanie listened.

Beanie asked with skepticism, "You mean you didn't know this building was full of hookers and pimps? My God, it's loaded with 'um."

Mama shook her head no, and swore, "Not until after we were deserted in front and saw women hanging from the windows, did I have any clue of who lived here."

Beanie offered mama a drink to calm her nerves. Mama knew full well that she should refuse the offer; one drink always led to another. However, in her depressed state, it was simply impossible for her to say no. Mama said timidly, "One little drink might pick me up a bit."

Beanie persisted, "Look here, blondie, don't be so damned depressed. You've got kids, and they can get a lot of work in this building."

By this time, mama had already started on her second drink, and was itching for her third. Between swigs she probed, "What kind of work?"

"Well, some of the girls in here have kids. Your girls could watch after them. Then again, when a gal goes downtown to meet a trick, one of your kids could go with her and act as a kind of lookout. They'd never suspect a child of being a lookout. Hell, they could pick up maybe five bucks if it was a twenty dollar date."

Mama said we were all wrong for that kind of job. "I really don't want my girls to grow up exposed to that sort of thing." Mama's statement was a bit ridiculous and somewhat sad. No matter how you looked at it, after what we had been exposed to around mama, there was very little difference between them and her.

Even so, Beanie was trying hard to be on mama's side. It didn't take her long to figure out our mama had a real thirst for the bottle. The door to Beanie's apartment was still open when Marion and I trudged up the stairs on our return from the store with our cleaning supplies. We looked in to discover mama slumped down in a chair at the kitchen table. Beanie told us to come on in.

I just stared at Beanie for a short moment before blurting out, "Are you a whore?"

She laughed loudly. "Kid, you are surrounded with 'um, wall to wall. We're not all that bad. You might even learn to like us. Now, as far as your mother is concerned, that woman loves you with everything she's got. You need to always let her know you feel the same. Say, I think you kids are likely to be able to make some good money for your mother here. What do you think about that, huh? Now, one of you go on and help your mother over to your place. I'll give you some food to take along. The other one stay here and I'll fill you in on how this neighborhood works. Your mother ain't feeling so well, so try and get some food into her, too."

Marion took mama and the food back over to our apartment across the hall while Beanie talked with me alone. "So what do you think, kid?"

"About what?" I asked.

"What I just told you, about making money here." Beanie sounded slightly aggravated, as if I were wasting her time.

"Do I gotta do the same thing you do, Beanie?" I inquired.

Beanie grinned, "No honey, you need to grow up some."

I liked her honest approach. I felt a real alliance spring up between us that evening.

"So what would I have to do to earn this money?" I was showing more interest.

"Well kid, it's sort of like babysitting, only you'd be doing it for whores."

My eyes turned twice their size. I couldn't wait to hear the follow-up to that. "Well, what do I gotta do?"

"One of these nights, we'll go to one of the big named hotels in downtown Detroit and, let's say, I got a trick on the fifth floor."

"What's a trick?" I was following along the best I could.

"Oh, come on; don't be so dumb" She was definitely getting annoyed. It's a guy that's gonna pay me for some pleasure he wants. "All you have to do is listen to me carefully, and you'll make five bucks without batting an eye."

"I'm listening, Beanie." She now had my undivided attention.

"You see, in these big hotels, they have chairs that sit against the walls. There are phones right beside them the bellboys use. The room my trick is in would be right around the corner; I'll let you know the room number before hand. If you see a copper or house dick snoopin' around, you pick up the phone and ask for my room number. It's so easy, there's no mistaking those guys for anyone else. So, you tell the operator to let my room number ring twice and then hang up. I'll do all the rest. One more thing, if anything happens, you gotta move fast."

Beanie enlightened me that the operators were in on the whole scheme. It was the pimp's job to pay them off weekly. If it was necessary, after I made the call, I was to go downstairs and wait for her outside the coffee shop.

Now I had the picture. "Boy, that's a cinch, Beanie." Instantly I felt a weight had lifted regarding the distressing financial situation we found ourselves in. There might be only five dollars left after the purchase of our cleaning supplies, but it looked as if I could do my part to make some money to help out mama.

Mama wasn't feeling particularly well the next morning. She had to be up at five o'clock to meet the people who were going to help her get a job at the Chrysler plant. I knew she felt awful, but I had my own troubles to worry about on the first day at *Little Bridge*, my new elementary school. *Bad Eye Bodie* was going to be the new kid in class that day, and I was sure someone was going to make fun of me because of the scar on my face. Being new at school made me really stand out; it seemed like all eyes were upon me. Kids can be cruel when another child is attempting to fit in. I overheard several whispered comments made about my scar and one about how scrawny I was. After school that afternoon, I settled the score. I wanted all the children to know I meant business. I tore into my insulters with all the rage I could muster. I released a lot of the anger I had building up inside of me for a long while. It took three teachers to pull us apart.

"Who started this?" A lady teacher asked.

"I did," I said.

"What reason do you have?"

"I don't need any reason. Being new here is enough of a reason for me. I just want those kids to know I'm the boss." I maintained my tough exterior attitude walking home, until the point where the school disappeared in the distance behind me. After that, I ran as fast as I could all the way to our apartment door. Inside I threw myself on the bed and sobbed. It was impossible for me to change myself or my looks. As a consequence of getting pushed off the pier at the lake, the scar I received on my face from landing on a nail had caused me emotional scars as well. I was too young to understand with time the scar would fade until it was barely visible. Nevertheless, while growing up, I was self-conscious about the scar for years. Because of it, I developed a real hang-up concerning my looks. It is quite possible the emotional scars went much deeper, and in many respects, would last for the rest of my life. I had a tendency to develop fixations about things that I felt were a direct result of my childhood problems.

We managed to adapt fairly well to our new surroundings. Nothing catastrophic happened either. I guess it was due in part to mama landing the job at Chrysler. Her previous experience at Oldsmobile in Lansing had made all the difference in getting the job. Secondly, mama was keeping her nose pretty clean at home. As for Marion and me, we were kept busy with school during our first months in Detroit. As it often happened, all our good luck was to end rather suddenly.

One morning, while getting ready to leave for school, I heard a faint tapping sound followed by moaning noises at our door. I opened up and was staring into Beanie's face, contorted by pain. I looked down and saw blood had saturated her nightgown and continued to drip, forming a small puddle where she stood.

"Beanie, what happened to you?"

"Please, Betty, quick. Get me a doctor."

I walked her over to her own apartment and helped her back into bed. Quickly, I ran downstairs and asked the manager of the building to call a doctor. "Beanie is upstairs bleeding to death," I sobbed.

I raced back upstairs and cleaned up as much of the blood as I could. Beanie screamed loudly in pain as I tried in desperation to calm her. A steady stream of blood continued to erupt from between her legs. I was unsure of how to help her. In desperation, I turned my attention to the blood; I couldn't wipe it up fast enough.

It seemed like an eternity, but the doctor finally appeared. When he entered the room, he casually walked over and sat on the edge of Beanie's bed. I'd seen that same look before on a doctor's face when everybody thought I would die with fever. His look was one of total apathy. I knew immediately that he wouldn't help her.

"What did you do? Use a hanger to abort it?" He growled.

Beanie shook her head no.

"Well, what did you use?"

"Quinine pills." She murmured.

He stood up, and with rage in his voice, fumed, "You go right ahead and suffer the consequences alone. I'll be damned if I help you. Maybe one day you whores will learn to take better care of yourselves." As he turned to leave the room, my presence caught his attention.

"How old are you, girl?"

"I'm nine, sir."

"I would advise you leave here immediately and go to school. She knows what to do. This is not the first time this has happened." With that, the doctor stormed out, slamming the door behind him.

My heart was breaking for her as I asked, "What can I do, Beanie? I don't know what to do to help you."

"Oh, Betty, I'll never forget you're being here for me like this. Please, just hold on to my hands tight and help me push."

Within minutes the baby appeared. I walked around and looked down between her bloodstained legs to see a perfectly formed, but a perfectly dead, miniature baby boy. In the state of shock I was in, it was like watching an accident happen in slow motion. Eventually, she passed the placenta. I had no idea what it was. I just stared and whined, "Beanie, *please* tell me what I am supposed to do."

After the passing of the placenta, Beanie's pain eased dramatically. Within minutes, she reverted quickly back to some semblance of her old self. "Oh, for Christ's sake Betty, you were bound to see something like this eventually, living in this place. Let me tell you another thing, if you don't get out of here soon, I might be helping you the same way someday. Now, stop crying and keep calm. Go get a bunch of newspapers and bring them back to me. Go quick."

I rounded up all the newspapers I could find. "Okay Betty, wrap that thing up good and tight and take it downstairs and throw it in one of the garbage cans outside the building."

"But Beanie, I can't... I mean, you can't do that. That just wouldn't be right?" I was repulsed by the thought of throwing a dead child in the trash.

"What do you mean, not right? What do you think I should do with it? Should I have it stuffed and hang it on the wall? Betty, go do exactly as I say. Don't you go tellin' nobody about this neither, especially not your mama. Now, go ahead and wrap it up!"

From the tone of her voice, Beanie meant every word. I went ahead and did what she told me to do. As I carried the package containing Beanie's aborted fetus downstairs, I felt like a murderer. I didn't just feel sorry for my family because of the way we lived, I felt sorry for Beanie and all the others who were victims of their own circumstances.

Poverty was so much more than being poor; it was a way of life. It wasn't only in a person's make up, it defined who they were. Years later, when I managed to pull my family out of poverty, I never once forgot where I came from. I managed to make millions during my career, but eventually lost it all. I think the constant fear of losing it that I carried around inside me actually made it happen. I know I made wrong decisions, but in some strange way, I think I lost everything I had because it wasn't meant to be in the first place. It wasn't who I was. My place in this world had already been decided at my birth.

The entire time I worked as a lookout for the hookers, we never got caught. Just like outsmarting the Feds with the booze, I took great pleasure in outwitting the cops for the young hookers in our building. It didn't take long for me to get close with a lot of them and to learn their stories. All of them fit pretty much into the same pattern. Hooking had been forced upon them by someone they at one time had trusted, or they had to turn to it because they lacked the education to make better choices. I liked them for their honesty. If it hadn't been for hookers during our first several months in Detroit, we would never have survived.

Chapter Five

The nightmare of Beanie's aborted child stayed with me. I was tormented by the vision of the dead child in my head. It made me want to run as fast and as far away from our self-imposed exile in this tenement building as possible. The faster we left the better. As fate would have it, mama returned from her job at the Chrysler plant that afternoon all happy and smiling. Mama's excitement made me momentarily forget about the bothersome mental picture in my head. "Come on, mom," I insisted, "what's happened to make you so happy? Please tell me."

"Betty, you are never going to believe this." She was glowing with pride. "They made me manager on my line at the plant. Can you imagine that?"

"That's great!" I hoped to bolster her confidence with my enthusiasm.

"I even got a raise!"

With more money available to us, my thoughts immediately turned to getting away from the whore house in which we lived. "Do you think we can finally afford to move away from here, mama?"

"Looks like it, honey. There'd been talk for several weeks about my promotion at work, so I nosed around for a new place for us already; it's on Vernon Highway. You'll be right across the street from your new school, Betty."

"You mean I get to go to Foch?"

"Sure does." My mother was in high spirits to see me so excited.

"Mom, you have no idea how happy I will be to leave this place behind us. I can't wait until I tell Marion the news. That means she'll be going to South Eastern High, right next door to Foch."

"I always told you things would improve, Betty. Nobody is ever gonna get the better of us."

"Mom, we have so little stuff to move, can't we go now? Please..."

Mama looked at me in a way that told me I wasn't getting the full story. There had to be a down side to all this good fortune. Nevertheless, I was so excited to be leaving this dump, I quickly dismissed my hunch.

Mother pried, "So what's the big hurry, Betty? We can wait a few days longer, can't we?"

"Please, mom, don't ask me questions. I just really want to get out of here. If we're gonna do it, why not now?" My mother had no idea the nightmares I had been living with over Beanie and her dead baby. After two years in this place, I often wondered if we would ever find a way out.

She didn't force me more on the matter. Mama must have known I had my own good reasons, or better yet, she felt guilty we had lived here so long. In two years, I never once mentioned she had originally asked us to hold out for a few weeks until she landed a job.

Mama merely shrugged her shoulders, and in a slightly passive manner said, "Okay, baby. When Marion gets home we can move on out. Will that be soon enough for you, your majesty?" She came back at me with a small jab.

"I guess I can wait that long," I said a bit sharply, as if to even the score.

"Betty, you need to know something right now. Don't go expecting too much. The new place is only a tiny bit bigger than this one. The good news is that you and your sister get to share a bedroom of your very own."

"Oh, mama, that's great news!" The more she revealed, the more impatient I became.

"It may not be a palace, but we will be living in a much better neighborhood, and you'll be close to school."

I was sold on the idea. In my mind, any place would be better than living here.

When Marion arrived home from school, mama and I already had everything packed. Marion wasn't happy we had gone through all her belongings in order to pack them. Mama and I were determined to keep the location and specifics of the new place a surprise. Our shared secret caused Marion to be slightly perturbed with both of us.

The exhilaration I experienced when Mama first told me about the new place was replaced by disappointment when I saw it for the first time. The building looked rather cold and uninviting. However, when I looked across the street and saw the beautiful soft rolling green lawns leading up to the front of Foch School, I felt much better. I imagined those lawns to be my own personal front yard.

Our new apartment was on the second floor, just as it had been in our old building. When we entered, the stairs and hallway were clean and devoid of bugs and foul smells. This time we weren't afraid to open the door. I was anxious to get in and see my new bedroom. Upon initial inspection, the living room appeared big in comparison with our old place. I bypassed the kitchen and went down a short hallway to the bedroom. Although it was on the small side, it was something Marion and I could call our own.

I went back in the living room to tell mother how nice the bedroom was. Suddenly, something dawned on me, and I stopped short. "Mom, but where are you going to sleep?"

"Right in here," she said as she opened two huge doors to reveal a Murphy bed.

"That bed is huge, mama!" I reacted with amazement because my mind instantly conjured up an image of mama forever getting lost in there all alone.

She looked back at me for the second time that day, as if I weren't getting the full story.

"Well girls, I hope you don't take this wrong, but the only real way I can afford this place is to have someone share the rent..."

I stopped her in her tracks. "Ah mama, how could you? Why didn't you tell us beforehand? I know, I bet because it's Gilbert Adams. Isn't it mama?"

"Look, I am all alone with no one. Who am I supposed to turn to when things get tough around here? Anyway, I love the guy."

"I kinda thought you had us to turn to, mama," Marion said. "I don't think you love what he does for you at all; I think you just love what he does *to* you." My sister didn't usually get involved in this kind of mud slinging, but she had been teed off since coming home from school to find we had packed all her stuff.

Those words had no sooner left my sister's lips, when in through the door walked Gilbert. He looked first at Marion and me, and then he turned to my mother. "Have you told them yet, Mabel?"

"Of course, they know. I also told them I love you."

I wanted desperately to walk out the door and never look back. I would run as far as I could get to make sure this was all left behind me forever. Instead, I laid into Gil. "My sister and I got so sick and tired of listening to the moans and groans you and my mother made every single night when you two were in bed. The funny part is, I don't even think my mother would let you do that stuff to her unless she got good and drunk first."

"Betty," mama started in.

"No mama," I snapped. "You two sound like some kind of farm animals at night when you're together. Please mama, not again. We don't need him here. Weren't we doing fine on our own? If it's the money, mama, maybe we can get our old apartment back. It wasn't so bad. Get rid of him, mama, he's no good!"

Gilbert had heard just about enough out of me. He lunged toward me from across the room. Mama jumped between us. "Please, Gil," she begged. "God, please don't hurt my baby. She's just a kid."

Gilbert pushed my mother out of his way. When his fist made contact with the side of my head, my body sailed way across to the other side of the room. I finally came to a stop when my head hit the radiator. As I lay there, blood trickled down the side of my face and neck, eventually disappearing somewhere down my collar and inside my shirt.

Mama sprung to life and began screaming at Gil. "You dirty bastard. She doesn't understand what we mean to each other."

"Like hell she doesn't. You are so stupid, Mabel. Remember the very first night I had you? You were grunting and snorting like a pig because you couldn't get enough of me then, and you still want more of me now. You were so damned drunk, you had no idea your little brat here stood in the doorway and watched everything. That's right, everything! All of a sudden, she comes in with a big butcher knife, aiming to plunge the thing into my chest. And do you know why? Because the little bitch is jealous, that's why. So don't you go tellin' me about your innocent little kid? I'm back here because you want me, and she probably does, too! Your innocent kid, my ass. Go ahead and admit it, admit why you invited me back here. You asked me back because sex and booze are the only two things you live for; the only things you care about in this world. You know I've got what it takes to satisfy you, woman. So wake up! She understands exactly what we mean to each other, and it makes her as mad as hell!"

Today, I realize, mama could not control her appetite for alcohol and men. Anyone with any form of addiction can understand her inability to help it. I know it well; I have been there just like mama. When an addict needs a fix, even the love for a child takes a back seat to the craving.

My mother was on her knees sobbing, attempting to wipe the blood from my face. I cradled mother's sobbing face in my hands, and after kissing her softly on the cheek, I said, "Never mind him, mom, you're not a drunk. You just have some sort of an illness because of the way we live. I'm gonna find a way to get you away from this life, and then you'll be cured."

Turning to look at Gilbert, without so much as a hesitation, I said, "You get out, or I'll call the cops. When they see what's happened here, you'll be sleeping in another bed alright; this time in prison. We got along without you just fine, and we'll do it again. I'll go sing on street corners to make money if need be."

I think it had been a good idea mentioning the cops, because that's when Gilbert grabbed his coat and made his way toward the door. He turned back for an instant and said only one thing before he walked out the door. "Goodbye, girls, it's been fun."

Marion had run off and locked herself in the bathroom shortly before I flew across the floor. I was glad she had not been involved in all of this. She wasn't like me. She was passive. In contrast, I always found it necessary to take matters into my own hands. Above all, I felt responsible to look after her and mama. Mama was usually too predisposed with a bottle or a man to take charge. Marion never took charge of anything; she never had the craving. In short, by process of elimination, the job became mine. You also have to remember one thing about my childhood; it wasn't normal by any stretch of the imagination. At an age when I should have been playing with dolls, I was helping hookers steer clear of the authorities and attempting to sober up my mother enough so she could report to work. It had such negative effects on me as a child; it was bound to have adverse effects on my life as an adult.

Mama never mentioned Gilbert again in front of me. After he left, she rapidly nose-dived in a dismal pattern of drinking day and night. It seemed as if that dreadful experience made her lose her will to live. To make matters worse, they opened joints that served 3-2 beer consisting of 3.2% alcohol, and it was legal. Most every night, I had to make the rounds at local bars to search for mama. While I was there, and before she fell on her face, I would sing a song or two. Before I propped mama up on her feet to walk her home, I would pick up the nickels and dimes that customers had thrown at me after each song. Some nights I managed to take home five to ten dollars; it all depended upon how drunk she got.

On Saturdays, I began singing on street corners in downtown Detroit. Folks seemed to like my personality, and enjoyed watching me as I belted out a tune. I could pick up as much as five dollars in change doing that. At the same time, I was trying to go to school, and making another five bucks a week doing housework for a German family. The word had gotten out around the neighborhood that mama was a drunk. At school, many of the kids weren't allowed to play with me because of it. My childhood wasn't really a childhood at all. The only kids that would be friends with me were tough boys. Some of the boys had parents who were so mean; they never wanted to go home for fear of what might happen. Mama might have been an alcoholic, but we never feared she might physically hurt us. She always loved us very much.

So this became my life. At night, I would drag mama home from a bar and try to get a bit of food into her. After I got her into bed, I would aim a fan in her direction in case she got the sweats. I would spend most of the night worrying if she would be well enough to make it to the plant in the morning in time for work. How she managed to keep her job at Chrysler is one of the biggest mysteries. Then, after arriving home from school, I never knew what to expect when I called out, "Mama, I'm home."

In October 1929, the stock market crashed. They said people were jumping from windows in office buildings and off of bridges. Millionaires the day before, were penniless the next. The good thing about being poor, if there can be any redeeming qualities to it; you don't have much of anything to lose. We lived in the slums and would probably always live in the slums, unless of course a miracle happened. Once again, my old dream of one day becoming a movie star rose from the depths to say hello. It was nice to dream, if only for a minute or two. My life was so full just trying to help support my family; I seldom had the luxury of dreaming dreams at all.

On one particular Sunday evening, mama woke up after being passed out in a drunken stupor for most of the day. She arose quite restless, so I went to the kitchen to get her a beer. After she guzzled it down, I returned her to bed. It was like giving a crying baby a bottle to calm it. When she eventually fell back asleep, I decided to wander around outside for some fresh air. Often times, I would go across the street and lay down on the vast lawn in front of school. Having my body come in contact with the cool damp earth invigorated me in a way that could flush away my bad thoughts. As I left the building, I came upon an elderly woman who asked me to help her across the street. I assumed she was blind by her deliberate and cautious movements. She took my arm, and as we walked across the street she said, "You are very sad, aren't you?

"Yes ma'am," I said without much reservation.

"I think you are hungry as well," she insisted.

"I sure am, but how can you tell, ma'am? I don't think you can even see me."

"I know because my heart takes the place of my eyes, my dear girl. Did you know today is Sunday, the day of the Lord? I'm on my way to church where we have enough food there to feed one-hundred children, just like you. Won't you come along with me?"

I wouldn't be missed. It was likely mama would sleep for several more hours, if not throughout the night. Besides, I had never been to church before. This elderly woman was so nice; I was drawn into going along with her. After a short street car ride, we arrived at a place called the Berea Tabernacle, a Pentecostal church. Before we went inside, the old woman explained that if a person believed in God hard enough, anything in their life was possible. We went in and sat down front. I remember feeling love all around me. The pastor was a man named Jesse R. Kline, but was called Brother Kline by everyone. His assistant, Ernie Eskaline, was a good looking young man. Years later, Brother Ernie became something of a famous minister in Africa through the church's missionary program.

As I sat through the church service, I wasn't quite sure what to say or do. Everyone sang their hearts out as people were asked to come forward to give their hearts to the Lord. Later, some men came out and began to lay their hands on sick people, asking Christ to heal them. The old lady I came with had been praying for the return of her eyesight in this church for years. This night, as hands were laid upon her in deep and devotional prayer for the return of her sight, she suddenly rose from her seat, and as she grabbed me, she said, "I can see you!" She wanted everyone to know a miracle had taken place, so she began proving it by describing the color of my hair, my eyes, and what I was wearing. The congregation went wild. Although the return of her vision did not last long, it is the words she said that remain with me today. "Betty, you were meant to see this happen. I am nothing more than an old lady. But you, my dear, are capable of picking up the cross and following Jesus throughout your life. Never forget what you have seen here today."

The commotion that erupted lasted for an hour. Everyone was coming up to kiss and embrace the old lady and me. The outpouring of love in church that evening was life altering for a young girl like me. At nearly ten years of age, I was open to most anything that meant change. Brother Kline and his wife could see I had become overwhelmed by the entire experience. I was taken downstairs to a prayer room where we went over everything that had happened that evening. I told them I had come along merely because I had been hungry, but now I was hungry for the Lord. Everyone in the room knelt and prayed with me for deliverance from my difficulties.

Afterwards, I was provided with food to eat. When I finally left the church that evening, I felt as if I were floating on a cloud. From that day on, I always tried to make it to church on Sundays. I started to take Marion along with me. She received the Lord wonderfully. Not only that, Brother Ernie became her boyfriend for a brief period. Over the time I remained involved, the church hosted ice skating parties, picnics, and countless other activities held all for us young people. The family I made at that church helped me to overcome some really lonely times in my early life.

At home, I prayed out loud in front of the bathroom mirror until my mother thought I had lost my mind. She would scream, "Oh, for Christ's sake, get the hell out of there and shut up." I was not about to explain what it meant to me. It probably wasn't possible to explain anyway. When she would turn to me and say, "Don't tell me any God would let us live like this." I could only kiss her and smile. I looked after mama, and now the Lord looked after me.

Amateur contests became the craze when a man by the name of *Major Bowes* started radio's best-known talent show, *The Major Bowes Amateur Hour*. Years later, the Bowes show became simply *The Original Amateur Hour* on both the radio and TV, and a few years after that, the TV show was hosted by *Ted Mack*.

As a consequence of the extremely popular Bowes show, local amateur shows started springing up in theaters and on local radio stations throughout America. I continued to sing on street corners and anywhere else I could take home some money to mama. Amateur shows were just one more opportunity, so I began to enter every one of them I could find in the Detroit area. There were never any big prizes. Usually, the winner would only receive a dollar or two. I didn't enter so much for the money as I did for the experience. Secondly, I always felt someone might see me performing, and that would be my ticket to fame and fortune.

Pretty much anything went at these amateur shows. They were set up specifically for the audience to get a real laugh. Guys were planted all over to hurl insults and to taunt the performer. If the audience booed you loudly, a guy with a great big hook would come out from the wings and yank you off the stage. The real fun for the audience was in the extent to which they could embarrass you. The local shows were often fixed with all kinds of stunts. At some contests, you had to eat a pie with your hands tied behind your back. The first one finished ran to the microphone to do their number. There were no rehearsals.

After arriving at a given time, you were shoved out on stage when it was your turn. You'd then tell the guy playing the piano what song you were going to sing and tell him in what key. I always stuck with one song, *Some of These Days*. I developed a song and a style, and stuck with it.

The amount of applause from the audience chose the winner. I really enjoyed the amateur shows, because I got the opportunity to try out different ways of getting the best reaction out of the audience. The applause was always my barometer of what worked and what didn't. Sometimes a singer could even develop a sort of following from one amateur show to the next. It was the first time people actually remembered who I was. Now, all I needed was for that special someone to come along and carry me off to stardom.

I managed to win fairly many contests. I'd take my bows, grab my money, and be on my way. When I rushed home to tell mama my good news, I was always prouder of the small amount I was paid from the contest than all the nickels and dimes I made on the street corners and booze joints. Unfortunately, mama was usually passed out. I seldom got to share my joy of winning with her.

This kind of thing went on for several years; it was my way of helping to put food on our table and booze in mama's hands. Mama had been laid off at the plant, and she would get work if and when she was able, but nothing secure.

By the time I was twelve, the *Great Depression* had a firm grip on our country. Families could not receive public assistance if a man lived in the house. In order for wives to receive government assistance for themselves and their children, men from the families took to riding freight trains across the country. *Hobo* camps were set up and the men were forced to take whatever temporary work they could find.

During this time, I also started to sing in many of the clubs throughout Detroit. Places like The Cave, The Nut House, and The Continental in downtown Detroit are where I really started to hone my craft. I think it was really more my style of singing, rather than my actual voice, that grabbed the attention of my audiences. Marion sang on and off in various places, but it seemed she was never as driven to do it as I was. Nevertheless, she had made enough of a name for her to earn some good money for an evening's work. Marion quit high school a year before graduation to help out supporting our family. She got a job at a local drug store, but it seemed she never managed to bring much money home from there after spending much of her paycheck on items for herself. A few years later, I dropped out of school after completing the tenth grade. I managed to convince Marion to join me in a singing sister act, but that didn't last too long. I guess our styles just weren't compatible on stage. After all, Marion had a much more refined singing style than I.

At fifteen, I felt I was on the verge of something big. Another contest came along. This one was really important; first prize allowed you to perform for an entire week at the Greystone. *The Greystone Ballroom* just happened to be the biggest and the best in downtown Detroit. I entered, and naturally I won. I was a big smash.

The Greystone had a bouncer by the name of Charlie Stanton. To me, he was the George Raft of Detroit. He was very sleek, almost patent leather sleek. Charlie chewed gum and looked at you out of the corner of his eye. I rode the street car down to the Greystone on Friday nights. When I arrived, Charlie would look at me and say, "Hiya, doll." Charlie was as high as a man could reach on my totem pole. He was beautiful.

I loved to stand around the bandstand and watch as the crystal prism slowly turned overhead. The sax section would blare out their notes, and Charlie would be standing up front watching everything going on in the place. The entire time, spotlights streamed down all around him. If kids danced too wildly, Charlie told them to get off the dance floor, and they listened. Charlie was *the* man.

Somehow Charlie Stanton claimed he knew the band leader, Tommy Dorsey. I was just this fifteen year old girl; who was I to question his connections? Besides, he promised that he could arrange an audition for me with Dorsey in Chicago. I thought if Tommy Dorsey could just get a look at my style, I might be able to make a really good connection. After I closed the gig I had won in the contest at the Greystone, Charlie offered to drive me to Chicago for the meeting. It was the middle of winter, and the roads were very icy as we slowly drove out of Detroit. After a few miles, I fell asleep while Charlie continued to drive. The next thing I recollect, my mother was looking down at me as I laid in a hospital bed back in Detroit.

Charlie had lost control of the car on the ice and was dead. I suffered a serious concussion. The press swarmed all around my hospital room in an attempt to interview me, but my mother kept them away. The newspapers refused to let the story alone. Every inference was made that Charlie had attempted to take a child across state lines for purposes other than an audition with Dorsey.

It had been a big scandal in the papers. I felt very guilty because my driving ambition to succeed had caused me to do whatever I thought necessary to get what I wanted. One of the deceiving things I found necessary to do was tell Charlie I was eighteen instead of fifteen when I first met him. You see, my burning desire to remove myself from the slum life I was living superseded everything. It's important to also mention, because of the insecurity I harbored over my dysfunctional relationship with mama and Marion, I figured if I could make it big, I could win more of the love from them I thought I was being denied.

Nevertheless, in this instance with Charlie, the price I ended up paying in my attempt to land an audition had been way too dear.

Now Charlie was dead, and I was laid up in a hospital bed. However, the worst part of all; I had allowed Charlie to have his way with me. I was young and foolish, and unable to say no in exchange for the help Charlie was going to give. I felt as if I had been a tomato, and Charlie squeezed the life out of me between his fingers. There's nothing you can do; no way to put it back together again. That's what can happen to a poor kid from the slums when you don't know any better. I prayed to the Lord for forgiveness.

In addition, at the age of fifteen, I began singing with three guys who had a small band. I don't even remember how I met Frank Winegar. He had a sax and a trumpet player, and I became the singer in his small band. We would do a show at the Rowe Hotel in Grand Rapids on Saturday nights. Frank was from Grand Rapids, so after the show, I would stay in the big two-story house he shared with his elderly mother. Often, we would do gigs in other places from Detroit to Lansing. The band liked my style. I would start out by singing quite calmly. After awhile, I would let loose by jumping high in the air and really begin belting out my song. I wasn't afraid to do much of anything when it came to my singing and dancing. The important thing for me about working with these guys happened one day when Frank casually suggested we all go to New York and try out our luck. Up until now, Detroit had been the center of my performing universe. Frank opened up my eyes to going after the big times, instead of waiting for them to come to find me.

When I approached the subject at home, mama really wasn't bothered by the idea of my taking off for New York. She probably realized I would go with or without her approval. I had always made my own small decisions; I was finally old enough to act upon my big ones. So with little hesitation, I and Frank's band of three were all in agreement. One pre-dawn morning, while the sky was still dark, the four of us headed off to New York City in a borrowed car, with a four-day supply of mama's fried chicken, and less than two hundred dollars between us.

Chapter Six

We drove into Manhattan on a crisp autumn morning. In no time at all, we had secured a few rooms so far uptown it was difficult for me to believe we were still in the same city. It was far off the beaten track, in a place where the bright lights and glamour did not abound, but the rent had gone easy on our nest egg. It took me a while to navigate my way around the city. It was so much bigger than any place I had ever been before. In spite of everything, without a doubt we were in New York, and I had no misgivings about our ability to find work and become a part of this vibrant city.

I began making rounds of every booking agent and nightclub in town. After a couple of weeks, I began to worry when none of us could come up with any solid leads. Swiftly, the money we had arrived with began to disappear. To ease my discouragement, I would take the subway downtown and walk around Broadway, just to feel like I belonged in this magical place. We diligently continued to make our rounds daily. Eventually, our determination paid off when an agent found us a job in a small club. The booking was secured for one night only, in order to try us out. If we fit in and were liked, an extended engagement was not only possible, but probable. Our audience loved us; we were an instant smash. Backstage we were taking a break between sets, and wallowing in praise from the club manager, when someone knocked on the dressing room door. As a man entered the room, we turned silent. I joked, "Boy, do you look official. What did we do, rob a bank?" Everyone in the room burst into laughter, but I instantly knew something was up.

"It's nothing, kids," the club manager said in an assuring manner. "This man here is from the Musician's Union. All he probably wants is to see your union cards."

As we looked at each other nervously, we all said in unison, "Our union cards, what union cards?"

The club manager's face turned ashen white. "Oh no, this ain't happening? I knew I should have checked... I could lose my club license over this."

The official from the Musicians Union spoke for the first time. "Calm down. Hold on just a minute. This isn't the end of the world. You three guys *do* need to be in New York for at least six months before you can apply for a union card. However, I'll tell you what. You're pretty damned good at what you do, so I don't see you having any trouble."

One of the guys from the band piped in, "But what are we supposed to do for money for the next six months?"

The union rep shot back, "Come on now, we have musicians like you three who come to New York every single day of the week. I always tell them the same thing. If you want this bad enough, I suggest you take any kind of job you can find. Do you boys know how to wash dishes? If not, you better learn. That's more than likely what you'll be doing for the next six months. Sorry gang, but those are the rules." With that he tipped his hat and left.

"Aw, come on, fellas, snap out of it. Maybe I can get a job with some song-plugger. They're always looking for people to sell their tunes. I've already met a few of them who like the way I sound. I'm sure one of them will give me a job. What do you say, huh?"

Frank, the piano player, said, "Okay, Betty. We'll hang around as long as we can. If things don't work out, we can always go home. We know we can find work there." Everybody shook hands in agreement. Somehow I got the feeling their determination to succeed was nothing like mine. As we said goodbye to the club manager, I had the strange feeling we had played our last gig together.

"You kids come back here in six months with union cards, and I'll give you work." The club manager had liked us from the start. I was happy we hadn't gotten him into any serious hot water with the union guy. It had been our one and only job together as a band in New York City. Leaving the club, all four of us headed off in separate directions.

I was not about to wash dishes in New York. A union card only applied to the musicians, who were required by law to secure one. I was free to go off and do as I pleased. Eventually, I got lucky and landed a job plugging songs. A *song-plugger* was typically a piano player employed by a music store to promote new music. The pianist played whatever sheet music was sent over to him by the store music clerk. Customers could select any title and have the plugger play it to get a feel for the music before buying it. At the place where I worked, we went one step further. The pianist would accompany me playing the selected song as I sang it. I sang pretty much all day, every day, except on Sundays. Saturdays were our busiest day of the week when people were off of work and out spending their hard earned money.

Jack, the plugger from our store, would make rounds in the evenings at clubs and hotels where bands played. He would take along a folder of new tunes in an attempt to familiarize musicians with brand new music and to sell it. Jack was a struggling composer of sorts; quite a brilliant and likeable guy. He hung around music types during his off time from the store as well. As a consequence of all this hobnobbing, he got to know the popular band leaders like Glenn Miller, Artie Shaw, Benny Goodman, and the Dorsey Brothers. In those days, some pluggers, like Jack, had a substantial amount of influence. After all, this *was* New York City.

One afternoon at work, Jack casually asked, "How would you like to meet Tommy Dorsey?" He looked rather proud of himself to be dropping a name so huge on just a kid. I was fifteen, but as before, eighteen better suited my endeavors while in New York.

"Are you kidding? When is he coming in?"

"No, he's playing at the Astor Roof. I'm going there for dinner, so he can take a look at some new music. Wanna be my date tonight, kid?"

"I'd really like to, but ..." I hesitated. "I don't have a gosh darn thing to wear to a fancy place like the Astor Roof."

"Well, that's easily remedied. We'll pop over to Saks after work. You can pick out whatever you need."

"Yeah, but, I don't have enough money, Jack." My face turned scarlet red. I was playing the helpless girl, and it embarrassed me to whine over such matters.

Jack assured me his intentions did not extend beyond friendship. He told me, "One day, kitten, you're going to be working places like the Astor Roof. I just want you to get a good look around the place before that happens. Don't worry about the dress, it's my treat."

Jack bought me a beautiful long white chiffon dress to wear that evening. It became my favorite dress ever. Going up the elevator at the Astor Roof, a dame and her husband, who looked really well healed, complimented me on my beautiful dress. I was floating on a cloud. In my head, I quickly said a prayer between floors. "Please let me act like a lady tonight, Lord, and please let Tommy Dorsey like me."

Exiting the elevator, I squeezed Jack's arm so hard, my nails dug right into his skin. He yelped, "Easy, kid, what the hell?"

"Sorry, Jack. I'm just afraid this is all a dream, and unless I hang on real tight, it just might all go away."

Jack laughed. "Okay, kid, let me prove to you it's not a dream. At the end of a number, we made our way over to the front of the bandstand. Tommy Dorsey smiled when he spotted Jack and reached down to shake his hand. Tommy's eyes looked me over from head to toe, as he said in a taunting fashion, "Hey, Jackie boy, sure looks like you're doing great tonight..."

I was planted in one spot, unable to move or speak. Jack said, "Oh, I'm sorry, Tommy, I'd like you to meet a friend of mine. This is Betty."

Tommy smiled. "A pleasure, I'm Tommy Dorsey... Jack, you really need to teach her a bit of English. What country did you say she's from?" Tommy seemed to be a really easy going sort of fella and somewhat of a comedian. "Hey, I'll join you at your table after this set. Try teaching her a few lines, Jack...and start with hello."

I couldn't get over meeting anyone as famous as Tommy Dorsey. As Jack and I walked over to our table, I was struck by the memory of Charlie Stanton, the bouncer at Detroit's Greystone, who once promised to get me an audition with Dorsey. My memory was bitter sweet. Even so, it was important at the moment that I stop acting like a little star stuck girl from Michigan, and start acting like a young lady. After all, here I was in New York City, and Tommy Dorsey was coming over to sit at my table.

When Tommy finally joined us, I was in little danger of passing out. This time I was sitting down. I was just beginning to feel a bit more comfortable, when suddenly, Dorsey leaned over and half-whispered into Jack's ear, "Hey, man, isn't this quail a little young?" I pretended not to hear.

"Sure she is," Jack whispered back, "but isn't she a beauty? And, brother, can she sing." I had the distinct impression Mr. Dorsey wasn't at all interested in my voice.

After a slight lull in the conversation, Tommy turned to look directly at me, and asked, "Say, we're having a few people over this weekend. Why not let Jack here bring you along? Jackie, you know where my place is up in Greenwich, don't you?" Jack nodded his head yes in acknowledgment.

Suddenly, I became very serious. "I'm sorry to bring it up, Mr. Dorsey, but what about your wife?"

Tommy laughed. He was having fun playing his little game with me. "Oh beautiful, rest assured, my wife will be there. She wouldn't have it any other way." He gave Jack a fast wink. "But of course, she can't be in all the rooms at the same time, if you catch my drift."

I had made a real fool out of myself. Not much could be said for my attempt to act like a lady that evening. As Jack took me home in the cab, he assured me Mr. Dorsey had not only found me to be amusing, but also charming in my naïveté.

Before dropping me off, Jack also imparted something that made me feel more comfortable about the entire evening. "I don't think Tommy Dorsey would invite anyone he didn't like up for the weekend, do you, Betty?"

Jack and I drove to Tommy's lavish home up in Greenwich, Connecticut. We enjoyed a wonderful and relaxing weekend with Tommy, his wife Mildred, and their two children. I even had the chance to sing a few numbers during cocktails before dinner. A few of the men guests in attendance showed some interest in my singing.

On our way back to the city from Connecticut, I told Jack a few of the male guests at the Dorsey's thought I had a really unique sound. "I think it's possible I might land a singing gig from one of them," I mentioned.

Jack suddenly turned his head in my direction. "Look at me, kid." With the stern voice of a father he started in, "Wake up little girl! Not one of those guys was interested in you for your voice. Do you get me?" Jack calmed down and continued on. "Look, doll, there are girl singers all over the place older than you who know every trick of the trade. You start messing in the big times, and you are going to get walked all over. Betty, you are way too young for this."

"I know, Jack, what should I do?" Jack's words made me feel like I had just been hit head-on by a truck.

"By the way, while we're on the subject of your age, just how old are you anyway, Betty? I didn't fall for you telling me you were eighteen from day one. You're lucky I'm not one of those thugs who doesn't stop and think first before acting. So what is it, how old are you anyway?"

I blurted it out. "I'm almost sixteen! *Satisfied?*"

Jack looked weak. "Jesus, Mary, and Joseph, what have you been thinking, little girl?"

"I'll tell you what you're going to do, and you listen to me good. I'm going to wait for you to pack up all your stuff, and then you and I are off to Penn Station. When we get there, I'll buy you a ticket, and your little ass is getting on the first train back home to Detroit and your mother. You need to forget everything you *think* you know about show business. I don't mean to hurt you, but you just don't have what it takes."

Never in my life had I received fatherly advice. It was the first time I ever remember not arguing back and ending up with things my way. Suddenly, I wished I had a father like

Jack. I had never seen him as anything but a friend, but now I knew for sure what he meant to me. As I bid Jack farewell, he kissed me softly on my forehead. Tears were streaming down my face as I stepped off the platform and boarded the train. I looked back and said tenderly, "See ya, pops."

Jack's eyes were glossed over with tears. As he waved goodbye, he said one final thing, "Someday Betty, maybe someday..."

I traveled in the coach car on my way home. The seats were made of wicker, not the most comfortable things in the world. Jack had bought me some cheese sandwiches at the station; I nibbled on them when I got hungry. Maybe Jack was right. My mother always said my plans to make it big were all a dream. As the train clacked its way toward Detroit, I had a lot of time to think. Although I had suffered a real setback, I told myself my resolve to make it had not changed. Whatever the future might have in store for me, I was ready. I almost managed to convince myself it was a good idea to return to Detroit in order to give myself a chance to regroup. No harm done. I had made it to New York. I had met Jack and Tommy Dorsey, and had enjoyed dinner on the Roof at the Astor Hotel. That's more than most people would ever be able to lay claim to in corny old Detroit. It seemed like it took an entire week for that train to get me home.

Mama knew I was coming. I had wired her from New York before I left. When the train came to a stop in Detroit, she was there on the platform waiting. I spotted her through the window from inside the train. A true feeling of love came over me for this tragic woman. I gathered up all my belongings before stepping down off the train and onto the station platform. Immediately, I spotted a familiar troubled look on her face; she was also half-loaded. My fuzzy warm feeling for her escaped through the top of my head and drifted off into space.

"Betty, Jesus Christ, I thought you'd never get here."

"Mom, what's the matter? Don't you feel well?" The role reversal was automatic.

"No, Betty, nothing as simple as that." She looked worried. "I'm almost afraid to tell you."

I instantly became annoyed, "Gilbert is back, isn't he?"

"No, that's not it. That's finished, baby. It's about your sister."

My own thoughts of New York and my life there flew out the window of the cab. "Tell me what happened. I promise, whatever it is, mama, I'll fix it."

"Well, it seems your sister, Marion, has taken up with a mobster. Worse than that, I think she loves the guy, *and* he's a married man. You should see the fur coat he's given her, and, oh my Lord, all those beautiful clothes..."

"Mom, when is she supposed to see this guy again?" I had already formulated a plan in my head.

"Why, tonight, honey. He's supposed to pick her up and take her to the club where she's working, I guess..." Mama had a hard time following my thought process when I moved too fast.

"Okay, the plans have changed. Marion will leave for the club early, and I will meet lover boy and set him straight about a few things."

"Oh, Betty, do you think that's safe?"

"There's only one thing that can scare me, mama, that's an audience."

When we arrived at the apartment, Marion was in the bathroom doing her makeup. I called in, "Hi ya, sis. Mama tells me you have a new boyfriend."

"Mama's been blabbing her big mouth again, huh? She doesn't like him, but I'm in love with the guy, and nothing or nobody is going to change that."

As I approached her in the bathroom, I noticed a real change in Marion. She now possessed an exterior toughness that wasn't there before I left for New York. I could smell booze on her, too, as I leaned forward to give her a peck on the cheek. "Marion, you know I love you. What's happened to make you so defiant? That's not you, sis. And why are you drinking so much? Can't you see what alcohol has done to mama?"

"Oh, come on now, Betty, knock off the bullshit. When did you get so high and mighty? You come in here acting like some little virgin or something. Next, you'll be telling me you were miss goody two-shoes in New York, huh?" Marion glanced over and looked at me squarely in the eyes. "I'll be damned! You didn't get laid in New York, did you?" Marion poked her head out the bathroom door and yelled down the hall, "Hey mom, we need to get Betty stuffed and send her off to the Smithsonian." Marion motioned for me to get out of the bathroom and then slammed the door after me.

I could see now why mama looked so concerned when she met me at the station. Mama didn't have any idea what to do; Marion seemed to be going totally out of control. Where men were concerned, my sister ignored any advice, choosing instead to dive in head first with both eyes closed. For the very first time, mama and I plotted together in an attempt to stop Marion from making the worst mistake of her life.

When Marion finally came out of the bathroom, mama said, "Marion, your boyfriend called. He's running late. He said you should go on ahead to the club, and he would pick you up after your show."

"*Now* you tell me!" Marion screamed. "Okay, I'm out the door, or I'll be late. Anyway, I don't wanna stick around and be the first one to see Betty's halo slip."

"Marion," I said, "your words can't hurt me. I know deep inside you are doing all of this to escape the slums, just like me. I understand, really I do. Now go, do your show, and break a leg." Marion didn't say a word as she walked out the door, but the tears in her eyes told me what I needed to hear.

Mama helped me fix myself up with some makeup and one of Marion's nice dresses. If I was going to be a stand-in for my sister, the least I could do is look half-way decent for the mobster. I also wanted to look as old as possible. My thinking was, the older I looked, the more serious he would take me. After all, I had a few things to say to this guy.

I no sooner finished getting all dolled up, when I heard a car horn blow. "Mama, is that him already?"

She ran over to the window and glanced down at the street in front of our building. "That's him alright. Hold on just a second, listen to this..."

I had no idea what she meant, so I stood perfectly still, almost holding my breath waiting for what might happen.

"Hey, tomato, it's me, big boy. You ready?" He hollered all the way up from the street.

Suddenly, I felt slightly unnerved. "Quick, mama, what's this lug's name again."

"It's Johnny. Good luck, honey," she muttered as she closed the door of the apartment behind me.

As Johnny opened the car door for me to get in, it took him a double take before he caught on, I wasn't who he was expecting. His jaw dropped as he asked, "Well, hello there, now who's this new doll?"

"Hello, Johnny. I'm Marion's sister, Betty. Marion is sorry, she had to rush off, but I really wanted to meet you anyway. I'm sure there's no problem if I tag along with you to the club, is there? Wow, this is some beautiful car you have here. I bet your wife really enjoys driving in it." I attempted to be sweet, but directly to the point.

"Hey, what are you gettin' at, pipsqueak?" Johnny acted surprised, but he knew exactly where I was going with this. He could sense right away that I was on to him, but he continued to play dumb.

"I just don't think my sister is right for you, Johnny. I bet your wife would feel the same way I do...right?"

"Your sister and I really got a good thing goin' right now. Besides, I got a lot of dough invested in her."

"That may well be, Johnny, but by the time my mother and I have a little talk with your wife, you may change your mind about deciding to see my sister any longer."

"Johnny looked over at me, and with a slight grin in the corner of his mouth that held the toothpick, he managed to mumble out, "Yah, sure, whatever..." It was just that easy. I knew then and there it was over between them. He hadn't been serious about my sister at all, he was simply playing around. Marion was the one who was going to be hurt over this. She would also be furious with me for a long time to come. It didn't matter, what I had accomplished was way more important in the long run. Anyway, she hadn't acted very cordial toward me in quite a long time.

I was surprised to learn Marion had become a regular at The Nut House. It was a cheesy joint, but it sure was popular. As it turned out, with my absence from the Detroit club scene, Marion had come into demand as a singer. Johnny and I were greeted at the door. We managed a table right down front because of who he was. Marion was in the middle of a song, but had seen us come in together. After her set was over, she stormed over to our table. "What the hell are you doing here with Johnny? I should have expected this out of you. Your first night back from New York, why not move in on your sister's territory, huh? Johnny, please get Betty the hell out of here, now."

Marion was really upset, and rightfully so. What I had done was pretty awful. Johnny got up and escorted me out of the club. Back in his car, he looked over at me and said in a playful manor, "You know, you sure are a lot cuter than your sister when you get mad."

"Don't start with me, Johnny," I barked. "Anyway, I'm not available. I'm lookin' to get myself out of this crummy town just as fast as I can."

Johnny was really being sincere. "No, I mean, I have no doubt you would do exactly as you said you would and call my wife. Wouldn't you, kid? Aren't you scared of nothin' or nobody?" It seemed as if he really wanted a straight answer.

"Yeah, I'm scared of an audience," I confided. "See, I aim to be this big star, I just can't seem to catch a decent break." Johnny seemed to be interested in what I had to say; at least he was listening. "Hey, look over there Johnny, it's the Continental Café. Take me in there, big boy. I wanna show you what I'm talking about."

The Continental Café was across the street from the Book Cadillac Hotel, the most exclusive hotel in Detroit. It was the hotel where Beanie had often pleasured her wealthiest tricks. I had frequented the place many times in the past acting as her lookout.

The Continental was a sleek nightclub, reportedly mob affiliated. I had worked the place on several occasions, and was always asked by the leader of the house band to come up on the stage and sing with them any time I came in. Johnny and I swept into the place like we owned it. When I was spotted, someone yelled out, "Betty, where the hell have you been? Get up there and sing us a song." It didn't take much persuasion to ever get me up to perform. I greeted the crowd as I walked up to the front. The band leader looked at me and said, "What'll it be, Betty?"

"*A-Tisket A-Taskit*, come on, boys, let's do it." I was all wound up from everything that had happened that evening. As I started in with the song, it felt really good to release some of my pent-up energy. Johnny was out there in the crowd too; I decided to really let them have it!

A-tisket a-tasket

A brown-and-yellow basket
I sent a letter to my mommy
On the way I dropped

I dropped it, I dropped it
Yes, on the way I dropped it
A little girlie picked it up
And put it in her pocket...

The crowd went crazy! I danced and jumped around like there was no tomorrow. It felt so good to be back on stage doing what I enjoyed most in life, entertaining.

A tisket- a -tasket
I lost my yellow basket
and if that girlie don't return it
I don't know what I'll do.

(Was it green?) No, no, no, no
(Was it red?) No, no, no, no
(Was it blue?) No, no, no, no
Just a little yellow basket
A little yellow basket...

I delivered exactly what everyone had expected from me. They all knew Betty didn't just get up and sing a song. I sang, I danced, and I climbed the walls. The only thing they didn't know is how far I'd carry it once I got up there. But, of course, neither did I. After the number was over, I was frazzled. I needed to sit one out, but promised the audience I would return later to do at least one more song. I searched for Johnny; I was anxious to see what he thought of my performance.

Johnny ran up when he saw me coming. "Christ, kid, you're like a rocket up there. With your talent, I could make a ton of money."

I looked at him with a nasty glare. "Is money all you lugs think about?"

The Maitre d' appeared out of nowhere. "Excuse me Miss Betty, there's a guy here who wants to meet you."

"What guy?" I hadn't been much in demand in New York. This sure came as a welcomed change.

"He's a big band leader, of a society band."

"What's his name?" What did I know of society bands? I was into the swing band style.

"His name is Vincent Lopez, and he asked if you'd be nice enough to join him at his table."

I wasn't sure how long this was going to take. I saw Johnny look down at his wrist watch. "Hey, Johnny," I said. "Why don't you go ahead and meet up with Marion. She'll be done singing at the club pretty soon. Please drive her home and be nice. You'll let her down easy, right?"

After throwing some money down, Johnny got up from the table and grabbed my hand. "See ya around, kid." He wasn't so bad, just not what my sister needed to get wrapped up with if she had any real intention of escaping from the slums.

The Maitre d' pulled out my chair and escorted me over to Mr. Lopez's table. He was sitting with a middle-aged, well-to-do looking couple. The other man rose to his feet when the Maitre d' introduced me, but not Lopez.

"Please, join us. Thanks for coming over. I wanted to talk with you." I sat down and Lopez introduced me to his friends, Mr. and Mrs. Haskell Bliss. "I can't tell you how much I enjoyed your performance. Your style is really different."

"Thank you, Mr. Lopez."

"I have a feeling you could make it in New York. That is, I mean, if you're serious about a singing career. Have you ever been there?"

I laughed out loud. Everyone at the table looked at me as if I had lost my mind. "Mr. Lopez, I just got off the train from New York a couple of hours ago. To tell you the truth, I was there looking to make it big in singing. I ended up back here. Does that tell you anything?"

"It tells me you weren't looking in the right place." Lopez expelled a forced little laugh. "Young lady, I like your spirit. I do believe you've really got something."

Mrs. Bliss quickly jumped in, "Well, whatever you have dear, I hope you don't give it to anyone else."

I laughed at the dame's comment, although I wasn't completely sure it had been a compliment.

Mrs. Bliss continued, "I don't understand how you stand that pace of yours. I have to admit, it wears me out just watching you."

Now I was sure it wasn't a compliment. It was okay though; Lopez seemed to like me a lot. I think he respected me for the belief he could see I had in my own talent.

"Look Betty, we're running a contest for a personality-girl singer. It's at the Fox Theater here, downtown. I would like you to be in it. I'll give you all the details."

I told Lopez, "Sure, I haven't anything to lose." He must have known what he was looking for in a girl singer; otherwise, he wouldn't have given me the time of day. After the way he reacted to my performance at the Continental, I was sure I could win the contest.

What happened after that is all a big blur. All hell broke loose the day I won the contest. It was difficult trying to tie up all kinds of loose ends in a few short hours. Mr. Lopez informed me we would be leaving early that evening en route to my premiere performance with the band at the Palace Theater in Fort Wayne. I already pleaded my case with Mr. Lopez to allow my mother along on the tour. Considering the fact I was really a minor, I don't think he could have made any other decision. When he asked nonchalantly how old I actually was, he turned slightly pale when I told him I was two months shy of my sixteenth birthday.

Marion had a steady singing gig at the *Nut House* in Detroit. Otherwise, I would have found some way to bring her along. I did manage to have Marion meet Mr. Lopez, and he even listened to her sing. Half-heartedly, he agreed to help find her a singing placement if and when that became necessary. Marion and I had become so competitive, I was glad to be leaving Detroit. I figured the town wasn't going to big enough for the two of us if we were intent upon pursuing the same path as singers.

Our leaving meant that Marion would have to find somewhere else to live for awhile. She said it really wasn't going to be a problem. I wondered what new guy she had on the hook to take the place of Johnny. I couldn't worry about it. Mama didn't seem to be in the least bit concerned. Of course, what mama thought was never a true gauge of how things really were. I was tired of making sure Marion was alright. She was a big girl now, and in many ways, she had a lot more going for her than I did.

The band had already boarded the train when our taxi arrived at the depot. Lopez's band manager met us and escorted us to our Pullman car. Mama turned to me, and with tears in her eyes said, "You promised me one day you would be a star so we could leave those horrible slums. Now look, sixty five dollars a week, Betty, do you know how much money that is?" I was really touched by mama's sincerity, especially considering the fact she was stone cold sober from the sheer excitement of everything happening so fast. She gave me a big hug before I went out to meet the boys.

Several of the musicians were sitting around with their instruments. When I walked in, impulsively the guys started to play. I joined in singing along in my own style. After the number finished, several of the guys broke into laughter. One of the guys in the group, Mike Durso, turned to me and said, "There's nothing wrong with your voice, Betty, but you're gonna have to change your style. We just don't play that kind of music."

I replied in an instant, "Don't worry, you will. After all, Lopez hired me after he heard me sing. That's why I'm here, fellas." I was waiting for reactions to what I had said, but we were interrupted by a porter who came down the aisle. I was informed Lopez wanted to see me in his drawing room. I hoped I hadn't come on too strong in front of the guys. I was the new kid on the block, so I had better mind my manners. I thanked the guys and followed the porter.

I knew the boss wanted to discuss a few things about my routine. I wanted to make sure he understood my true excitement and my genuine appreciation for being selected to sing with the band. In my own mind, I couldn't help think how wonderful it was that mama would never have to spit another upholstery tack at the Chrysler plant. It was all too good to be true. However, in just a few moments, I was to learn what it would cost me to sing with the Vincent Lopez Orchestra. Everything in life has its price. I should have known, when something seemed too good to be true, it probably was.

I'd never been in a drawing room; just the name made it sound fancy and important. The porter opened the door and let me in. Lopez was propped up in bed with lots of pillows. He was looking down at a hand full of papers, and still more were scattered on top of his bed. He wore what looked like a velvet smoking jacket. I was pretty impressed. When he heard me enter, he looked up and smiled. "I see you found the train all right. Did your mother get settled in?"

"Yes sir, Mr. Lopez"

"And how are you feeling tonight?"

"Well, I'm just about the happiest girl in the world, sir, thanks to you."

"Good, Betty. I'm so glad, because now I want you to show me how appreciative you really are."

"Any time and any place," I said with confidence. "Actually, Mr. Lopez, that's part of what I wanted to talk to you about. I want to make sure you understand exactly how grateful..."

"That's fine... I just, I mean, I've done some checking into your background and..."

"Whatever you found, Mr. Lopez, I know I can explain."

"That's not... What I meant to say is, from your disagreeable living conditions, I'm sure you must have seen, or been exposed to, well, one would assume that you've been around a lot of sex."

"Boy, have I ever!"

"So you pretty much know what's going on?"

"Yes, sir, and you don't need to worry one bit. That's why I'm so glad to have this opportunity you've given me. I'm here to work, and work hard. You don't have to give it a second thought. I have absolutely no intention of getting involved with any of the guys in the band; I give you my solemn..."

He interrupted me again, "I wasn't really referring to the band. What I was trying to say is, well, we all have to pay a price for things we want... You do understand that, don't you, Betty?"

I looked at him with a puzzled look. His voice got very quiet. Then he spit it out, "Have you ever gone down on a man, Betty?" He shoved his papers aside and threw back the covers from his bed. "If you want to sing with my orchestra, then you'll have to learn to take care of this."

He pushed me to my knees. Everything that had made me not trust men in my life came rushing into my head. There was absolutely nowhere left to turn. My mother was counting on me. For a long time, I had been out to get what I needed to save my mother and myself, at whatever the cost. Now it was time to pay up. I knew what I had to do, and I did it.

When it was over, he cautioned me against ever saying anything to my mother or anyone else. He also told me to stay away from the guys in the band. "If they're nice to you, Betty, they're only after one thing." If I could have gotten away with killing him that night, I would have. I knew I would never be young again after that first night on the train.

There was little doubt, I wanted to run, fast and far. Somehow, I always ended up doing that sort of thing throughout my life. When things didn't go exactly my way, I was ready to throw in the towel and run. Despite what had happened with Lopez, I stayed. I had been hurt, humiliated, and most of all, deceived. Nevertheless, this was the opportunity I had been waiting for. If I played my cards right, Lopez would be a mere stepping stone to my stardom. Then, I would turn my back on this greasy little man for good.

We arrived in Fort Wayne, the place where I was to sing with the Lopez Orchestra for the very first time. After a quick rehearsal that morning, Lopez took me to breakfast at a place called The Berghoff Gardens. It was *the* spot for entertainers in Fort Wayne.

"Would you like ham and eggs, Betty?" Lopez asked.

"No thanks, I'd like a really big steak." At lunch I ordered a second steak, and equally enjoyed my third at dinner after our evening show. I knew Lopez was curious about all the steak. I had already seen him look a bit funny when I ordered my second of the day.

Lopez couldn't stand it a minute longer and abruptly asked, "Betty, what's with this steak kick of yours? Is it a high-protein diet of some kind?"

"No, Mr. Lopez. I'm just so sick and tired of hunting for tiny scraps of meat in stew. I promised myself, if I ever made enough money to afford it, I would eat steak at every meal." Lopez was fascinated by my adolescent reasoning.

My matinee debut with the band didn't go very well. I had been accustomed to audiences going crazy and jumping to their feet at the places I worked in Detroit. I had gone all out for this afternoon crowd. When I finished to very little applause, I nearly died. Lopez dismissed it by saying it would take time for me and the band to work together as a team.

Lopez called the band together before the evening show, specifically to go through my numbers. He asked me to tone down my movements. I think the guys in the band were already starting to complain. After all, I had gone and laid into them the previous night after leaving Detroit. Mike Durso, the trombone player, warned me I needed to change my style. I basically told the band that they needed to change their music. How stupid could I have been? I understood and agreed with what Lopez was saying, but to tone my performance down was easier said than done.

For the evening show, I purposely held back. I toned my act down considerably. It had been a very difficult thing for me to do. The audience reaction wasn't any better than it had been for the matinee. Still, Lopez was patient with me. He made excuses to bolster my confidence. "It's a really tough town, Betty. They can't relate to our type of music." It was obvious to me; something I was doing was causing all the problems. When I became so frustrated, and about ready to toss in the towel, Lopez would say, "Wait until the next show, Betty, you'll wow them then."

When I tried to wow them the next time around, something always came along to stand in my way. It was my bad luck other acts or celebrities in the show always seemed to outshine me. At the Earle Theater in Philadelphia, multi-talented headliner, Benay Venuta, stole all the thunder. I even tried changing my outfits. I bought a blouse, skirt, and saddle shoes to give a boost to my jitterbug image. The outfit earned me less applause than before. Now I was really confused. Lopez seemed to have liked when I sang and danced like crazy; after all he had hired me. Now, he wanted me to tone it down; in essence, stopping me from being who I really was. I became totally disheartened.

At the end of our run in Philly, I had the distinct feeling this was going to be my last date with the band. I just wasn't making it. I could see it in the eyes of Lopez and the band members. Sure enough, Lopez took me aside and said, "Betty, I'm going to give you enough money to take you and your mother back to Detroit. You're just not performing the way I saw you. I've had nothing but complaints about your work from the start, I just couldn't see letting you go until now."

All I could think of saying is, "That's okay." Not until Lopez walked away did I begin to sob uncontrollably. Mike Durso was close by and saw me crying.

"Betty, what's the matter?" There was compassion in his voice.

"I shot back, "Lopez just canned me!"

"Kid, don't feel too bad. It's happened to many girl singers before, and it will happen again." Mike gave me a big hug that showed me he really cared. "I know... Let's go out together and have one hell of a meal before the last show."

I was overwhelmed. This had been the first kind words spoken to me by a member of the band. I wiped away my tears and said, "Okay, Mike, what the heck, it's my last night. Anyway, there's nothing more he can do to me now."

Mike took me to a really lovely restaurant. As we sat and relaxed, I found I could tell him more about myself and my situation. I explained how I was disappointed in myself for one real reason, I would not be able to keep the promise I had made to change my mother's life. I also told him I was really fearful of Lopez, although I tried never to show it. I didn't say a word about the things Lopez had made me do in order to keep my job.

Mike reached his hand across the table in a show of friendship. "Betty, let's have a drink together. It just might pull you out of your blues. Hell, you might be able to go back there for your last show without any fear at all and really be able to show them what you can do."

"Mike," I confessed, "I've never had a drink in my life."

"That's okay. It won't hurt you, Betty. It'll probably just loosen you up."

He didn't know my mother was an alcoholic. We had really kept that under wraps since I joined the band. Mama was on her best behavior because everything was new, and for a change, she was happy. To tell the truth, I was afraid to have a drink; alcohol was such a poison in my family. Considering I was losing my job, and would have the painful job of explaining everything to mama, I threw caution to the wind and said yes.

Mike ordered us something called B&B. It was a small little cocktail on ice; mild to the taste, but I found out it packed a real punch. The first one made me feel warm all over, so I decided to have two more after dinner. It didn't really get me drunk; instead I just lost all of my inhibitions. I couldn't wait to get back to the theatre and give my final performance everything I had.

The band was tuning up as we walked through the door from dinner. Out on stage, I sat in my usual place. Only after the curtain rose, did I decide to change what I had been doing since I started with the band. I went ahead and made believe they were a swing band. I began clapping my hands wildly to the rhythm of the music. Lopez glared over at me to see what I was up to. Suddenly, it was like a whole new setup. When it was time for me to go down to the mike, the audience was already with me. For a change, they were witnessing a singer get into the song before she even sang it. The audience was primed. I jitter-bugged my way on down to the mike to start my song. Instead of just singing *The Dipsy Doodle*, I kicked up a storm with *The Dipsy Doodle*. I shouted, stomped and shrieked. I jumped on the piano, off the piano, and then turned a few somersaults for good measure.

During the sixteen bars where I didn't sing, I screamed out, "Clap along," and the audience did! I ran back to the bandstand and tossed all their sheet music into the air. "They ought to know it by now," I shouted out. Then I went over, picked up Lopez, and swung him around to the rhythm of the music. After I was done, I plunked him back down. I danced back over and launching a flying tackle at the microphone before finally finishing my song. For the first time since singing with the band, I felt the love of the audience swell up over the footlights and take aim directly at me. The applause was deafening. Their eyes twinkled as if to say, "More, kid, please sing more. Don't you know we're on your side?"

It has always been difficult to explain, but at that moment, the crowd actually loved me. If it had been possible, I would have gone down those steps and kissed each of those people in the audience. I made my way back to my seat and sat down. The powerful exhilaration I felt deep within me was just too much to comprehend. I looked over at Mike Duro with tears in my eyes and noticed he also had tears in his.

If all of these special circumstances had never come together in the way they had that evening, I would have been finished. Nevertheless, they did, and the band that never cared for me was now applauding me. Lopez, who had almost managed to destroy my inner being, hugged me and said, "Betty, you were just great! Make sure you do that every show."

When Lopez came over to congratulate me again back stage, everybody was still riding high from our triumphant show. Mike Duro and a few other guys from the band came over to share in the joy. Automatically, everyone began discussing what it was that had made the show so great that evening. The guys all agreed that in order for the band to continue successfully into the future, it was necessary for things to be changed. After what he had just witnessed on stage, Lopez was ready to listen. He realized swing was the new style, and the potential it had for the band. Slowly, because of that night and my performance, the Vincent Lopez Orchestra would never again be the same.

We had kind of a rough start in New Orleans at The Jung Hotel's Tulane Room. After bumping into him on the street, Lopez invited Cary Grant to our opening show. The crowds went wild for Cary, which pretty much ruined the opening for the band. My performance that evening was lost because of the hoopla over Cary, but for the rest of our play date in New Orleans, I started to come into my own. The rough edges started to become more polished. Lopez, despite our past differences, really *taught* me how to become a professional.

When we opened at the Royal Palms in Miami, one of the headliners was Scottish actress and singer, Ella Logan. She appeared in several Broadway shows in the 1930s. Lopez suggested I watch her carefully on stage. He must have known exactly what he was talking about, because I managed to learn a lot about stage style and presence, just from observing her. It wasn't that I wanted to copy anything someone else did, but just by watching the way they did it, I improved my own act. My confidence grew with every new date we played. I began watching other seasoned performers and absorbed everything I could. Suddenly, other singers started watching me for tips, especially when I performed *The Dipsy Doodle*.

Ella Logan and I became very close friends. She became my method teacher. I noticed how she would vary her movements each night according to the reactions of the audience. What I learned just from watching her proved invaluable to my singing career, not to mention how essential it would be to my movie career when I eventually reached Hollywood.

One night, Ella Logan got sick, and was unable to do her show. Lopez knew she had taught me her routines, and asked me if I thought I could go on and do them. This was really the big time. It made me really nervous, but I agreed. For the first time in my career, I went out on stage in a head-liner spot. I was surrounded by all those beautiful lights; I still love them to this day. The spotlight was pink, the borders were magenta and blue, and they enveloped me totally. I sang with all my heart, and used every move I had learned. I was a success that evening in Miami, but I knew nothing you do can make you anybody until you do it in New York.

I was really excited when Lopez told us we might be ending our tour in New York. That's the place I really wanted to be. Billy Rose expressed interest in having us for his new show at the *Casa Manana*. Before we got to New York, we did a series of one-nighters to keep us on our toes and to assure we were in top shape when we got there. Lopez also approached me about changing my professional name to something else. At the time, I was going by the name Betty Jane Darling. Lopez was into numerology and wanted a name that had just the correct rhythm and number balance to attract attention. The name he came up with for me was *Betty Hutton*.

With Vincent Lopez, 1939.
Photo: Betty's private collection, The Betty Hutton Estate

Taken during the Lopez Band days, 1939.
Photo: by Murray Korman, NY, The Betty Hutton Estate

Chapter Seven

Since that triumphant evening where I realized my singing breakthrough, Lopez made some style changes in his music. It had been a turning point in my career and a new start for the band. Lopez came up with something he called, suave-swing. It was a funny phrase, but pretty much summed up what it was - a little less sophistication and a bit more swing. It was his way of coming half way for all of us without completely compromising himself. All this change was in preparation for our opening at *Billy Rose's Casa Manana*.

The Casa Manana was housed in the old Earl Carroll Theatre at Seventh Avenue and Fiftieth Street. Earl Carroll was a theatrical director and producer who built the building, and had named it after himself. He demolished it in 1930, bought the adjacent building, and rebuilt it as a bigger theatre and movie palace. Unfortunately, the weekly running costs proved too huge, and foreclosure followed. By 1933, the property had become a nightclub. Billy Rose took it over for his Casa Manana in 1936 because of its great location.

During the afternoon rehearsal for our opening night performance, I was tense. All these well-known professional stars from vaudeville and the club circuits made me feel uneasy about my own abilities. This was something I learned to live with throughout my career. One moment I was on top, enjoying all the love and adoration the audience could shower upon me. The next minute, I was wondering how the hell I managed to make it as far as I had. It was difficult, considering all the great talent out there defusing mine. It was all fear on my part. Fear that I wouldn't make it, and that I would be rejected. I also had a constant fear I would end up right back in the slums where I had started.

The new show at Billy Rose's featured the talents of comic actor, Lou Holtz, torch singer, Helen Morgan, dog trainer, Paul Sydell, tap dancer, Georgie Tapps, ballerina dancer, Harriet Hoctor, and of course, the Vincent Lopez Orchestra. Rehearsals started with Lou Holtz, the emcee of the show, introducing the wonderful Helen Morgan. She starred as Julie LaVerne in the original Broadway musical production of *Show Boat* in 1927, and became a wildly popular torch singer. She walked on to the stage in a beautiful white gown, carrying her signature long white handkerchief. She walked right up to the mike, looked directly into the spotlight, and didn't move as she sang her biggest hit, *He's Just My Bill.* The way she could hold an audience was extraordinary. She finished her song and turned to gracefully exit, but instead, after a few steps she fell right on her face. I screamed and ran toward the stage. I was sure she had tripped on the hem of her dress and had hurt herself. Lopez caught me and quickly pulled me over to the side. He whispered, "Betty, leave it alone. She's a drunk."

The first thing I thought of was how much she reminded me of my poor mother. It was obvious no one understood her, or even cared to. Billy Rose yelled, "Get her off the stage and sober her up. Goddamnit, if she's like this tonight, she won't open." Helen was treated exactly the same way my mother was treated when she was drunk, with contempt. The stage hands helped Helen off and into her dressing room. Immediately, Lou Holtz returned and continued in with his jokes as if nothing had happened. It was one of the first lessons I had learned about the toughness of show business; the show must go on. I ran back to Helen's dressing room and knocked on her door. When I entered, she looked up at me with eyes that seemed as terrified as those of a trapped animal. I hugged her tightly and said, "Helen, tonight you are going to be just great." She made me promise to keep an eye on her so she wouldn't drink too much. I said a little prayer out loud as I continued to hold this wounded woman in my arms. Helen went on stage that night, and she was fine, but eventually time took its toll. Helen Morgan collapsed onstage during a performance of *George White's Scandals of 1942* in Chicago, and died of cirrhosis of the liver in October 1941. She was forty-one years of age.

Opening night was spectacular; our show was very well received. I felt so lucky to be a part. Mama and I were backstage peeking out through the curtains. What we witnessed was the biggest, most fantastic crowd we had ever seen. My unbelievable dream had become a reality. Mama and I were standing on one of the most famous stages in New York City at the time.

Mama was with me every night at the theater. It got to the point where I couldn't leave her by herself. The few times I did, it took me hours to go from bar to bar at night to locate her. One time, I found her drunk and bragging to all the folks in the place about me. I could have died. I didn't dare to leave her home alone; there was no telling what she might do. From then on, I had a house seat for her every night. She knew to behave herself in the club. We befriended the waiters and other staff we met backstage. We used to shoot craps with many of them at the rare times when we had minutes to spare. They all loved my mother, and when I wasn't around, they did me the favor of watching her like a hawk.

It was about this time I found a red fox coat in a pawn shop. Tears form in my eyes as I recollect it, I knew immediately mama would love that coat. On sixty-five dollars a week, it was awfully difficult to come up with extra money. Even so, I was able to make small payments of five dollars each week until mama had her fur. When I finally got to put it across her shoulders, I remember vividly the look of joy that washed over her face. Mama actually managed to stop drinking for two entire days because she was so pleased.

We had been working the Casa Manana for several weeks, and I was a pretty big hit on the bandstand. However, one fateful night, the opening act for the third and final show of the night, a group of jugglers, didn't show up. Everyone backstage was frantic. Lou Holtz ran to Billy Rose and told him the bad news. Billy Rose swore in several languages, "God damned show people. They're no good, you can never trust them."

Lou Holtz calmed him down and said, "Billy, I've got one hell of an idea. Why don't we put Lopez's girl singer on?"

"Have you lost your mind, Lou?" Billy Rose grumbled. "How can a girl singer open the show?"

"Have you watched her, Billy? When she gets up there to sing, no one even gets out on the floor to dance. They just sit with their mouths open and watch her!"

Naturally, Billy hadn't seen me. He never stayed for the end of the show, which is when I was on. He had no idea I was even alive. However, tonight he was desperate. I happened to be onstage finishing up my song from the second show of the evening, when down the isle came Billy Rose. I'll never forget his walk. It was the kind of walk that said get out of my way, I'm important. No wonder he was known as "The Little Napoleon of Showmanship." Billy pushed through the crowd and came to a standstill right where he could watch me. He looked me over as if I were a prize cow at a Wisconsin county fair. He watched me for a minute, then turned his head to Lou Holtz and nodded yes. I watched them the entire time I was singing, but had no idea what was in the works.

When our set was over, Lou rushed over to Lopez and explained what was going on. Lopez was the one to inform me I was slated to open the show. The opening act is really fairly insignificant, since it is mainly intended to warm up the audience while they are finishing up their dinner. I became very worried. Here I had been given a real chance, and yet, I figured no one would even pay any attention to me. I felt the cards were stacked against me in this unique opportunity to finally prove myself. All I could do is kneel in prayer right there behind the curtains, and ask the Lord for his help.

One by one, the waiters in the place descended upon me backstage with hugs and kisses, and wished me the best of luck. Word sure got around the club fast. Suddenly, I had a revelation. I turned to the head waiters and asked them to keep all the other wait staff off the floor while I performed. My request was strictly against the rules. Waiters were required to finish up the food service by clearing the tables during opening act. They knew exactly what I was asking. If there was no clamor of dishes or staff rushing back and forth, it would be much easier for the audience to give their full attention to my performance.

I asked the Maitre d' to sit my mother at her usual table where I could keep an eye on her. When the opening fanfare started to play, I took a deep breath and walked out on to the stage to do my number. There were no spotlights on me. Instead, all the house lights remained on, presumably to afford the waiters the time to finish up the food service. I began singing, *A-Tisket, A-Tasket*. I might not have been the greatest singer in the world, but I sure as hell was the loudest. The audience couldn't help but look up at me from their meals and pay me notice. Then came the eighteen bars where the singer usually sat down to allow the band to show off their stuff, but I didn't sit down at all. Instead, I jumped around and danced like mad. I threw the music into the air and yelled, much as I had done on what was supposed to have been my last evening with the band. Well, to my amazement, the house lights went down and up came the spots. Billy Rose was no fool. He must have cued the light men to catch me and attempt to keep me in the spot. I came back to the mike and finished up my number. After it was done, everyone stood up and applauded. However, it was clear from the audience response; they didn't want me to leave the stage.

Suddenly, there were screams for more from the crowd. I turned to Lopez and told him to cue *The Dipsy Doodle*. The spotlight focused in so I was the only thing they could see on stage. This time there were only eight bars left of the band's playing before my singing, so I ran back and picked up Lopez and swung him all over the stage. Lopez was big and round. Seeing him fly around the stage caused pandemonium in the theatre.

Every time I took a bow and started to exit the stage, there were cries for more. I looked at Lopez for guidance, but all he could do is shrug his shoulders.

One of the guys in the band yelled out, "Hey Betty, why don't you sing the new number. The great lyricist, songwriter, and musician, Sammy Cahn, had written a song for me. It was a take on *Old Man Mose Is Dead*, called, *Old Man Mose Ain't Dead*. I had never before performed it in public. I looked toward Lopez, who once again simply shrugged his shoulders. After it was over, the crowd again went wild with applause, followed by calls for more.

I didn't know what to do. I had gone through all my really good rehearsal numbers. What I did next came to me spontaneously. The curtains were about thirty feet high. I took a good hold of the big red velvet one, and with a running jump, I swung myself out over the crowd and landed back perfectly at center stage. I released the curtain and was standing there in a position which made me look like a ballerina in a graceful bow. Then, I ran as fast as I could off into the wings.

Lou Holtz hurried out on stage after me and raised his hands to quiet down the crowd. When it was finally still enough to speak, Lou started, "Ladies and gentlemen, you have witnessed something truly amazing here tonight. When something this extraordinary happens to someone in show business, we say *A Star is Born*." Mom had joined me back in the wings where we fell into each other's arms. I had no idea at the time how this one performance would set the wheels of my career in New York into motion. For now, I was simply full of gratitude to have been such a great success. For me, this had been a most spectacular debut into New York Theatre.

Everyone was making such a big deal over my performance; I assumed they were going a bit overboard. There was one really significant thing that worked in my favor that evening. Everyone who was anyone in New York miraculously seemed to have been in the audience to watch me that night. Someone came up to me backstage to inform me, Walter Winchell, the famous and influential columnist, was out front raving about me to Billy Rose. After I dolled myself up, I was invited out front to mingle. It was a real thrill for me to be introduced to everyone. One of the first people I was met was Orson Welles. He was a really big name since his radio drama series, *Mercury Theatre on the Air*, had successfully launched in

New York the previous year. His broadcast of *War of the Worlds* would soon cause widespread panic on Halloween night in 1938. Mr. Welles was anxious to introduce me to a man seated at his table, *Bernard Baruch*. Baruch was a high profile public figure. He was a financier, statesman, and a presidential advisor who split his time between New York and Washington. He did his best thinking in Central Park. It was not uncommon to see him discussing government affairs with other people while sitting on a park bench. It became his trademark. Incidentally, Billy Rose had begun his career as a stenographic clerk to Bernard Baruch some years before. It seemed as if all the influential people you met at Billy Rose's belonged to his exclusive little set. This Mr. Baruch would influence my life in a way that no other ever could. He became my mentor and a true father figure to me for all of my life. He possessed a big booming voice which always filled me with joy. He said, "Dear Miss Hutton, great doors swing on tiny hinges and great stars are born. Those very doors have opened for you tonight. I am so happy to have been here to witness it."

I couldn't stop talking with Mr. Baruch. We established an instant rapport. I told him I had made it only through the tenth grade and, consequently, it was difficult for me to meet people who I felt were so superior to me in every way. People who were educated and those who possessed intelligence, charm, and wit were beyond my reach. Since this man had dealt with me in a fatherly fashion from the start, I asked him for his help. I pleaded with him to teach me how to talk to famous people, and how to act like a proper lady. Mr. Baruch turned to me and said, "My dear child, if you can do what you did on that stage tonight with any warning, you must realize that you have superior, innate intelligence. Regardless, I would be most happy to help you in any way I can." He overwhelmed me. Here, one of the greatest minds, and an advisor to presidents, is telling little Betty June Thornburg from Detroit, Michigan that he would be happy to help her.

Mr. Baruch told me he had a favorite bench in Central Park where he went every morning to feed the pigeons. All people seeking his advice, even Senators, came to speak with him there. "Why not come tomorrow around two o'clock. It will give you time to rest, as I'm sure you work late." Even his understanding and appreciation for my working hours touched my heart. With tears in my eyes, I picked up his hand and kissed it.

I became very close with Mr. Baruch. In the following months, I tried to extract all the knowledge from him I could. He would take me to dinner and dancing where we would talk away the hours. On one particular evening, he took me to a fine Italian restaurant. After our meal, the waiter asked me if I wanted a demitasse, to which I replied, "No thanks, I would prefer to have some coffee." I thought Mr. Baruch was going to fall from his chair to the floor laughing. It had been a good lesson for me. No matter how much you think you know, there is always something you don't. It was becoming easier for me to meet and to converse with people, thanks to one fantastic and sometimes boring thing Baruch made me do. He made me read the entire New York Times, stem to stern, every single day. I had to read the entire paper, want ads and all, and he would quiz me to see if I had complied. Believe me, it was no small task, especially on Sundays! Even so, what it did was evoke within me the desire to read more and more. He told me that if I read the Times every day, I would always have something to add to a conversation at a party. That little trick has never once let me down.

Mr. Baruch was a brilliant conversationalist. Talking with him over the course of time gave me the confidence I needed to overcome the fears my lack of formal education instilled within me. I once told him, "Mr. Baruch, when they use those great big words, hours on end, at some party, I don't know what they are talking about." He laughed and admitted, "Neither do they."

I studied with Baruch until I left for Hollywood. For many years after, when I was in New York, I would meet him in Central Park. He would allow me to absorb his knowledge and grace as we sat and shared a bag lunch. I will never forget the tremendous positive influence he had over my young adult life.

Years later, after my film career, I followed Judy Garland with a show at the Palace Theater in New York. When I got out on to the stage, right down front sat Bernard Baruch. When I stopped and talked to the crowd at a certain point in my show, I introduced him. Before I did, however, I made quite an eloquent speech. I did it for him, and I wasn't scared to speak any longer. I used all the right words, because they were words that came from my heart. After the show, Baruch came backstage to see me. I could see he had been very proud of me. He said, "Betty, if I were a little younger, and you would be my speech writer, we could run for the presidency of The United States and win." We remained friends until his death in 1965 at the age of ninety-four. I still read the New York Times with all the warmth in my heart just for him.

At that moment, a head waiter came over to tell me Billy Rose wished to see me in his office. I thanked everyone I had been talking with, and excused myself from Mr. Baruch. When I entered Billy's upstairs office, all the cast were already assembled. Billy was giving notes on changes we wanted members of the cast to make for the next performance. When he was finished with everyone, they all turned and exited. There I stood alone. What could he possibly want to say to me? I was not a cast member, only Lopez's lowly girl singer. Billy looked me in the eye and said, "Well young lady, I want to tell you, tomorrow night you go on right before closing number." I was speechless; second to last is starring bill. I just stood and stared at him. "Another thing, your name is going up on the marquee. But, do me a favor. When you swing on my curtains, for Christ's sake, don't tear down my theater."

After a few weeks of playing on the starring bill, I approached Billy Rose about money. I was still only getting what I received from Lopez, sixty-five dollars a week. Now I was not only singing for Lopez, but I was also doubling as headliner for Billy Rose. I told him in all sincerity, "Billy, you know I am a big hit here. I feel I am drawing in a large portion of the crowd. Would you consider giving me one hundred dollars a week?"

Billy Rose turned and looked at me, as if I had lost my mind. "You should be paying me," he shouted. "Don't you realize, if I had not put you in the show, you would still be a band singer?"

"But, Billy, look at all the publicity I'm getting. Almost everyone is coming in to see me after reading Winchell's column. Besides, I really need the money," I argued.

"Listen kid, Winchell comes into Billy Rose's Casa Manana because I'm the famous one here. So you need to understand, I get the credit for putting you in the show in the first place."

I wanted to belt him one for a split second, but I realized what he was saying was the truth. It still didn't resolve the fact that I was living in a walkup flat, all the while being toasted as the hit of New York, with little if anything to show for it.

It may seem unusual, but at this same time, I really started to miss my sister, Marion. I think my measure of good luck and moderate success gave me the confidence I needed to again include Marion in my life. By this time, Marion had also adopted my stage name of Hutton. I already had succeeded in convincing Lopez to ask The William Morris agency to represent her. They had managed to get her bookings in several spots throughout the country. However, I saw a potential for trouble, because Marion was all alone. Mama didn't like the idea of Marion floating around out there unaccompanied; not to mention the fact that she missed her terribly. After a lot of finagling, I finally convinced Lopez to let Marion join us in our show. It had not been easy to get him to agree.

While doing the show for Billy Rose, Lopez also booked club dates and other events on our off nights. Naturally, I never got an extra dime; it was all for him. If that weren't enough, he and I appeared in a series of four one-reel musical shorts. One was done for *Paramount* and the other three were for *Vitaphone*. So, in addition to three shows a night at Billy Rose's place, I had to be up at six in the morning and rush out to Astoria Studios in Queens where we filmed the shorts. During that period of time, I developed insomnia. I rarely slept more than three hours a night. This is something that would plague me throughout the remainder of my life. I think at this point in my career, I just had too many things constantly running through my head. Whatever the reason, it was an impetus for my eventual pill use.

After a successful run at the Casa Manana, Lopez asked Billy Rose to let him out of the show because of a prior commitment he had to play the Piping Rock Club at Saratoga. By this time, Marion had arrived in preparation to work with us, and Lopez included her in our trip Upstate.

Somehow, I thought with having my sister around, I could recapture the old times back in Michigan. It's funny how things never stay the same, and what happened once, can never be duplicated. In some instances, it can even backfire on you. The owner of the Piping Rock liked me, but he took a bigger liking to Marion. When Lopez told me, I experienced a real fit of jealousy and walked out. Before returning to Detroit, I told Lopez I had no idea when I would be back. After four short days in Detroit, I was more than ready. What had I been thinking? Had I been ready to trade my new life in New York for Detroit? It was one of those big blunders I stepped into without even stopping to think beforehand. I had a tendency to do myself in. It was a life-long pattern for me, and a source for much of my own undoing. All I can say is that I must have been crazy with jealousy.

They preferred Marion, and that was fine. I found Detroit as boring and as derelict as ever, so I got on the train and rejoined the band in Saratoga. Vincent let me know in a very kind way he hadn't appreciated the way I had walked out. I really couldn't blame him. He welcomed me back, but not without letting me know what a great job Marion had done in my absence.

A few days after my return, the club closed down for the remainder of the season because of some problem that had put the casino out of commission. The William Morris Agency found an opening in Montreal for the band. Lopez was paid in full for the balance of our run at Saratoga. The man was rolling in dough, but he never once shared any of that overage with me, or with the band to my knowledge. I was peeved. Again I felt like spreading my wings. I left the band to audition for a show in New York. I figured Lopez could get along just fine with Marion. I didn't get the part in New York; I hadn't put my heart into the audition. I reluctantly returned to the band and to an annoyed Lopez in Montreal.

We moved on to Boston where I opened with Marion and the band at the Ritz-Carlton Roof. Glenn Miller was playing Boston at the same time, and had his eye out for a girl singer. In the past, there have been several differing stories how Marion came to be the female vocalist with Glenn Miller, but mine is the real deal. Someone told Miller to come over to the Ritz-Carlton to hear me sing. I had no desire to sing with another big band. I wanted desperately to become a movie star, not to live out the remainder of my career as a girl singer. The unfortunate thing about girl singers is that they rapidly turn into old girl singers. I definitely did not want that to be my fate.

I came down off the bandstand and joined Glenn at his table so we could talk. I believe he was ready to steal me away from Lopez, but I had other ideas. If Miller would take Marion off my hands and out of my hair, both Marion and I would end up winners. I asked Glenn to stick around to hear Marion; she was slated to sing next.

I knew right away that Glenn liked Marion more than he liked me. Marion was never the entertainer I was, but she had a more relaxed singing style, and possibly Glenn Miller sensed she might be easier to handle. After all, my bombastic personality was ever-present. Actually, I think Lopez let her go because he thought it would make life easier for all of us. I loved my sister, but I believe I could love her more from a distance.

Glenn and Helen Miller became Marion's legal guardians. They treated her like their own. Glenn was like a father to Marion. After all, she never had a decent one she could remember. In 1942, at the peak of his civilian career, Miller decided he could better serve those in uniform by joining the war effort. After being accepted in the Army, Glenn's civilian band played their last concert in Passaic, New Jersey in the autumn of 1942. While traveling from England to France to entertain U.S. troops who had recently liberated Paris, Major Miller's plane disappeared in bad weather. His body was never found. Marion suddenly found herself between a rock and a hard place concerning her singing career. She never really found a place to put her talent after that. She did not possess the drive to pursue her career. Luckily, she seemed to be born a natural housewife and mother.

During the time Glenn Miller and his orchestra were regulars at the Pennsylvania Hotel in New York; my mother was deeply hurt she was never allowed in to see my sister perform. Glenn was afraid my mother would cause a scene with her drinking. It was difficult for me to forgive Marion for not insisting that her mother be allowed to attend. I think it's funny, other people in the place could be drunk, but my mother would seemingly have been the only one to be singled out.

As Vincent and I drove away from Boston on our way to New York, the great hurricane of 1938 swept up the East Coast and blew the roof off the Ritz-Carlton behind us. We had left at the right time. Heading into Manhattan with Marion once again out of my life, I was hoping things might be able to return to normal.

A great vaudeville show was put together at the Shubert in Newark. The cast included the likes of comedy team, Abbott and Costello and silent film star, Estelle Taylor. I became the surprise hit of the show. My reputation as *America's Number One Jitterbug* was really catching on. In addition, Lopez and I had managing to mend our personal relationship. I only hoped it would last.

When we later played the Paramount Theater on Times Square, I guess my head had grown a bit too large after my sweeping success in Newark. Actor John Boles was plugging his latest film at theaters around the country, and he and I were on the same ticket at the Paramount, with him as headliner. I demanded that my name be in lights on all three sides of the marquee, but above that of John Boles. Lopez asked me to reconsider what I was asking, and insisted people were coming to the Paramount to see John Boles and not me. I wouldn't give in, and eventually Lopez got my egotistical demand approved.

It would be impossible to ever meet a better looking man, or one who possessed more suave and sophistication than John Boles. How I ever decided I could upstage someone like him was a major miscalculation on my part. I had insisted on closing the show, a spot reserved for the headliner. After the very first show, and the tremendous reaction to Boles from the audience, I regretted my decision. I went to Lopez and humbly asked him to seek a reversal of the billing. The audience had liked me just fine, but they had *loved* John Boles. Lopez was happy I admitted my mistake. He attempted to help me soothe my damaged ego. For the moment, everything was fine between us, but that was not to last long.

Slowly, things between us began to deteriorate on both a personal and business level. Our disagreements became more frequent, and were often aired in public. One of our last huge arguments ended with Lopez giving me too much of a shove on stage, which sent me sailing across the dance floor. I attempted to make it appear as part of our routine, but I knew it was nearing the end for both of us. Lopez had already taken on an additional girl singer by the name of Ann Barrett. He had snatched this girl from another orchestra, readying him and the band for my inevitable departure. He had even taught Ann to copy some of my mannerisms and to imitate my style. For me, that was the final straw. Teaching another girl what came to me naturally was a personal affront. I knew I was being replaced, but I wanted out at the same time.

After a short engagement at a place in Detroit, I performed my last passionate song with the Vincent Lopez Orchestra. I threw a big party for my family and friends in the city where I had first met Lopez. In retrospect, it was a farewell party for us both. I have no idea why I hung on for a few additional months, before calling it quits and returning to New York. It was a bittersweet parting of the ways. I had been with Lopez for so long; it was difficult cutting the cord. Nevertheless, I had met people along the way I knew could help me. My aspirations now turned to New York legitimate theater. I was heading home to New York, and hopefully on to Broadway.

Chapter Eight

I informed my mother that I was calling it quits with Lopez. Naturally, she thought I was crazy. When I set my mind to something, as many people can tell you, it was to be the final word on the matter. In addition, since Billy Rose refused to pitch in any additional money, above and beyond the sixty-five dollars a week I was receiving from Lopez, I decided to end my association with him as well. I quit Lopez and Billy Rose in one fell swoop, with hardly a dime in my pocket.

I didn't make this rash decision totally without something to back me up. I had made friends with Abe Lastfogel and his wife Francis; they were there to fall back upon if I needed to. Abe was an important agent and long-time president of the famed William Morris talent agency. Both he and his wife liked me very much, and I never hesitated to seek their advice. The Lastfogels would take me to *Lindy's* in Times Square to eat, a place famous for its cheesecake and for all the theatrical stars that congregated there at night. I loved mingling with the

Broadway crowd, and being there with someone as influential as Abe Lastfogel was a real plus.

Lastfogel told me, in no uncertain terms, I was capable of making one thousand dollars a week playing vaudeville dates. That was pretty much all I needed to hear. Billy Rose sent me jeweled bags and wonderful notes, all in an attempt to lure me back into his fold. What I never could understand, he never once mentioned a single word about money.

There was no way I was going back to Billy Rose, much less to Lopez. Abe told me the only way to get at Rose was to beat him at his own game. I'm not sure how I interpreted that back then, but I did know I wanted to be that special someone I was being told I was by so many. While I was being heralded as this shining new star on the New York scene, as America's Number One Jitterbug, we'd been living in a coldwater walkup. That had become a real thorn in my side, and it was going to change. I decided to move mama and me into a room at the luxurious Astor Hotel. It was there I had been introduced to Tommy Dorsey by Jack the song-plugger. Somehow, the Astor had stuck in my head as the epitome of "having arrived" in New York City. Only a kid with my amount of nerve could make such a rash decision.

It was a stretch to make a go of it financially while living at the Astor. In addition to our rent being several days behind, mama and I took up cooking in our room as a means to conserve money. It was a strictly forbidden practice. I would put a towel beneath the door to help hold in the cooking odors. Obviously, that was of little help. We were reported to the manager, and I was called down to his office. I wasn't too worried; my upbringing had prepared me for weaseling my way out of tight situations.

The manager turned out to be a really wonderful guy. I'll never forget him; he only had one arm. He was familiar with my stint at the Casa Manana, so it came as a real surprise when I cried to him about not having enough money for the rent. He said, "But you are a really big star, aren't you?" I told him Billy Rose had never paid me a single cent. I stressed the fact that I was capable of making one thousand dollars a week on the vaudeville circuit, but Lopez refused to give me my arrangements. Without them, I was unable to get work. I begged for his indulgence for a while longer. I was told to put an extra *damp* towel under the door to help trap the odors, and to make payment, as soon as I had it.

After hearing my story, the kind Astor manager called a friend on my behalf. This friend, Abe Berman, just happened to be one of the finest show business attorneys in New York City. An appointment was made for me to meet Mr. Berman in his office the following afternoon.

Mr. Berman was a very patient and understanding man. As I explained my story, I paced up and down in his office. My nervous energy would not allow me to sit. I told him about the seemingly iron-clad contract I had signed with Lopez. Not only did he withhold my arrangements, but it seemed he was entitled to twenty percent of everything I earned for life after I left him. What's more, he claimed ownership of my stage name, Betty Hutton. I thought it strange, as I was laying this entire story out on the table, Mr. Berman kept watching my every movement like a hawk. After I had exhausted my complaints, he finally opened his mouth and said, "Betty, wait just one moment. I have a phone call to make."

Abe Berman made a call to B.G. DeSylva, a man who just happened to be the biggest producer on Broadway at the time. I stood right there as Mr. Berman said over the phone, "Buddy, it seems I've found your Florrie for *Panama Hattie*." How could I once again be lucky enough to find myself in the right place at the right time? As I left Mr. Berman's office, I said a little thank you in my head to the Lord for intervening in my life at a time when I needed him so desperately.

I met with Buddy DeSylva, and indeed the part was mine. He had seen me perform at Billy Rose's place. I was told I would be second lead to Ethel Merman in a new show, *Panama Hattie*. The show was still being written, and it would take almost a year to get it to the stage, but I was headed to Broadway. When we finally did open the show, Buddy was the only producer on Broadway to have three hits running at the same time. I didn't realize it then, but Buddy and I were to become inseparable friends.

Mr. Berman took my case against Lopez in front of a judge. The court decided Lopez's contract with me was so one-sided in his favor; it was ruled null and void. I suddenly had my name back, and I was not required to pay Lopez a percentage of my future earnings. The best think of all, I ended up with my arrangements. Now I could work and bring in some well needed cash before the show opened on Broadway. William Morris started booking me across the country, but I still needed a band to back me up.

It just so happened, Harry James, one of the greatest trumpet players of all time, decided to leave Benny Goodman to have a try out on his own. The moment I heard the news, I arranged a meeting with him. In all honesty, we really hit it off. The man was the complete package. A handsome man who really knew how to blow his horn sent me over the top! When I heard his band play my arrangements, and he heard me sing, we knew we belonged together.

For us both, it was love at first sight. I fell so madly in love for the very first time, it was crazy. He was the first man who really understood the depths of my pain and the responsibility I had to my mother. None of this mattered to Harry, he loved me unconditionally. Every single note he played behind me onstage was a caress. We couldn't keep our eyes or hands off each other. Now I came to the realization what sex should be. It wasn't anything dirty, like I had seen in my childhood. Up until now, it was an experience I thought I could only have with an audience. Not the sex, but the love I felt. Don't get me wrong, Harry was tops in the love making department, every single touch from the man sent me into orbit.

Due to all this sudden stability in my life, I began to perform better on stage. And boy, we played everywhere. I actually began to grow up. I became a woman. I thought I would do anything for Harry. That is, until Harry confided in me his dream one night, after we made mad, passionate love. He wanted to take me to Hollywood and play the Palladium. He knew we would be a big hit there together. After that, he wanted to buy a ranch in California and settle down. My heart sank like a stone. "But Harry, you know I'm going to do a show on Broadway for Buddy DeSylva. I really want to be a stage actress."

Harry was furious as he jumped from the bed. "You'll just have to choose between me and your career," he said with anger.

"But, Harry," I pleaded. "This has been my dream for my entire life, and it's just beginning to come true for me."

Harry got dressed and walked out of the room and my life forever. I leaned back on my pillow while the tears flowed freely down my face. I never saw him again. My heart broke over my loss of Harry. As a consolation, I told myself no man could take the place of my beloved audience. And yet, I can still hear Harry behind me playing that lovely Gershwin tune I sang so often, *But Not For Me.*

They're writing songs of love, but not for me,
A lucky star's above, but not for me
With love to lead the way,

I found more clouds of grey,
Than any Russian play could guarantee.

It all began so well, but what an end,
This is the time a fella needs a friend,
When every happy plot,
Ends in a marriage knot,
And there's no knot for me.

By this time, and after the success I had enjoyed with Harry, I was living in an apartment on Central Park. Of course, my mother was still with me. Marion was pregnant and had moved in with us. I was supporting my family. It was a familiar role I was playing, one I had played before.

Thank God I had made those movie shorts with Sammy Cahn. I was approached by Gertrude Macy and Stanley Gilkey about a show they were producing on Broadway. They had seen me in a few of the musical short movies I had done with Lopez and at the Casa Manana, and wanted me for their new show. The original musical revue they were producing was called, *Two for the Show.*

We rehearsed for six weeks in New York. It was a funny little show, a series of musical numbers and sketches, all jumbled together to make an entertaining evening. After we were comfortable with the show, we were ready to take it to try-outs in Boston at the Shubert. Try-outs started toward the end of January 1940, lasting for five nights. We brought it back to New York where we opened on February 8, 1940, at the Booth Theatre. The show ran for almost four months, during which we did 124 performances. The cast included such notable actors as Eve Arden, Keenan Wynn, Alfred Drake, and Richard Haydn.

John Murray Anderson was staging the production, with direction by Josh Logan. I quickly developed a real crush on Josh Logan. I started following him around backstage, bringing him coffee, and in general making a real pest out of myself. I managed to corner him one night and asked, "Josh, don't you ever stop to look at me?"

"Sure I do, kid," he said. "And I want you to know you're doing a really great job."

"No, I mean, why don't you look at me the way I look at you?"

He put a brotherly arm around my shoulder and said, "Betty, you're just a young girl, and I'm really flattered by your attention."

After that, Josh remained pleasant, but kept his distance from me as often as possible. That same year he became engaged and got married.

It was John Murray Anderson who encouraged me to have confidence in myself on the Broadway stage, because he believed in me. He had nicknames for everyone. Mine was Tisket, after my big hit song, *A-Tisket A-Tasket*. I will always remember the way he called me Tisket; he had such an endearing quality to his voice when he said it. I wanted so much to please in the beginning; I was just a flurry of movements that no one could understand. Still, John had all the confidence I would work my way into my parts and be a real hit.

I did several great numbers in the show. I had some real fun with the *Calypso Joe* number. However, my biggest was with Keenan Wynn, who was a real genius when it came to comedy. The number was called, *Little Miss Muffett*, a funny take on the children's nursery rhyme. I played little Miss Muffett and Keenan played the spider. The number put a halt to everything for a few moments in the theatre while the audience howled. On another occasion, in a sketch with a ballet scene, the lead dancer was late entering the stage. The orchestra played the introduction music to the number several times, and still the actor didn't appear. I figured something had to be done. I stepped out on the stage and announced the guy had ripped his pants. The crowd went crazy with laughter.

I will never forget my opening night on Broadway. It was almost as chaotic as giving birth. The band struck up the overture, and instantly I froze. My mouth went dry as the stage manager prompted, "Come on, kids, you're on." Thank God, I didn't have one single line of dialogue in the entire show. It gave me time to concentrate on my songs.

As I stood in the wings ready to go on, suddenly I heard the familiar voice of John Murray Anderson behind me, speaking softly in my ear. "You can do it, walk out there proudly. Remember, they're no different from you. They would give anything to be in your place." I think he gave me a slight nudge, and there I was onstage doing what I dreamed of doing all my life.

Just as John Murray had predicted, I was well received. The reviews were overwhelmingly good. I was singled out as *the* sensation of the show. Anderson called the cast together after the show and said, "I want you all to know, and I don't want any grumbling, because tonight Tisket is the hit of the show." Keenan Wynn and Eve Arden hated me because I was such a success.

If I had thought *Two for the Show* was big time, I had no idea what the big league was until *Panama Hattie*. I walked into the 46th Street Theater, all excited for the first day of rehearsals. I was grateful to be working alongside Ethel Merman, the biggest musical star on Broadway, and Buddy DeSylva, the most successful musical producer of the time. It was my intention to play it cool from the start. I wanted to be cautious and observant, a great way to avoid making many mistakes and few enemies. I wanted to make absolutely sure I stayed on the good side of Merman, the star of the show. I must confess, I was completely in awe of her at first sight; after all, she was a great star. It wouldn't take me long to realize, however, there was not a bit of warmth that emanated from her entire being.

Panama Hattie was written by Buddy DeSylva and Herbert Fields. Merman plays Hattie Maloney, a brassy nightclub singer relocated to the Panama Canal Zone. After cleaning up her act, she tries to fit into the upper-crust world of the man she loves, an officer in the armed forces. The only thing standing in her way is his clever young daughter. Matters are made worse by three wacky sailors and the need to foil a plot to blow up the Canal. I played Florrie, a local good time girl. I was excited to play the role. Up until this time, all I had done was run on stage, sing a song, and run back off. Having a character to create on stage was challenging. You have to know your character and carry it throughout the show. Others in the cast included, Arthur Treacher, James Dunn, Phyllis Brooks, and Rags Ragland. June Allyson was in the chorus and was also my understudy. Additional girl chorus members were Betsy Blair, Lucille Bremer, and Vera-Ellen.

Merman was going with Sherman Billingsley at the time, the owner of *The Stork Club*. It was *the* hottest and ritziest place to be seen in New York City. The heavy bronze door to his club on East 53rd Street swung open to admit only the chosen few. The real entertainment at this club was the patrons themselves. I had never been inside, but it appeared as if the curtains were suddenly going to open up to an entire new glamorous world for me, all due to my association with the show.

Merman wore a bracelet on her arm made up of square cut diamonds that spelled out: *Merman & Sherman*. The damned thing looked like a headlight! Everyone got caught up in the Merman and Sherman thing, it was unavoidable. I was so astounded at the attention this man gave to her, at one point I truly believed if I could be like her, I just might live happily ever after. The love I desperately sought, I saw through her eyes. I didn't even stop to realize until much later, Sherman was a married man. Their affair was public knowledge only among circles of the elite. It began to trouble me greatly; fame and fortune should afford those people fortunate enough to have it a certain degree of happiness and contentment. At least that's the way I saw it at the time. I think that's the way the public saw it, and probably still does today. I came to know it is seldom true, with the odd exception.

Every single day of rehearsals, Sherman Billingsley would send not one, but two trucks of food over for the cast. I don't mean just food, I mean gourmet cuisine. Waiters in dress uniforms set up tables with crisp linens and silver, so we could dine in comfort and elegance. Thanks to the work Baruch had done with me, I was no longer afraid *to use the wrong fork at the Stork in New York!*

Cole Porter had written the score for the show. We took turns meeting with him in his suite at the Waldorf where he would work with us individually. I didn't like the man from day one, nor was I thrilled with his songs. They just weren't me, with the exception of the one I was to do with Arthur Treacher. Even so, who was I to say this wasn't a good score. So, I decided to really turn on the personality to make sure the stuff worked in my favor. It's funny, when the show was made into a movie a year or so later, almost half of Porter's numbers had been replaced. The troubled production was completely re-filmed after a terrible preview, delaying its scheduled release by almost a year. One review started in by saying the movie was merely the leftovers of a musical comedy.

Everyone was saying, "Yes, Mr. Porter" this, and "Yes, Mr. Porter" that, all over the place. It was so ridiculous. I remember being repulsed by the man. His suite at the Waldorf was cavernous. He lived on one side, and his wife on the other. He was gay and his wife was a lesbian. I had no trouble with that; many of the guys were gay in the chorus and everywhere else throughout show business.

One of my favorite things to do after the show was to go down to The Village with guys from the chorus. They would take me to clubs where gay guys performed in drag; you would swear they were women. I sure as hell got along better with them then I did with some of these so-called stars who had the idea in their own minds that they were way more important than they actually were. What I didn't care for was the fact that Porter and his wife married to put up a socially acceptable front. In the slums, we learned really fast that you *were* who you *were*.

Phyllis Brooks was in the show. Phyllis was the first civilian woman to travel to the Pacific during World War II on a USO tour, something I did later as well. At some point, Phyllis had been going with Cary Grant. There was a rumor that Cary and *Brooksie*, as he called her, were going to get married. Then suddenly, without warning she got dumped. Cary had confided in her that he liked men; naturally she was devastated. Cary and I met and became friendly years later in Hollywood. It was when I was buying the very first house I purchased in Brentwood. Cary and I were in a bidding war over that house, and I won. He refused to go any higher than the sixty-five thousand I ended up paying for it. Years later, the worth of that house was in the millions. Cary Grant and I remained close friends. We would go to the fights together on Saturday nights in Los Angeles and have ourselves a ball.

Rehearsals at the theatre went along well. Robert Alton was the choreographer. He would always point with his foot and say, "You, go over there..." The man never used his hands. He was wild, and I adored him. We started our blocking of the show upstairs, even before we got down on the stage. Merman was like a machine. She had her blocking marks, and she could hit them every single time. We rehearsed for six weeks solid. Almost everyone seemed to get along just fine. My part wasn't great, but I loved the cast. Arthur Treacher was a thrill to work with. He was so tall and I was so small, I just knew we would be a smash.

Merman managed to keep a distance from me. I admired her so much because of her talent, and tried desperately to win her friendship. Just when I thought that friendship might develop, she had a big altercation with Billingsley. Suddenly, the entire cast was barred from the Stork Club. I got so damned mad; I marched down to his club and demanded to see Sherman. After quite a wait, I was allowed into his office. I let him know that just because he had a fight with Merman, there was no reason to ban the entire cast. From that moment on, Sherman and I became fast friends. I think he had been impressed with my boldness. He explained his wife had put her foot down, and naturally Merman was furious.

After their breakup, Merman became quite bitter. Her performance in rehearsals was never affected. She was one of the toughest broads I have ever seen. Sometimes I wish I had just half of her steel veneer, it might have helped me better cope with some of the things I blew in my career due to my inner weakness.

Walter Winchell became a personal friend of mine during this time. He and Broadway columnist, Louis Sobol, would pick me up at the theatre after rehearsals and take me to dine at *Twenty-One*. I loved Walter dearly. Everything seemed to be going so well in my life, and especially in the show.

Walter Winchell really enjoyed dancing; every night was like New Years Eve when he took me. We would go to The Stork Club, a place where I was treated like a star because I was in the show. Walter and I would do the rumba; he was the best damned dancer I ever saw.

One day, Walter called me up and told me to get myself ready, there was someone he wanted me to meet. Upstairs at the Waldorf, after ringing the bell to a suite of rooms, a gruff looking individual motioned for us to enter. We were no sooner seated, when the bedroom door swung open to reveal one of my childhood idols, the wonderful *George Raft*. Directly behind Raft walked a beautiful blonde gal, she was stacked like a double-dip cone. She proceeded to the front door and exited without a word. I immediately sensed she was a hooker. God, how I wished I had looked like that!

Walter introduced us. Raft was a most charming man. I was in awe, being in the presence of such a famous star. He poured us a drink and sat down right beside me to talk. "So, I guess we're all going out dancing. Walter tells me you're really good at it."

I was speechless. The thought of being whirled around a dance floor like Carole Lombard, by none other than George Raft, was a dream I had not yet even imagined.

Walter, George, and I hit every hot spot in town we could think of. We ended up at *El Morocco* where they played nothing but tangos and the rumba. I closed my eyes when dancing with him. It was truly like a dream, with his body so very close to mine, I felt exactly like a movie star that evening.

Buddy DeSylva and I also became very close. He had a secretary by the name of Marie Valentine. I always had to go through her if and when I wanted to talk to Buddy. At least I had the smarts to know when she was around; I had better play up to her. Buddy and I dined together quite often just steps from Broadway at the famous Dinty Moore's on West 46th Street. There we would sit and talk for hours.

We opened in New Haven on October 3rd. The theatre was completely full. There were so many encores called, the show lasted way past midnight. A few days later, on the 7th, we opened in Boston. Again we were a smash. The two last minute additions to the cast before leaving New York were Pat Harrington and Frank Hyres. The three of us did a number called, *Fresh as a Daisy*. We couldn't take enough encores for that number. I was always afraid they were going to take it out of the show for two reasons. First, the two men in it were in so many other numbers, everyone was afraid they were being over used. Second, the number worked so well between us three; I think a few people thought it detracted from some of the other more important numbers in the show that were performed by cast members who figured they were more important. This left me totally unprepared for the number that eventually did get cut at the very last minute.

I loved my number with just Arthur Treacher called, *They Ain't Done Right by Our Nell*. I knew that number was safe because it was the only real number Treacher had in the show. The only other number I had was called, *All I've Got to Get Now is My Man*, but that was more of an ensemble number.

Before opening night in New York, there was a dress rehearsal for all the lighting guys. This was the time all the markings went down on the stage. The next night was a benefit performance; it was like a dress rehearsal, but with a live audience. This particular night, Arthur Treacher and I had the hit number in the show. I looked up at Buddy in his box seat, and he was beaming. I could not have been happier if he had handed me the moon.

The night after that was the real thing, opening night. The critics would be there, as well as the elite of show business and the glamour set. I was wonderfully excited on my way to the theatre that evening; all ready to get to my dressing room and prepare for the start of the show. As I walked around backstage, people were running in all directions; excitement was running high. I walked into my dressing room, and there, attached to the mirror was an envelope. In it was a note that read:

Miss Hutton:

This is to notify you that your number with Arthur Treacher has been cut from the show.

B.G. DeSylva

Sobbing uncontrollably, I ran out and asked the stage manager, "Where is Buddy, I need to talk to Buddy DeSylva?" After a frantic search, I finally located Buddy. I looked at him and screamed, "Buddy, why?"

He took me to a quiet corner. When I was calm enough to listen, he explained, "Merman has that kind of power, it's in her contract, Betty."

I said, "Buddy, if you take out that number, I can't go on. My heart won't be in it. If she had to do this, why not when we were out of town with the show or even last night, but why do it now?"

Buddy knew the pain I was in. The decision had been made, nothing could be done. Buddy pulled me close, and in a half whisper confided, "Betty, I am going to head up production at Paramount Studios in Hollywood. You are the first to hear this out of my mouth. If you promise me you will go on tonight, and will stay with the show for a year, I will take you with me and make you a movie star. You are young, one year to you will make no difference."

Buddy and I shook hands on the deal. I knew his word was his bond. At the time, it was difficult to comprehend what Merman was doing to me that night was my actual ticket to stardom. As I walked back toward my dressing room, I happened across Merman. I looked at her and said, "Ethel, I'm scared to death. I don't know if I can make it out there tonight. Do you ever get a little scared?" I guess I was hoping my admission of fear would somehow garner some feeling of compassion from deep within her.

Merman remarked quite nonchalantly, "Fuck 'um! If they were as good as me, *they* would be up here." With that, she turned and walked away.

As I watched her saunter off, I knew for sure she possessed no heart. I went and peeked out at my beloved audience. The scent of perfume and the gentle roar of casual conversation from the opposite side of the curtain calmed me considerably.

Panama Hattie ran from October 30, 1940, through January 3, 1942. The show lasted for a total of five hundred and one performances; the first show in over a decade in New York City to exceed the five hundred consecutive performance mark.

At *Billy Rose's Casa Manana* in New York City, 1939.

Photo: Betty's private collection, The Betty Hutton Estate

The early days in New York City.
Photo: Betty's private collection, The Betty Hutton Estate

Publicity photo from *Two For The Show*, Broadway 1940.
Photo: Betty's private collection, The Betty Hutton Estate

From *Two For The Show* 1940 with actor Willard Gary, 1940.
Photo: Courtesy Ben Carbonetto, photographer unknown

With Arthur Treacher in *Two For The Show,* 1940.
This was the "big" number that was cut from the show by
Merman on opening night. Photo taken during try-outs in Boston.
Photo: Courtesy Ben Carbonetto, photographer unknown

Publicity photo from *Panama Hattie*, Broadway 1940.
Photo: Courtesy Ben Carbonetto, photographer unknown

Onstage with *Panama Hattie*, Broadway.
Photo: Courtesy Ben Carbonetto, photographer unknown

Panama Hattie, Broadway.
Photo: Courtesy Ben Carbonetto, photographer unknown

My sister Marion and I, post Broadway.
Photo: Betty's private collection, The Betty Hutton Estate

With Ethel Merman and songwriter Jule Styne, post Broadway.
Photo: Courtesy Ben Carbonetto, photographer unknown

Chapter Nine

Buddy DeSylva was now *the* man in my life. He was the one who was there to watch over and guide me. I really needed that sort of a crutch at the time, and have always required that kind of support throughout my career. Buddy took care of me, much as Lopez had done, but without owing payback. Buddy was so successful; he didn't need to take advantage of me as Lopez had. I knew things were going to be better this time. After all, I really liked Buddy DeSylva. More importantly, I respected him.

Buddy had every intention of keeping his promise to me, of that I wasn't worried. Early in 1941, after William LeBaron left his post as vice president in charge of production at Paramount, Buddy DeSylva was asked to replace him. When LeBaron handed down his hefty salary to start his own independent film unit at Fox, Buddy was there immediately to take over the reins.

I got a call in New York from Buddy out on the West Coast. He asked me to take a screen test for the studio. Since he was new, he was making every effort to play by the rules as they were written in studio policy. Taking a screen test scared the hell out of me. "Buddy, I've gone that route once before, and it didn't work. Remember, I told you about the screen test I did for Fox when I was with Lopez," I protested. "They died my hair dark and managed to spoil my looks on camera. That was that, it put an end to my one and only screen test."

Buddy shot back, "Betty, the studio insists upon it. If you agree, and the test goes well, the studio will sign you at $750 a week.

I knew I had one over on Buddy, and I was ready to use it. MGM had bought the rights to Panama Hattie. It was Buddy's property, but he sold it. Paramount wouldn't allow him to bring in any of his own work when he arrived to head production. I suppose it could have created a conflict of interests. They wanted to cast Ann Sothern in the lead role Merman had played on Broadway, and wanted me to repeat my role of Florrie, at a really hefty weekly salary. The best part of all, I wasn't required to take any screen test; they were already familiar with my acting ability from having seen me in the part in New York. After passing this all by Buddy, he was ready to bargain. I was signed on at $1000 a week for my appearance in one film, with no screen test. If I wanted to work at Paramount as a contract player after that time, I would have to screen test. With the deal made, it looked like I was on my way to Hollywood.

I left Panama Hattie on Broadway in June of 1941, before the end of the run. June Allyson had been my understudy. I worked with her after the show and whenever else we found the time so that she could learn my part. Then, when I was out with the German measles, (what other kind of measles could you get at the advent of WWII), June Allyson took over my part in the show. Buddy wasn't happy; I was spending too much of my time and effort on her. He said to me, "Betty, you never take a chorus girl and teach her anything."

"Buddy," I protested, "I think you are wrong. She's a really sweet girl." I went ahead, in spite of what he said, and taught her everything I knew. I never could understand it, but when I finally did quit the show, despite knowing my role well, she didn't get the part. From that time on, June Allyson never again gave me the time of day, even during our successful days in Hollywood.

The girl who did step in for me was Ann Barrett, the one who took over for me as girl singer in the Lopez band. I hoped for her sake, after the show closed, she would move on to something totally different. I didn't want the poor thing spending the rest of her career following me around and acting as my stand-in.

Mom and I took the train to California. I remember how foreign everything seemed when we arrived in Los Angeles. It was warm in Southern California, and the air was dry. I remember there were orange trees when you got off the train, it smelled so wonderful. Union Station, with its Spanish architecture, was unlike anything I had ever seen before. It was new and clean, having been built only a couple of years earlier. For that matter, most everything in Los Angeles looked new in comparison to the East Coast. People seemed a lot friendlier too, and things didn't move at the frantic pace they had in New York City. I knew I had come here to work, but I couldn't help but feel I was on some sort of an extended vacation.

I thought all of Los Angeles was beautiful until I got my first look at Paramount. The studio was like a fantasy land all wrapped up in a small town. Everything a person required was right there within the walls of the studio, making it unnecessary to ever leave the place. It was the best studio to work for; there I found safety and structure. Everywhere, people called you by your first name, and expected the same in return. Somehow it all worked, and worked well. It was a family, and I really loved working and being there.

The year before I arrived, in 1940, Paramount agreed to a government ruling which blocked booking and pre-selling of films. In a nut shell, it stopped the practice of collecting up-front money for films not yet in production. Because of that new ruling, Paramount immediately cut back on its production. During the war years, the studio went from sixty or more pictures a year to about twenty. Despite the production decrease, war time attendance numbers at theaters went sky high. With men off to war, their women stayed home alone. A slew of feel-good, pro-American war theme movies bought these lonely women to theaters in droves. A roster of fresh new faces at Paramount like, Bob Hope, Alan Ladd, Veronica Lake, Paulette Goddard, and myself helped boost theater attendance as well.

During the War, Paramount and its associated theater holdings made more money than ever. Because of it, the Federal Trade Commission and the Justice Department decided to reopen their case against the five integrated studios. On top of everything, Paramount also had a monopoly over Detroit movie theaters through an off-shoot company called United Detroit Theaters. That was all the government needed. In 1948, a Supreme Court case, The United States v. Paramount Pictures, Inc. ruled that movie studios could no longer own movie theater chains. This decision broke up Paramount's long standing monopoly, and effectively brought an end to the enduring Hollywood studio system. With the loss of the theater chain, it became necessary to cut studio-backed production, and Paramount Pictures went into a fast and steep nose-dive. The studio was forced to let go of its contract players and to begin making production deals with independents. By the mid-1950s, all the great names at Paramount were gone, with the exception of DeMille.

For now, the studio was safe. With the war on the horizon, Paramount continued to make money. Under Buddy DeSylva's control, they concentrated on turning out nice, light-hearted comedies and musicals. Paramount was great at tailor making their films to get the best of use out of their catalogue of actors. It looked as if I had fallen into a tub of butter, lucky enough to land right in the middle of a studio like Paramount.

It wasn't necessary for Buddy to tailor make a role for me in my very first film. *The Fleet's In* already had a part that I could fit into perfectly. The role of Bessie Dale was a young woman who wore her heart on her sleeve, along with possessing a real comic side. Paramount already had funny lady, Cass Daley, but she usually capitalized on making fun of her own flawed looks, and played everything on the screen off of that fact. This role called for a fresh looking girl comedian who had a certain amount of vulnerability and attractiveness which would allow the audience to really like her as a person. I had exactly what was necessary to fill the bill.

In the film, a young William Holden gets a picture taken with movie star, Betty Jane Rhodes, while simply attempting to obtain her autograph. The photograph circulates among the fellas in the fleet, and immediately he gets the reputation of being a lady's man. A challenge comes with it, to see if he can get a kiss out of a San Francisco club singer going by the name of the Countess of Swingland. Dorothy Lamour plays the Countess, a beautiful woman known for being quite icy and unapproachable. A lot of money is riding on the bet placed by Holden's pal Eddie Bracken. I play the Countess' best friend, Bessie Dale, and I set all my sights on the Bracken character. I was twenty years old when I made this film. If you still don't know where this entire movie is headed, it doesn't matter one bit. It's merely a slim plot to hang a lot of nice songs on.

Paramount's top female box office draw at the time was Dorothy Lamour. She was about 28 years old in the picture, and at the very top of her form. William Holden was only around 24, but somehow he seemed to possess a lot more maturity. Watching him, you get the distinct impression that he is being wasted in a light-hearted comedy.

Dorothy Lamour had no illusions about her acting or singing ability. Once asked by an interviewer if she had ever studied acting or singing, she replied, "No, can't you tell?" During World War II, Dorothy was known as "the *bond* bombshell" because of the tireless effort she made in selling United States War Bonds. In tours around the country, she was credited with selling nearly $300 million in bonds. She was so popular and so valuable to the effort; the Government put a private railroad car at her disposal when she went out on a bond tour. Dorothy and I became fast friends. I will always love her for the friendship she immediately showed to me in those early days. As a matter of fact, Dorothy later hosted the baby shower held for my first child at Steven Crane's famous *Luau* restaurant in Beverly Hills.

The Fleet's In was the first of several films in which Eddie Bracken and I appeared together. Bracken and I developed a long standing competitive stance toward each other. If we had a scene together, we would try to outdo one another. I don't think it ever caused any real harm. On the contrary, I believe it went far in making what we were doing together on the screen even better. In a typical scene from the movie, Bracken and I are confronted with an enormous flight of stairs to my San Francisco apartment. Bracken lifted me into his arms and began the steep ascent. The scene dissolved to us finally walking in the door, but this time I was carrying Bracken. That was really funny and clever comic relief. We were good friends, but I'm sure he was not all that happy with the instant success I managed to achieve. After all, Bracken had been around for a couple of years. Regardless, his tentative nature, together with my aggressive energy, instantly made us a popular duo. Eddie Bracken was always a very capable funny man. What made him great was his lack of fear at playing the blundering character that always seemed to do himself in. Our rapport in this film was the impetus for us working together time and again onscreen.

I was told it wasn't easy trying to film me during the shoots. First to blame was my untrained on-camera acting ability. I just didn't have it. Second, my enthusiasm made me unable to tone myself down. I guess the cameraman just couldn't keep up with me. It didn't help I was unable to hit my marks. Buddy had a solution, as he always did when it came to me. He had three cameras follow the action, that way we were covered. Buddy didn't want a lot of takes of me. He suspected I was giving it all I had my first time around. It was the spontaneity of my actions he wanted to capture.

What really made this movie was the songs and music, together with one of the most popular bands of the era, Jimmy Dorsey's Orchestra and vocalists, Bob Eberly and Helen O'Connell. Credit for the music went to the director of the film, Victor Schertzinger. The lyrics were created by the brilliant lyricist, Johnny Mercer. *The Fleet's In* was unfortunately the last effort of Schertzinger. He died unexpectedly in his sleep from a heart attack at the age of 53, just before the movie was completely finished. Because of his death, the film wasn't released until January of 1942. Schertzinger had directed 89 films, and had composed music for more than 50 of them.

Several songs from the movie were instant successes. *I Remember You* was very enthusiastically received. The song, *Tangerine,* by the Jimmy Dorsey Orchestra, with vocalists, Helen O'Connell and Bob Eberly, was released by Decca Records. It became the most popular song from the movie. The record first reached the Billboard magazine charts on April 10, 1942, and lasted fifteen weeks. It peaked at number one.

If You Build a Better Mousetrap was the first song I performed in the film. It was a real novelty number. I jumped around so on stage, that by the end of my number, the curls they had piled all over the top of my head started to fall completely out. If the routine had gone on only moments longer, we would have had to do a complete retake to shore up my hairdo. I came off a bit laughable in the number. In my opinion, it was due to the outrageous clothes they made me wear. Even so, nothing was as bad as the clown clothes I wore in *Arthur Murray*. I had a contraption on my head that looked like rabbit ears. Years later, when I saw the film again, I remember feeling rather foolish. What I failed to remember was that the costumes had been carefully chosen to make me appear as a buffoon, and to completely offset the beauty and stylish clothing worn by Dorothy Lamour. After all, she was the star of the movie; as such, she needed to be set apart with the ultimate in style to make sure her star blazed brightly. The fun part of the song happened when I plucked rubber-limbed Gil Lamb from the audience. I dragged him up on stage and proceeded to toss his pencil-thin body all over the place. It was a gimmick that really made the entire number.

Funny enough, my stand-out number was the song, *Not Mine*. It was a reprise of the serious love song sung by Dorothy Lamour in front of William Holden. I sang mine as a comedy bit with Eddie Bracken, but I came off as sincere and sweet, nonetheless. I started getting fan mail at the studio telling me how touching my interpretation of the song had been. I sang, "It's somebody else's moon above..." When I got to the part, "But not mine...," I would sing it with a big droopy bottom lip and sad eyes; like I was about to burst into tears. I guess the heartbreaking manner in which I played it, although comical, completely caught everyone off guard. In doing so, I made a real impact. I guess it showed I had heart, as well as comedic talent.

The third song I performed was also a novelty number, and was once again backed by Jimmy Dorsey and his great Orchestra. *Arthur Murray Taught Me Dancing in a Hurry* was so popular; it actually increased the business for the real Arthur Murray. In 1938, the first Arthur Murray dance studio franchise was opened in Minneapolis. Although Arthur Murray had been around for quite a while, after we recorded the song for the movie, his business really started to boom. Four short years after the release of the song, there were a total of seventy-two Arthur Murray Dance Studios across America. That surely says something about the power film has to influence public desires and attitudes. Arthur Murray continued on for decades as an important American company. *Arthur Murray Dance Studios* were certainly an American trend-setter, in that they are the second oldest franchised company in America. The company's long-standing influence can be seen in the former pupils it can boast, such as, Eleanor Roosevelt, John D. Rockefeller Jr., Elizabeth Arden, and Jack Dempsey. Incidentally, the oldest franchise in America is *A&W*. The root beer company was started way back in 1919.

All in all, for my very first film, I had quite a substantial part. I made an instant bang with the movie going public. Paramount did not immediately promote me to a major star. Buddy had a plan, and it was going to take time for me to earn my stripes. They did realize one thing, they wanted to keep me. In December of 1941, I was signed to a seven-year contract. No screen test had ever been required! On my road to stardom, I had to make two more movies before I became Bob Hope's leading lady in *Let's Face It,* in 1943. Following the release of *The Miracle of*

Morgan's Creek in 1944, I was indisputably a major star. With the release of *Incendiary Blonde* in 1945, I had displaced Lamour as Paramount's number one female box office attraction.

Star Spangled Rhythm was my second film, and was put together in response to the war effort. Shortly after the attack on Pearl Harbor, the US rallied like never before. A large part of recruitment to the war effort was due to a cooperative media, particularly movies. The White House asked the studios to rush some feel-good films into production, and this was Paramount's initial offering. Many of the Hollywood studios produced such films during the war, generally musicals, and frequently with flimsy storylines. In addition to their entertainment value, they were used as a tool to encourage fundraising as well as patriotism. We started shooting in mid-July of 1942. The entire film was shot in thirteen days, between filming at Paramount's studios and on location at the Naval Training Center in San Diego.

This is a special film based on cast participation alone. The plot, all centered on activities at a movie studio, is what allows for cameo appearances by virtually every star at Paramount Pictures, as well as some of the studio's major directors. The slender plot involves the efforts by modest studio doorman, Pop Webster (Victor Moore), to pass himself off as a Paramount bigwig executive for the benefit of his sailor son, Johnny (Eddie Bracken). When Johnny shows up in Hollywood on shore leave, Pop and the studio's switchboard operator, Polly Judson, the role played by me, go to the extreme to maintain the illusion for Johnny and his sailor friends. Luckily, the real studio boss is out of town. So well loved is Pop, virtually everyone on the studio lot is willing to help out with the charade. Plot doesn't really matter here; it's just an excuse for a lot of studio stars to show up in one place and perform.

One of the highlights of the film was a scene where I struggle to gain entrance to the studio by climbing over the back wall. This was done with inept help from acrobat comedians, Walter Dare Wahl and Company. Wahl, his silent partner, and I end up in all sorts of strange contorted positions in our efforts to mount the wall. It turns into a really funny slapstick routine. When we previewed the scene, Eddie Bracken wasn't at all happy. The whole wall-climbing thing hadn't been in the original script, and I guess it took him by surprise. Buddy DeSylva was the one who bore the responsibility for including the scene in the film. I doubt anyone was going to argue with him. It caused some major animosity, since it more or less stole the show.

I had only one song in the film, but it was a really sizzling number I did all by myself. It was called, *I'm Doing It for Defense.* I sang it while driving in a jeep full of sailors at about one hundred miles an hour. It was not an easy shoot. We hit a landing wrong while making a jump with the jeep and one actor was thrown from the vehicle. The rest of us were really shaken up. In this particular instance, it wasn't my fault if they couldn't keep me in the camera during shooting. At least no one can say my one number in the movie wasn't exciting!

Another song called, *Hit the Road to Dreamland*, was set in the dining car of a train. It was sung by Mary Martin, Dick Powell, and the Golden Gate Quartette. It's a catchy number and a real show stopper. I recorded the same song in 1956 and did really well with it.

The big hit song from the film was, *That Old Black Magic*. That song received an Academy Award nomination in 1944 as Best Original Song for Harold Arlen's music and Johnny Mercer's lyrics. Robert Emmett Dolan was also nominated for Best Score.

Variety summed it up best when it said of the film and its efforts, "Except for a few gags, *Rhythm* has essentially nothing new in it. But neither has a Christmas tree. Yet both bring good cheer because of the way they're dressed up. The whole thing, as Harry Tugend has written it and George Marshall directed it, is fresh, alive and full of bounce."

Star Spangled Rhythm premiered in New York City on December 30, 1942. America flocked to theaters to see it. Paramount had jumped on the wagon by producing its first wartime morale boosting film, the first of many.

I had received fourth billing in my first film, *The Fleet's In*. Now, in my second movie, *Star Spangled Rhythm*, I received equal billing along side Eddie Bracken. I was working my way up the ladder, and I wasn't even really trying. I certainly never attempted to walk over the top of anyone else as I worked my way on up. I suppose Buddy was the one to do the dirty work for me. I was still naive concerning the politics and hierarchy of the industry. I was young and eager to do my very best at whatever came my way.

It wasn't until much later, I would come to realize all the behind the scene manipulations Buddy did in my favor. Buddy had predicted I was going to be a star long before I even arrived at the studio. Whether or not I was his pet project, I cannot judge. I do know, he believed in me wholeheartedly and was there to guide my every movement. I do feel that I had something to do with my own success. I also know I had a universal appeal, both men and women audiences liked me. The men adored me because I was like their daughter or a carefree sister. Women were not intimidated by me in the least. I think my humor and natural acting approach were automatically disarming to them.

A lot of people presumed I was sleeping with Buddy. After all, it was no secret; he was closely guiding my career. Sleeping with him couldn't be farther from the truth. Buddy and I had a healthy respect for each other.

Our friendship had started out as business, and although we became close friends, our relationship stayed as one based upon our business association. I think I was almost like a daughter to him. He enjoyed watching me grow into the kind of actress he had envisioned I could become.

On January 4, 1943, less than a week after the opening of *Star Spangled Rhythm*, was the official release of my third movie, *Happy Go Lucky*. This was again a lighthearted musical comedy. "When you have a winning formula, you stick with it," was Buddy's motto. The Mary Martin character, Marjory Stuart, is a beautiful young woman who works in the hatcheck room at a Manhattan nightclub. Dreams of being a rich socialite take her on a cruise to the Caribbean, all in an effort to land a rich husband. Posing as a wealthy debutante, Marjory makes friends with Bubbles Hennessy, my character in the film. I am a good-natured singer who's on board to meet up with my boyfriend, Wally Case, played by Eddie Bracken. Along with Wally is his friend, Pete Hamilton, played by Dick Powell, a beach bum who possesses little more than charm and personality. Bubbles, Wally, and Pete soon realize that Marjory is hardly a member of the social elite, but they like her enough to play along at her game of snaring the man she has her eye on, a stuffy, but rich, Alfred Monroe, played by Rudy Vallee. To complicate matters, just as the Mary Martin character starts getting somewhere with Rudy Vallee, she and Dick Powell realize that they've fallen for each other. Naturally, I had been teamed up again romantically with Bracken. Our match continued to be a winning twosome on film.

This was my first movie to be released in color. Everyone working on the film was excited about it. I had a great musical number in the film I would be identified with forever, *Murder, He Says*. It was a wonderful number because I could play it up to the hilt. The music was written by the talented, Jimmy McHugh. The lyrics were by the most wonderful man, Frank Loesser. Frank and I became great friends. We even dated at one point. I loved the man, his talent for writing, and his humor. The other song I had in the film was called, *The Fuddy Duddy Watchmaker*. It didn't have the commercial appeal of *Murder*, but it was a fun song to perform, even so. The movie had a much tighter story line than my first two films had. Every scene led well into another. At the end of the film, everything tied together so well, there should have been a big pink bow around it. I was allowed to wear attractive clothes for a change, and although I was still goofy in the film, it was a more sophisticated humor. The well written songs and the great lyrics went far in making the film a real success.

I think for the first time, I might have been slightly difficult to work with in a film. Since it was my third movie, I was prepared, or at least felt comfortable to do some things in my own way. Up until this time, I always waited for direction to guide me where I was supposed to go with the material. I had enjoyed working with George Marshall so much on *Rhythm*; I was a bit put out by the director on *Happy Go Lucky*, Curtis Bernhardt. He was new to America, having only arrived a few years earlier from Germany. Europeans have a completely different style in film making. If you look at later films made by Bernhardt, most of them were of a hard-boiled realistic nature. I really don't think he had a very good handle on comedy, particularly American comedy. I suppose I became a bit cocky for the first time. Buddy came to see me between scenes and asked, "Who told you to do it that way?" Of course I had no answer for him, I had made the decision to do whatever it was I had done on my own. When I felt I was in the right, I went with my instincts, no matter the cost. As an actor learns their craft, I believe you make judgment calls concerning the things that work and things that don't. I was merely exercising my new found knowledge. It was the first time I was pulled aside for what was more than likely considered being difficult. It may have been the first time, but it certainly wasn't going to be the last.

During the war years, most of the era's biggest stars made a war picture. Many Hollywood stars even served in the armed forces. Others went on war bond tours when they were between films, or worked at the Hollywood Canteen where servicemen and women mingled with the stars. I entertained troops at the Hollywood Canteen, a place where I sang *Murder, He Says* about a million times. Bob Hope once joked that if they were to put a propeller on me and send me off to Germany, the war would be over by Christmas. By 1944, I was receiving seven thousand letters every single week from servicemen around the world. Troops voted me the girl they would most like to spend a howling furlough with.

In today's world, the President can spend taxpayer money during wartime without consulting the taxpayer. It was different during WWII. In the early 1940's, the war cost an enormous amount of money. To pay for it, the US Treasury and President Roosevelt asked Americans to invest in *War Bonds*. Issued by the U.S. Government, they were first called Defense Bonds. The name was changed to War Bonds after the Japanese attack on Pearl Harbor. They were for the purpose of financing our military operations. An emotional appeal went out to citizens by means of advertising. Even though the bonds offered a rate of return below the market value, it represented a moral and financial stake in the war effort. The advertisements started with radio, newspapers, and magazines. The Treasury eventually advertised the sale of these War Bonds through national bond tours.

In 1943, I joined a group on a three week War Bond Tour with Hollywood film stars, all in an effort to enhance the advertising's effectiveness. Together with me on the tour were, Greer Garson, Judy Garland, Mickey Rooney, Fred Astaire, William Powell, Jimmy Cagney, Harpo Marx, and Lucille Ball. Everyone on that train was from MGM except for me; I was the only actor from Paramount.

During this time, I was seeing a man by the name of Charles Martin, and I was head over heels for the guy. Martin had been a screenwriter in Hollywood, and was previously seeing my good friend, Joan Crawford. Martin was now in New York writing scripts for radio. When our Bond Tour arrived in New York, Charles, and I got together. It didn't take long for me to decide he was the one. During a show at Madison Square Garden, I got a hold of the microphone from the public-address system, and announced to the entire place that Charles Martin and I were getting married. I even called Louella Parsons back in Hollywood. She felt really great by being the first to hear the news on the opposite coast.

The very next day, on September 19, 1943, Louella reported the following in her newspaper column, "Betty is so attractive and vivacious that you get the idea she has actual beauty, even though her features are not the classic type. The Paramount publicity department swears by her because she is never temperamental and is always ready to do whatever they ask. I know myself how cooperative she is. On five minutes notice, I asked her if she would go to the Hollywood canteen with me. She went and so captivated the service men and had such a good time herself that she promised to go every week with me. Betty, who is with the Hollywood War Bond Victory Caravan on a bond selling tour, telephoned from New York to say she is going to marry Charles Martin in January. He was formerly a scenario writer in Hollywood and was seen often in the company of Joan Crawford a few years ago. He is now writing radio scripts and will arrive in Hollywood in six weeks. Just before the blonde Hutton left for New York, she said she would make up her mind about marrying him..."

As it turned out, Martin didn't care about me the way I felt about him. After it was over, I felt foolish. I decided to make it look as if the marriage had been somewhat of a publicity stunt. That worked, but I was truly crushed. My luck with men wasn't good, but I kept trying.

The real love affair that shattered my world when it never materialized was with a handsome man I met on the set of the movie, *Let's Face It*. *Sidney Lanfield* was the director of the picture, but also a married man. We hit it off immediately when we met. We would plan to meet, and then rendezvous at *Charley Farrell's Racquet Club* in Palm Springs. *The Racquet Club* was one of the most popular celebrity hangouts and retreats during the 1940s and 50s. It was a place for stars to come and let their hair down, and to escape the pressures of Hollywood. Sid and I took full advantage of the place. We would arrive separately. A few hours after checking into our individual cottages, we would "accidentally" bump into each other in the *Bamboo Lounge*, the hub for all the activity at the club. I'd say, "Sid, it's so lovely to see you here. How have you been?" Sid would say something like, "Betty, I can't believe it. Well, you just never know who you are going to run into when you come out to Palm Springs." Because I was an actress, I assumed I was getting away with our charade. It probably wasn't all that necessary, everyone else there was probably up to the same thing as us.

Because Sidney was a married man, I was warned by a few close friends that what we had going together would never amount to anything, but I wouldn't listen. I went along with it because Sid told me his divorce was all set and right around the corner. A few weeks went by, then a few months, and still no divorce. By 1945, this bright girl finally realized he had been stringing her along. I cried bitter tears for weeks. It seemed every time I got to bat with some guy, I would strike right out.

The War Bond Tour took us to many cities all over the country. During our time between cities on the train, Harpo Marx and I taught Lucille Ball what to do on a comedy stage. She hadn't any clue. At MGM, she was lost on the back lot. When they did give her a part, it was in some straight role for which she wasn't well suited. Less than a decade later, when she landed her television show with Desi Arnaz, everything she put into practice on the show was what Harpo and I had taught her.

On the tour, we visited many theaters where free movie days were held with a bond purchase as the price of admission. Any city that agreed to subscribe to at least one million dollars was added to our whistle-stop agenda. In all, more than three hundred American cities and towns were visited during seven tours to promote War Bonds. The *Stars Over America* bond blitz, in which 337 stars took part, surpassed its quota and netted almost nine hundred million worth of bonds.

Not everything good came from the War Bond Tours. Actress Carole Lombard, then the wife of Clark Gable, died on January 16, 1942, when the DC-3 plane she was in crashed in the Sierra-Nevada Mountains west of Las Vegas. She was returning to Hollywood from a bond tour. She had been home to her native Indiana, and held one of the first and most successful war bond drives in Indianapolis. She raised almost two and one half million dollars. Her last words to all the people just before boarding TWA flight number three were, "Before I say goodbye to you all, come on and join me in a big cheer, V for victory!" All twenty two passengers on board died, including Carole's mother.

Lombard was dead at the age of thirty-three. The grief-stricken Clark Gable quickly joined up and became a gunnery officer in the Army Air Corps. Carole Lombard was posthumously awarded a medal from Franklin Roosevelt, as *the first woman to be killed in action, in defense of her country, in its war against the Axis Powers.*

In my next film, I played the female lead opposite Bob Hope. The movie, *Let's Face It,* was based upon the Broadway musical of the same name. Once again, Cole Porter's musical work, originally intended for the Broadway stage, gets watered down and all but disappears to make room for onscreen comic charades. Although Jule Styne and Sammy Cahn wrote and added new musical material, which was better suited to my taste, none of the songs were of any lasting consequence. In the end, this film wasn't about the music at all; it ended up as little more than a vehicle for Bob Hope's off-the-wall antics. That, in itself, wasn't a bad thing. The flimsy script, and even Bob himself, simply couldn't fully pull it off. An actor is only as good as their material allows them to be. One good thing; I got glamorized with new makeup, new hair, and an Edith Head wardrobe to take on the lead role, a first for me in a movie.

The story centers around three neglected wives who hire a trio of lonely GIs as their weekend escorts. Bob Hope is one member of the threesome, engaged by the wives in order to make their philandering husbands jealous. I play Hope's fiancée who runs a fat farm, the place where the three husbands dump their wives so they can run out and play. As always, complications arise when the three women's husbands show up unexpectedly, along with the soldier's own irate sweethearts, at a country home at the same time.

The movie opened in New York on August 5, 1943. In the same week, *The New York Times* said, "Although no one can do more with poor material than Bob Hope, there are limits. But if Mr. Hope's batting average has slumped, it still gathers enough laughter to make an amusing warm-weather caper. Perhaps most of the difficulty lies in the fact that *Let's Face It* was a rather undistinguished musical to begin with. All too often the material tries too strenuously to be funny."

In my opinion, Bob Hope and I clicked very well on camera. It's a real shame we never worked together on material written especially for us, in contrast to something watered down to accommodate us. Bob let me know the match between us didn't work. "Kid, you are too good, and we are too much alike." I took it as a compliment. In his own way, he was threatened by my commanding nature on the screen. I was okay with that. Bob needed someone to play *off*, instead of playing *with* on the screen. If the movie had been a real success, I guess the story between us might have turned out completely different. Bob and I remained life-long friends. It wasn't as if our paths never crossed again, the war effort kept us close. I did many Armed Forces radio program episodes of *Command Performance* with him throughout the 1940s. Years later, when I got myself into financial trouble; he was the one to come to my rescue. He was a lovely man for whom I will always hold a special place in my heart.

Between 1940 and 1944, Preston Sturges wrote and directed a series of seven comedies for Paramount Studios. *The Miracle of Morgan's Creek*, a blaring satirical farce about the home front during World War II, came near the end of that run. The movie was so well received; Sturges got an Oscar nomination for his screenplay of *Miracle* in 1944. Sadly, he was also nominated in the same category for *Hail The Conquering Hero*. That put him up against himself that year, and caused both of his nominations to essentially cancel each other out. Sturges lost the Oscar to Fox's biographical film, *Wilson*.

For whatever my performance lacked in *Let's Face It*, I was surely back on track in *The Miracle of Morgan's Creek*. For the first time in a movie, I was left vulnerable without my usual musical production numbers to fall back on.

Therefore, I knew I would really have to crank up my comic acting skills and fine tune my timing. Most of all, I would have to create a rich characterization of a young woman struggling against the social attitudes of the time.

I play Trudy Kockenlocker, a small town girl, who attends an army dance and later discovers she got married and impregnated during that same evening. The problem is I don't remember who I wed. Eddie Bracken plays the local 4-F boy who has always loved me. I trick him into marrying me to help me out of my unfortunate situation. Naturally, things get complicated when we actually do fall in love. My difficulty is eventually put right by *the miracle*, a Christmas birth of sextuplets. It's really intended as a spoof of the nativity story, yet it manages to be sweet and uplifting at the same time.

Preston Sturges treads in this film where other directors feared back in 1944. There were so many objections from the censors; Sturges began production with only ten approved script pages. Preston knew and freely admitted, "If you keep it funny, the censors will never be able to touch it." Miraculously, he did manage to squeak this film by the film control board. Still, for all the manipulation Sturges went through to get this controversial subject matter made, the basic idea that my character got drunk and slept with a soldier comes across loud and clear in the film. Sturges brilliantly carried on from there to make the most of the panic and desperation of the situation, turning it all into a fast-paced chaotic comedy.

Because of the problems with the film censors and the few approved script pages to start out with, Preston Sturges more or less made things up as we went along. He proved to be a wonderful man to work with. He reminded us we were all professionals, and as such, we all knew what needed to be done to make the movie work. Sturges would work on the next day's scenes the previous night. When we all arrived at the studio the next day, he would hand us what we were going to do that day. We would sit around for awhile and discuss the movie and the direction it was headed. By this time, it was fast approaching noon. Preston owned the popular *Players Restaurant,* the place where we would usually take our lunch break, or he would have the fabulous food sent in so we really couldn't complain too much about sitting around. Finally, in the afternoon, we would get around to shooting a few scenes - twelve to fifteen minutes a day, tops. Yet, for those of us in the cast, it was great fun getting to make things up as we went along. No one else ever let us do what Preston did, he trusted us. It was all very casual, but quite time consuming at the same time.

Right from the beginning, Buddy told me this movie wasn't good for me. You see, Buddy wasn't all that fond of Sturges from a business standpoint. He just couldn't hit his schedules. Buddy warned me, "Eddie (Bracken) is going to walk away with this picture, Betty."

I protested, "Buddy, I don't have to sing and dance in this one. I finally get the chance to really be *me* up there on the screen."

Buddy shot back, "Yes, and who are you, Betty?"

"I don't know, but there has to be something else to me besides singing and jumping all over the place," I added defensively.

Buddy must have been in one of his honest-to-God, tell-all moods that day. He informed me Eddie had no intention of making another picture with me if I sang a song in it. Shortly after, there was a preview at the studio to view some of the scenes shot from *Miracle.* I tried never to go to the "sneaks", as they were called; I was uncomfortable watching myself onscreen. Afterwards, Eddie came to see me in my dressing room all happy. The comment cards from the sneak-preview had been tallied, and shown Eddie to be the clear favorite in the film. He looked at me and said, "Betty, thank you for making me a star."

"What?" I questioned him with a suspicious look on my face.

"Betty, I got all the notices from the sneaks."

"That's great Eddie." So it seemed as if Buddy had been right. Eddie would walk away with the film.

When the movie opened, it was me who received most of the critical acclaim. It was the craziest thing. In retaliation, Eddie went in to see Buddy and demanded, "I never want to be in a picture with her again. When she sings, forget it!"

Years later, Eddie asked me to come to Washington D.C. for a special showing of *Miracle*. As we sat in the theater and watched it, I laughed hysterically. After the screening, Eddie asked, "What was with you and all the laughter?"

I confessed, "I've never seen the whole movie before, Eddie." He was unable to comprehend that. Even so, while we were talking, I decided to confront him. "Why did you do that, why did you say you would never be in another picture with me, Eddie?"

"Betty, it was probably one of the worst mistakes I have ever made in my life." He had a true look of remorse on his face.

Still I wasn't satisfied. I wanted more of an explanation. So, I continued to plead my case. "I can't understand how you could do that. I loved you so... We were so great together, Eddie."

"I just had this thing, Betty. If I was in another movie with you where you sang, I was pretty much through."

I persevered, "But I didn't sing a single note in *Miracle*, Eddie." I was trying hard to extract from him the true reason.

"I realize that now, Betty, I was wrong."

So that was that. "I was wrong" was as much of an explanation as I was going to get. I dropped the subject. I believe I was giving him the third degree in an attempt to get back at him in my own little way. I knew deep in my heart the *real* reason he had done it. It goes to show how insecure we all can be about our careers as actors. Very few possess the ability not to allow comments from fellow actors to affect them. Ours is a relatively cut-throat kind of business.

Although shot in 1942 and early 1943, *The Miracle of Morgan's Creek* was withheld from distribution until Paramount had a slot in its schedule to release it. When the film was officially opened on January 19, 1944, it was such a huge hit; there was literally standing room only for many performances. The National Board of Review nominated the film for Best Picture of 1944, and honored me with the award for Best Acting for my performance in the film.

The year 1944 was a busy one for me. In that same year, I signed with Capitol Records. The Capitol Records Company was founded by songwriter, Johnny Mercer, in 1942, with the financial help of Buddy DeSylva, and the business insight of Glenn Wallichs, owner of Music City, at the time the biggest record store in Los Angeles. Music City record store opened in 1940, and was located in Hollywood, on the corner of Sunset and Vine. It was the leading music store in all of Southern California. In February of 1942, Mercer and Wallichs met with Buddy DeSylva at a Hollywood restaurant to ask if Paramount Pictures would invest in the new record company. DeSylva said it wasn't possible, but that he would. Buddy gave them a check for $15,000 to help the company with its startup. Capitol was the first West Coast label, competing with RCA-Victor, Columbia, and Decca, all New York based companies.

My recording career came as sort of a bonus offshoot to the movie making. It was something I had never really thought about or expected. It came so easy for me. It's not because it wasn't hard work to put down a great recording, I just went into the recording studio with a good attitude and did it.

Toward the end of April, *And The Angels Sing* was released. This was my sixth movie. Even though I was billed third behind Dorothy Lamour and Fred MacMurray, the critics somehow managed to say I walked away with the picture. I believe it had a great deal to do with my outrageous show-stopping number, *His Rocking Horse Ran Away*. *The New York Times* said, "If the whole show were up to this number, it would be a sensational affair." This became one of the numbers to be closely associated with me for the remainder of my career. The marvelous lyrics to all the songs in the show were written by Johnny Burke, and all the music was composed by Jimmy Van Heusen. This musical team really knew their stuff. They were on the same genius par with Frank Loesser. *Bluebirds In My Belfry* was my other catchy novelty number solo. This had to be some of the best music I did in any of my films. At least *The New York Times* seemed to think so, when they also commented, "At least Hutton makes up in energy what the writers failed to provide." All the numbers bounced along throughout the picture, and once the film was over, people actually left the theaters humming and whistling the tunes.

I play one of the four Angel sisters who manage to get themselves all wrapped up with unscrupulous bandleader, Fred MacMurray. My character gets swindled out of money by MacMurray, who needs it in order for his band to get traveling money to an engagement in Brooklyn. The sisters feel duped, and trail him to New York City to retrieve their money. Some funny things happen, and several musical numbers manage to get performed along the way. The story line was not meant to be involved, it's merely fun and entertaining; a real reason for a lot of great music. The four-sister act sings several songs in great harmony including, *The First Hundred Years* and *Knocking On Your Own Front Door*. To be sure, movies like this raised the spirits of war weary citizens during the 1940's.

His *Rocking Horse Ran Away* was so successful, Johnny Burke and Jimmy Van Heusen had a special rocking horse jewelry pin created and presented it to me. From it, a chain led to a little boy who appeared to be holding on to the horse's reins. You pinned both rocking horse and boy separately from each other, so it appeared as if the boy was in flight after having been thrown from the horse. It is a lovely piece, and I have it to this day. I had given it to my dear and wonderful friend, Judy Rector, from Newport at some point, but she eventually returned it because of the significance it has to my career. The pin is solid gold and both the horse and boy have diamond eyes.

To close out 1944, *Here Come The Waves* opened on December 18th. This snappy wartime musical starred Bing Crosby and me. Bing plays Johnny, a popular radio singer, who joins the Navy to escape his out-of-control fans. After enlisting, he is ordered to aid a Wave recruiting drive. There he meets me, or both of me, I should say, since I play identical twin sisters, Susie and Rosemary. One is a shy and quiet redhead, the other a bold and sassy blonde. Part of Johnny's duties is to stage a musical show, but in the process he falls hard for one sister, but can't tell one from the other. With the confusion of identities and the Wave recruiting show to put on, a comic plot is concocted, and musical numbers are sure to follow. This is the film in which Bing Crosby and Sonny Tufts introduce the Academy Award nominated Johnny Mercer and Harold Arlen song, *Ac-Cent-Tchu-Ate the Positive*. My decent solo number in the film was, *There's A Fellow Waiting in Poughkeepsi*. Bing had been great to work with, but he came on set when he felt like it. That was tough on the crew. The effect it had on the outcome of the picture may well have been detrimental.

The film was not all that well received. I was praised for my dual characterization, yet I was chastised for being too over the top as the boisterous blonde twin. It looked as if 1944 had started out with a bang, but was ending on a sour note. I had progressed to the point where I knew you couldn't win them all. The positive aspects were undeniable; I was at the height of my popularity and had the reputation as a major star. I was now drawing five thousand dollars a week in my contract with the studio, placing me in the upper echelon of actors at Paramount. I was a success, but my private life had been put on almost permanent hold. I was paying way too much attention to my career. Maybe it was time I started looking around. Nevertheless, the type of money I was making, and the celebrity I had attained, made my odds of meeting someone with whom I could be compatible, and all the while remain non-threatening, a bit unlikely.

Shortly after arriving at Paramount.
Photo: Paramount publicity, Betty's private collection

With my wonderful friend Dorothy Lamour.
Photo: Betty's private collection, The Betty Hutton Estate

The cast from *Happy Go Lucky*, 1943.
Photo: Paramount publicity photo, Betty's private collection

War Bond Cavalcade returns home to Los Angeles after 10,091
miles through 16 American cities in 21 days.
Photo: Pictorial Paradise

Performing at The Hollywood Canteen, 1943.
Photo: Betty's private collection, The Betty Hutton Estate.

Hamming it up with Eddie Bracken on the set of
The Miracle of Morgan's Creek, 1944.
Photo: Paramount photo, Betty's private collection

Reading fan mail in my Paramount dressing room.
Photo: Paramount photo, Betty's private collection

The *Rocking Horse* pin Johnny Burke and Jimmy Van Heusen
had made for me after the great success I had with their song.
Photo: Betty's private collection, The Betty Hutton Estate

Wonderful display outside a New York Theater
Promoting *Here Come The Waves,* 1944.
Photo: Betty's private collection, The Betty Hutton Estate

Chapter Ten

Like the previous year, I was sure 1945 was going to be equally demanding. During the war years, when you weren't busy making a movie, you were more than likely occupied with something attached to the war effort. I had so many things in the works, I actually felt relieved when *Incendiary Blonde* opened in New York at the end of July. After all, we had finished the production of it more than a year before. It was always strange when a picture you had worked so hard on was held back from release. By the time the film was ready to open, you were already so involved in some other project. Consequently, you had practically forgotten about making it. However, the fun part was still there to enjoy when hype over the movie really got going with interviews and celebrity appearances.

Incendiary Blonde was the biopic story of prohibition-era nightclub performer, Texas Guinan, who rose to fame from a boisterous performer in a Wild West Show. She went on to become a singing and dancing Broadway star, movie actress, and ultimately to the owner of a famous 1920s New York City nightclub. I play Texas Guinan, and carry her through her various careers and failed romances. The whole thing is in Technicolor, and tied together with fine music written by Robert Emmett Dolan. *Incendiary Blonde* earned him a nomination for an Academy Award for best music-scoring of a musical picture in 1946.

Arturo de Cordova caused me much heartache in the movie by playing my love interest and business partner. He also managed to cause me much personal heartache, due to the dreary and lackluster manner in which he played his character. Why, oh why, was I never afforded a decent leading man in at least one of my movies? When it had originally been announced the film was going into production, Alan Ladd was slated to be the male lead. Then, when we were just about to start filming in Arizona, Barry Sullivan, who had been named after Ladd, was assigned at the very last minute to another film. That's how we ended up with Cordova, by process of elimination.

Most of Cordova's films were made in his native Mexico where he had become a major motion picture actor. He achieved film success in Spain as well. Having lost Rudolph Valentino in a 1924 contract dispute, Paramount was forever on the lookout for a new Latin lover type, and so it happened, they signed Arturo de Cordova to a contract. All I can think is somehow, something got lost in the translation to English; I never understood the supposed appeal, much less his mediocre acting ability.

A few of my songs were real winners. *It Had to Be You* and *What Do You Want to Make Those Eyes at Me For* were real standouts, and forever after associated with me. The number *Row, Row, Row* was beautifully choreographed by a guy named Danny Dare, with whom I had worked on several of my earlier pictures. His best known work was in the movie, *Holiday Inn,* where he staged the dance numbers. For some reason, whenever *Incendiary Blonde* is mentioned, or clips are shown, that's the number that invariably comes up. Before I start singing *Row, Row, Row* in the film, I turn to the bandleader and say, "Okay Freddy, don't hit any high notes, I've got a new corset on. It's tight, too!"

I have to admit, I did look great in that beautiful midnight blue sequined strapless gown by the marvelous *Edith Head*. My god, how I wish I still looked like that! It wasn't an easy job staying fit for the camera. I actually had to take a couple of weeks off during the making of the film, just so I could fit into those beauties. My normal weight was around 125 pounds, but for the camera, I had to get down to about 112; my face always appeared too full if I was at my regular weight. I also needed a rest. After thirty-eight costume changes and all the different hairdos, I was extremely exhausted.

In early 1945, I was excited to participate in a USO tour of the Western Pacific. I had enjoyed being involved with the War Bond Tour, but now I wanted to step my involvement up a notch and be with the boys who were actually fighting for us. We had not gone into war of our own free will; we were forced into it. There had been no alternative. I wanted to go and entertain the boys who were as bewildered as I about how this all came to be. The tour took us to places I had never even heard of. We ended up doing fifty thousand miles in eight weeks. We made countless stops in our quest to visit as many of our boys as possible, on islands and atolls in the Mariana group such as Guam, Saipan, and Tinian, the Marshall Islands, the Gilbert Islands, and Iwo Jima in the Ogasawara Islands.

It's hard to imagine, but our guys were fighting an enemy in the Pacific who didn't mind dying. Japanese pilots made dive-bomb attacks on our men, a practice which made little sense to any of us. How the hell do you battle an enemy who doesn't give a damn for their own lives? There is never justification for war, but our troops were over there in the middle of it, and I was anxious to be with them.

The real reason I went was to let the boys know America really cared. What better morale booster can you offer our boys but a visit from home? They gave me a General's uniform to wear. In the event I was captured by the Japanese, my rank was supposed to offer me a degree of protection from their persuasive methods of interrogation.

I found the General's helmet useful as a prop to provide me with a degree of disguise so I could surprise our boys when I approached them. Often they really were *just boys*. Many had peach fuzz faces and appeared barely old enough to be out of high school, much less a world away from their homes and families. I would crawl right down into the foxholes on my hands and knees. When I approached, they would turn and point their guns in my direction. When I got close enough, I would remove the helmet and my golden locks would tumble down around my shoulders. This is when the real fun began. Usually tears of joy flowed unashamedly down their cheeks as they recognized who I was. Someone would cry out, "Betty, you're Betty Hutton. Oh my God, you're here!" This was indeed one of the greatest thrills of not only my career, but of my entire life. Nothing else, no other feeling in the world, could possibly compare with how I felt inside bringing joy to those young men. Everyone would gather close as we exchanged hugs and kisses. Most often, I would sing a few bars from one of my songs, or one they might request. It was difficult for those boys to believe a popular movie entertainer would crawl down into a hole to perform just for them. It wasn't crazy to me at all. I wouldn't have exchanged the precious minutes I had with those guys for anything. I did it as much for me as I did for them, but who actually received the most from the exchange is anyone's guess.

I wasn't expecting anything in return for visiting our boys, but years later when I opened at the Palace on Broadway in New York, God had something in store for me that indirectly rewarded me for my efforts. I was truly blessed when a large group of parents of boys from the war came to see me. Suddenly, I came to the realization these were parents of boys who perished during the war and never returned home to their families. They came backstage to see me, and each of them took me in their arms and kissed me, as if I were their very own. You see, they simply wanted to hold me, the girl who had held their sons. I had been the same age then as their sons were, and by taking me in their arms, they felt as if they were connecting with their own beloved sons. At that moment it hit me, I knew visiting our men overseas was one of the most important things I could have done, and would ever do, in my life.

I will never forget until my dying day how damned hot it was on those islands in the Western Pacific. It was truly a living hell for everyone. Along with the enemy, we were forced to fight against all sorts of fungi and bugs that were capable of invading your body because of the extreme heat and humidity.

The lovely clothes I have taken along with me for the boys to see literally fell apart on my body. If you didn't shower regularly, you were asking for trouble. The real trouble was in finding a place for two girls to shower surrounded by all those men. I had taken a girl named Virginia along with me to entertain our troops. She was a wonderful dancer. A few of the more industrious men erected a shower for us out of corrugated tin that they more or less wrapped around us like a stall. They also rigged a few large empty food drums into water taps by putting a series of holes in the bottoms of the cans. The boys probably drew straws to see who would stand on platforms to hold the water drums up above our heads.

Whichever guys got the job were on their honor not to sneak a peek down at us. I'm not sure they always kept their promise, but then, *we were there to entertain the troops.*

As we exited our makeshift shower, a G. I. was stationed on either side with an enormous towel to wrap around us. At the same time, the rest of the battalion stood at attention watching every move we made. They were supposed to be assembled there for our protection. It really was a hilarious sight to behold. I'm so fortunate I was an actress; I could play it to the hilt and still act sweet and innocent. All the men managed to keep their composure and a straight face to avoid us any undo embarrassment. But what the hell, we knew they all got a good eyeful, but we never minded in the least. It was one call to duty that you had better believe not one of those guys minded getting assigned to. To make matters even funnier, our clothing was laundered for us, and our underpants could be seen up on a line appearing almost like a camp flag waving in the breeze.

The very worst part of our stay with the troops was in having to use the latrine at night. It was mandatory for us to be escorted by an armed soldier, as the islands were never completely secured. Most often, Japanese were hiding everywhere around us. It was always unfortunate if you had to use the toilet for the particular purpose that usually involved sound effects. I always tried to hold it, but by the time we left Iwo Jima, I felt like a big balloon full of gas. Upon exiting the latrine, a soldier stood there and saluted you; I felt so completely foolish.

It's probably common knowledge, movie stars don't poop. In the rare event one might, by accident, it should be known by all, it smells exactly like roses. I managed to keep my dignity by carrying a can of deodorant that I used to generously spray the latrine before and after each use.

For a brief time, while I was in there anyway, the place managed to smell almost like a rose garden.

I was forever proud of my involvement and participation during the war. Years later, I received countless letters and photographs from service men who remember having seen me entertain them. As the years passed, and the older both I and the soldier became, the weepier the letters got. The letters mostly lamented the wonderful days of our youth, even though we were caught in the middle of that horrendous war in the very primes of our lives. I made phone calls when possible to many of the servicemen I received letters from. Naturally, it would take quite some time to get them to believe I really was who I said I was. The other part of the time we spent was in sharing tears. Tears of sadness for our lost youth, but mostly tears of joy we were still around to talk about it.

When I returned home to the States, I recovered for a short time from an illness I had contracted while on tour in the Pacific. I believe the doctors said it was amoebic dysentery. I had actually spent some time in an American army hospital in Saipan, but managed to complete the remainder of the tour. After I was feeling better, I was off in the other direction. This time, I was headed off for a six-week USO tour of European army camps. I cut it short, since I still wasn't feeling perfect, and returned home in August.

While I was in Europe, I received a cable from the man I had been seeing. Ted Briskin and I met at a restaurant on Rush Street in downtown Chicago named the Singapore, shortly before the USO tour to Europe. I saw him while I was sitting and eating spare ribs, of all things. I was working on my second or third rib when I looked up and saw him at another table staring at me. I thought maybe I had made a complete mess all over my face eating ribs, but that wasn't it at all. Someone introduced us, and we actually went out dancing that very same evening. I was almost sure he was a married man; no one would let someone like him stay single for long. Nevertheless, he wasn't, and for me, he was the one. We courted and fell in love. Teddy accompanied me to New York to see me off on the European tour. The cable Ted sent was a marriage proposal which simply read, "Please send size of third finger, left hand."

Before heading home from Europe, the word had gotten out. In an interview, I was asked about my impending marriage to Teddy. I answered by saying, "I don't know if we will be married right away, or after I return to California." They got a real kick when I added, "It all depends on what happens when I see him."

Upon my arrival back in the States, Teddy was there to meet me in New York with a colossal square-cut diamond ring. We continued on to Teddy's home town of Chicago. There we were married on September 2, 1945, in the Camellia House of the Drake Hotel. I was 24 years old, and this was a first marriage for us both. I wore a smart gold wool suit with a yellow hat made from real orchids. Wearing flowers on my head was a fashion statement; one I borrowed from my lovely friend, Dorothy Lamour. Another dear friend, Lindsey Durand, from Paramount's publicity department, was my maid of honor. Teddy's older brother, Philip, stood up as his best man. A reception was held immediately afterwards, and by that same night, we had already left to honeymoon in Miami. I was sure if we went straight back to California, they would put me back to work at the studio immediately.

Louella Parsons reported about our marriage, "It was love at first sight for Betty Hutton and Briskin. I've talked to a lot of newlyweds in the many years I have been writing on movie marriages, but I doubt if I ever have seen any couple as ecstatically happy as Betty and her Chicago groom, Ted Briskin. Ted is young, he's good looking, and best of all he's as crazy about Betty as she is about him, and that's saying a lot."

We were in love, and I wanted to keep it that way. At 27, Teddy was already the president of the Revere Camera Company of Chicago; his family was made of money. I made it clear right from the beginning, I had no intention of giving up my career. Since Teddy was self-made, I didn't see any problem. We both had our own career paths to keep us occupied. The times we weren't pulled in opposite directions would be quality time for us to share together. The only problem that I saw was in dividing our time between Hollywood and Chicago, as we had agreed we would do. In short, I needed to be in Hollywood most of the time. With Teddy's business being headquartered in Chicago, somehow I knew our division of time wasn't going to work out as well as we had expected.

We arrived home to California on September 22, 1945, with plans to live in the house I had purchased in Brentwood not long before our marriage. My mother met us at the train station in Pasadena where we arrived on the Santa Fe Chief. Mother had a reception planned for us in The Sun Room at the Beverly Hills Hotel the following evening, so as not to exclude our West Coast friends and family entirely from our wedding festivities. I introduced Teddy to my friends by saying, "I could never find anything like him in Hollywood. I had to go all the way to Chicago... some town that Chicago."

Teddy and I did really well in the beginning. Everything was so new between us, it took time just getting acclimated to sharing your life with someone else. After about six months of marriage, Teddy became pretty annoyed with the attention I was paying to my career instead of him, and wanted me to quit. Our arguments about it could get pretty heated. I would head to the studio and the privacy of my dressing room; there I would cry my eyes out for hours. We kept apart for awhile, but shortly thereafter, we came to a compromise, or I should say, Teddy did. I still refused to budge concerning my career, telling Teddy I couldn't abandon it for him or any other man. Teddy gave in, and said he understood. He opened a camera company in Santa Monica as something to keep him busy while I was off doing my thing. He even made me vice president of his new company. It might have been solely for the publicity my name could afford his camera sales, since the media were following us closely. Teddy told them we had reached a compromise and was sure we would be happy from then on.

In November 1946 was the birth of our first child, Lindsay. Having a child changed our lives together. At least we didn't fight as much. I did my best to be home more, but a lot of that choice was out of my immediate control. I loved my family, but I was married to my career, first and foremost. I know now that sounds crazy, but I think I was a bit crazy when it came to my career. Teddy had no idea what I had gone through to get where I was. There had been countless years of singing on street corners, poverty, abuse, and lousy breaks. No guy could ask me to give my career up after all of that.

In 1948, Candy, our second child, was born. Teddy and I were hanging in there. Things weren't getting better between us; they were actually going in the other direction. I was kept so busy at the studio; I really didn't have time to do one thing or the other when it came to dealings at home. The nannies and the maids took care of the children in my absence. Oh sure, there were good times, but they were few and far between.

By February of 1950, I filed for divorce from Ted. He wasn't happy with my career, and in all honesty, I understood him. I just wasn't in the least bit capable of facing up to the fact that he was right. By April, we had a provisional divorce ruling, but again we stalled the inevitable. The decree was halted in July. Things continued to get so ugly, that by December, I filed a second suit, this time charging him with extreme mental cruelty. Ted was ultimately motivated to make a public statement in which he said, "I can't stand a bossy woman".

There were seven movies between the time we got married, and the time our divorce was finalized in January of 1951. That, in itself, was enough to send any husband packing. It was all about my career and my refusal to make any compromises. My mother told the press, "Betty isn't fooling anyone. The reason she works so hard is that when she's out there singing and carrying on entertaining people, she feels as good as anyone in the entire world." My career was my whole life, and I couldn't help it.

I should never have married; I just wasn't any good at it. I had three more cracks at it until I finally got the hint. Even that was fine, my career compensated me in ways a husband never could. It's my children I feel terrible about. They really suffered. They never even got to know me, because I didn't know myself. I sure as hell didn't give them what they needed, and I know now what they needed was me. I was too busy making a living. There were so many people who depended upon me, I couldn't possibly quit working. Nobody forced me to stay working; I was the selfish one who just wouldn't give it up. I made the choice to select my career over my family, and I live with that realization each and every day I spend without them.

That wonderful gown from *Incendiary Blonde*, 1945.
Photo: Paramount photo, Betty's private collection

On the Island of Saipan, 1945.
Photo: Betty's private collection, The Betty Hutton Estate

Entertaining the troops was one of my most
rewarding, but challenging assignments.
Photo: Betty's private collection, The Betty Hutton Estate

My wedding day with Ted Briskin, September 2, 1945.
Photo: Betty's private collection, The Betty Hutton Estate

Early married life was bliss!
Photo: Betty's private collection, The Betty Hutton Estate

Me, with my mother, sister, and new husband, Ted.
Photo: Betty's private collection, The Betty Hutton Estate

Teddy and I with Mr. Entertainment, Bob Hope.

Photo: Betty's private collection, The Betty Hutton Estate

Chapter Eleven

It seemed as if I alternated between making a halfway decent movie and a real stinker. *Here Come The Waves* had been bad, and immediately after, *Incendiary Blonde* was good. Well, it was my turn for a bad one again, and that's exactly what I got with *Duffy's Tavern*. Fortunately, I can't take total blame for the movie; I only had a minute part in it. It was another one of those huge extravaganzas, with a paper thin story line, which made it easy for Paramount to gather in one place a veritable who's who from their acting roster. The film opened on September 28, 1945, and was an attempt by Paramount Pictures to cash in on the wildly popular radio situation comedy of the same name. It featured Ed Gardner, recreating his role as Archie, surrounded by a throng of Paramount stars playing themselves. Archie begins recruiting the stars to donate their services and assistance when their neighborhood bar is in danger of closing. Radio's *Duffy's Tavern* didn't translate well to film, and the picture fizzled at the box office. I did have a great musical number in the film, *(Doin' It) The Hard Way,* which I sang in a psychiatrist office skit with *Billy De Wolfe,* but it had little if anything to do with the story line. Nevertheless, it was another fine song by one of my favorite winning duos, Jimmy Van Heusen and Johnny Burke.

By this time, Buddy DeSylva had already stepped down from his post as production chief at Paramount. He had suffered a stroke and was having a difficult time trying to make a comeback, but he remained in the game. His first independently-produced project was *The Stork Club,* and he did it with me in mind. Buddy wrote the screenplay, completing it before his illness. My last film had been bad, so if my memory served me well, I was in line for a hit. From what we all saw in the script Buddy presented; this movie was going to do the trick.

The real *Stork Club* had been one of my old haunts during my New York days. *Ethel Merman* was going with owner *Sherman Billingsley* while I was in *Panama Hattie* on Broadway. Buddy DeSylva had once been barred from the Stork Club, but he was still ready to offer Billingsley big bucks for screen rights to use the name and likeness of the club in his movie production. I had become friends with Sherman years before, so when he heard I was to star in the film, he allowed Buddy to use the name of the club. If any money was exchanged for the usage rights, I would be really surprised. After all, Billingsley was in line to make millions off the publicity the movie would generate for his establishment. At one point, rumors flew that Billingsley's Stork Club financed the making of the movie as a sort of feature-length commercial. I doubt it highly; Sherman's club was always surrounded by much speculation and rumor due to its exclusivity.

Paramount's New York office moved in on the club with their cameras, shooting everything from the kitchen to the ladies' powder room. They rushed the pictures out to Hollywood so the crews could get busy building a duplicate nightclub in the studio. The Paramount Stork Club looked so convincingly real, Buddy invited Sherman Billingsley out to see it. When Sherman arrived, a party was held for him in what looked like his own club, but without a roof. If you are unfamiliar, sets are built without ceilings so lights and a host of other equipment can function from above without any type of hindrance.

The movie was in production between April and June of 1945. In the movie, I play a hat-check girl from the club who rescues what appears to be a tramp from drowning in a lake. However, the tramp, played by wonderful Irish character actor Barry Fitzgerald, is actually a millionaire. In appreciation, he anonymously provides me with a bank account, a luxury apartment, and an unlimited charge account at a department store. When my orchestra leader boyfriend, played by Don DeFore, returns from overseas, he thinks I'm a kept woman. I end up spending all my new-found wealth to help him become famous. It's a totally predictable feel-good movie, with one of those plots where people jump to conclusions and romantic problems automatically follow.

The movie was released a few days after Christmas in 1945. I had instant success with two songs from the film. The first one, *Doctor, Lawyer, Indian Chief*, featured music by Hoagy Carmichael and lyrics by Paul Francis Webster. I recorded this song with Capitol records, and it was on the music charts for an incredible twenty weeks. It sprinted to first place on the singles chart during the week of March 2, 1946, and stayed there for two weeks. It is probably *the* song most associated with me and my career. The other song from the movie that I also did very well with, was *A Square in the Social Circle*. It was written by my great friends, Jay Livingston and Ray Evans. It was the "B-side" of the record, with *Doctor, Lawyer* being on the "A-side". How about that, two hits for the price of one!

It was a lovely film, and I enjoyed making it. In the end, however, ownership of the film was somehow vague enough to allow it to slip into the public domain in 1982. That's the reason the picture has been released by virtually every mom and pop operation who have the money to shell out on decent DVD reproduction equipment. They cut the film to disk and sell it as if they owned it. It's sort of sad, but public domain laws allow exactly that.

By the end of 1945, I was thoroughly exhausted from my hectic schedule. I took several months off to recoup my physical strength and mental well being. When I returned to the studio in January of 1946, I tried my best to go back with a renewed attitude. I guess it must have been a major change, because everyone at the studio was buzzing about it. I had decided while on hiatus that I needed to stop trying to carry all the weight of a film on my own shoulders. I got so involved; I actually started worrying about things that should only be the producer's burden to carry. I had been agonizing about the electricians, prop men, and every minuscule detail behind the scenes. As a consequence of all the stress, I was becoming a nervous wreck. It was really beginning to wear me out.

Everyone was talking about the "new" Betty. I was back and raring to go in a new, restrained sort of way. I hoped to tone down my career to the point where I could reach a new happy balance and become more of a dramatic actress. I guess, in a way I was being selfish, but the comic roughhousing was starting to get to me. Although it was the comic Betty Hutton that got me to where I was, and it was exactly what my fans had come to expect, I knew deep inside I couldn't keep up that kind of a pace forever. I was getting older, and somehow it didn't seem altogether appropriate.

Shortly after my return to work, I became pregnant with our first child. By the end of summer, I was as excited as any expectant mother ever could be. I took things easier by spending some well needed time at home preparing for the baby. *Cross My Heart* was the next movie of mine slated to be released, but it had finished production a year earlier. We worked on *The Perils of Pauline* while I was pregnant, but production was started in February and wrapped in May. I was happy to spend the critical months of my pregnancy off the set. The baby wasn't due until sometime in November.

I had a great time getting the nursery ready. I managed to get a Walt Disney artist over to decorate the room. It turned out beautiful, with painted animals parading down the side of one wall, and then continuing across the floor and up the opposite wall. I spared no expense in the preparations. The media got a hold of the story, and naturally they wanted to come over and photograph the room for a magazine layout. I went ahead and gave them exactly what they wanted. I made it sound typically Betty Hutton for the press when I said, "Trust me to make a production out of it." It was exactly what they had anticipated from the girl who never knew when to say quits.

In May, the same month we finishing up work on *The Perils of Pauline, a* new musical opened at the *Imperial Theater* in New York. It had lyrics and music written by *Irving Berlin,* and book by brother and sister team, *Herbert and Dorothy Fields.* The show was called, *Annie Get Your Gun,* and it starred *Ethel Merman* in the title role. I went to New York to see it, and fell deeply in love with the role of Annie Oakley. This was a part I just had to play in the hotly anticipated movie version. I went back to Hollywood and talked to Buddy about it, but I couldn't get any real enthusiasm out of him; his health was still so tentative.

My eleventh film, *Cross My Heart* opened on January 10, 1947, to poor reviews. I play Peggy Harper, a compulsive liar who'll do anything to help her attorney fiancé, Oliver Clarke (Sonny Tufts), get his struggling law practice going. When it looks as though an unsolved murder case will be Oliver's ticket to legal success, Peggy compellingly confesses to the killing. It gives her boyfriend the opportunity to prove her innocence, thereby strengthening his reputation and law practice. Of course, things don't go quite as planned. The New York Times reported, "But a lie is not the only thing you can't hide; you can't hide a weak script, and here one is." There were cute moments in the film, but it wasn't a solid enough project to make an impact at the theaters.

I must have either forgotten about this picture, or intentionally wiped it from my mind. When I was reminded of it years later by my friend in Palm Springs, I must have had a blank or puzzled look on my face. My friend, Mike, turned to me and said, "You know, Betty, it's the movie where you sing so pretty in front of the courtroom, the jury applauds, and the judge lets you out of the murder rap..." I broke down in a fit of laughter at the premise. My laughter must have been contagious, because suddenly we were both hysterical. Even after going through clippings to include mention of it here, I recollect nothing but the songs. I can tell you one thing; I must have done some brilliant singing to get myself out of a murder rap!

I had three songs in the movie, *That Little Dream Got Nowhere*, *How Do You Do It*, and *Love Is The Darndest Thing*. They were all by the very talented team of Johnny Burke and Jimmy Van Heusen. They were great song writers, but neither their songs nor my singing them could help save this little movie.

Our first child was born on November 23, 1946. We had a baby girl, and we named her Lindsay. She was beautiful. My sister, Marion, came to see the baby, but for some reason, she just had to make the comment, "She looks like a pink chicken." Marion was not happy with my success, and at that moment, I resented her for transferring her disfavor for me onto my lovely child. I had no clue at the time that Marion was drinking to such excess. I think the reality of everything was too overwhelming for her. Her dissatisfaction started after Glenn Miller was killed, and she was never able to recover her career. Because I made it so big, there was a lot of jealousy on her part. She confessed to me, "Betty, I have never been able to deal with it."

In April of 1947, an article written by the popular reporter, Bob Thomas, who covered the Film Industry for the Associated Press stated, "You'd better get acquainted with Betty Hutton, because you're going to be seeing a lot of her. She will soon be one of the most important stars in Hollywood, because Betty is a cinch for high honors after she is seen in her next movie, *The Perils of Pauline*. When she arrived in this town, she could do little but make funny faces, throw herself around, and sing a loud song. By sheer energy and concentration, she has developed into an accomplished actress and can sing and dance anything that might be required."

This article helped bring people out in droves to see *The Perils of Pauline,* which opened on July 4, 1947. The movie is a musical comedy, based loosely upon on the life of Pearl White, who leaves a New York sweat shop to join a theatrical troupe. Eventually, she winds up in Hollywood, the most successful silent film actress of her day. It was shot in Technicolor as a wonderful period piece, but was criticized for being little more than a fictionalized account of Pearl White's rise to fame. Hollywood was blamed for hyping the story up in order to showcase my comic and singing abilities. Nevertheless, in those days, films were made more for their entertainment value than they were for their historical accuracy. In spite of the criticism, the film was a huge box office and financial success. So much so, the studio immediately sought additional biographical projects for me to star in. Sadly, none of those movie ideas developed beyond the talking stage.

I played Pearl White, and actor John Lund is the aloof, unemotional object of my affections. The cast also included the wonderful, Billy De Wolfe and William Demarest. Constance Collier plays my female colleague and mentor in the movie. She got very sick during filming, and they wanted to replace her. I was so in love with Constance, I told them *no*. I guess my clout on the set finally meant something; they waited until Collier was well enough to return to the set and continue filming.

I loved all the songs I had to sing in the movie, probably because they were all written by the wonderful and talented Frank Loesser. *I Wish I Didn't Love You So* was nominated for an Oscar for best music-original song for Loesser in 1948. Also from the movie were, *The Sewing Machine*, *Rumble, Rumble, Rumble*, and *Poppa, Don't Preach To Me*. My renditions of all the songs were well received. Frank Loesser was a musical genius and good personal friend. I was always so proud to perform his music.

The Perils of Pauline was one of the films Paramount attempted to package, along with seven-hundred others, to dump in a sale to Universal in 1958 for television distribution. However, because of some unrevealed legal complications, *The Perils of Pauline* was inadvertently excluded from the original television package. In the end, the copyright was apparently never renewed, and the film sadly fell into the public domain, just as *The Stork Club* had.

By the middle of 1947, I was pregnant with our second child. My pregnancy caused me to lose out on the starring role in the *Warner Brothers* film called, *Romance on the High Seas*, with music and lyrics by Jule Styne and Sammy Cahn. For the part of Georgia Garrett, Warner Bros. inquired about borrowing *Judy Garland* from MGM, but Metro's policy at the time was not to lend Garland out to other studios. Warner Bros. then acquired me in a loan-out deal with Paramount, but before filming started, I had to bow out because of my impending motherhood.

Newcomer Doris Day attended a show-biz party where she met lyricist, Sammy Cahn. At Cahn's urging, Doris sang *Embraceable You* for the party goers. There at the party to hear her was, Michael Curtiz, director of the upcoming film. Curtiz asked her to test for the leading role of Georgia Garrett. Doris Day recalled that in her screen-test song, *A Rainy Night in Rio*, director Michael Curtiz initially instructed her to move around in the frenzied style of Betty Hutton. Since Doris was testing for her first movie role, she was probably rather naïve, and likewise, not amused. She suggested she perform the number in her own, more dignified manner. She got the part anyway, and with, it launched her very successful film career.

We had already finished up the production of my next film, *Dream Girl*, by the time I became pregnant. I was just coming down off a successful film, so I was prepared for my inevitable stinker. *Dream Girl* turned out to be that and more! I was miscast in the role, and I must admit, I never really fully understood the character. If Buddy had still been at Paramount, I'm quite sure he would have never allowed me to appear in such a film. I missed Buddy and his guidance. I felt like I was floundering without it. In hindsight, this was the beginning of the end for my film career. As soon as I hit the top, I was already poised for the decline. There were a few really good movies left to make, but those were outside of the norm. I knew I had been fortunate to have had someone like Buddy around to attend to every detail of my career, but I had become spoiled. Without his help, I felt I was now losing my edge.

In *Dream Girl*, I play Georgina Allerton, a girl who periodically escapes her humdrum existence by retreating into elaborate daydreams. The role was made popular by

Betty Field in the Broadway hit by her husband, Elmer Rice. Georgina is a chronic daydreamer, whose uncontrollable imagination leads her into all sorts of fantastic situations.

A New York Times reporter said about *Dream Girl*, "According to our information, Paramount paid a lot for the screen rights to Elmer Rice's play, more than two-hundred thousand, in fact. But, according to our observation, it has kissed both coin and *Dream Girl* good-by. Director Leisen has forgotten that motion pictures should move along and not bog down in soggy stretches of back and forth talk. It must be stated that Betty Hutton is a dud as the poor little millionaire's daughter who goes wandering in cuckoo-land. In those scenes when she tries to be poignant, she is drearily artificial."

Another reporter remarked, "Just so the audience doesn't miss anything, the producers have added a voiceover narration to explain what has just been seen. With all this going against *Dream Girl*, Betty Hutton emerges unscathed, delivering a lot better performance than her material warrants."

For lack of anything good to say about the film, or my role in it, I answered with the following, "It takes a tremendous amount of concentration to project yourself into all these different roles, but I love it. It's a challenge." What a bunch of bunk that was! I was trying to conceal the fact the film stunk, and so did my acting in it.

Ready or not, the movie opened on July 27, 1948, and the crowds stayed away from the theaters in droves. The only thing good I accomplished in the film was in keeping Edith Head on the payroll. Director Mitchell Leisen had a long-standing feud with my friend the costume designer, and refused to work with her. I insisted on keeping her on the film, and won.

I really hated failure. I was fearful that at some point my career would be snatched out from underneath me, and be taken completely away. Was it in the cards, or just in my head? I could only hope I had paid my dues with this disaster of a film, and my next role would be a good one. Coincidently, in my next movie there was a song I was going to sing, and I couldn't help feeling it had relevancy for me now. The song was called, *(Where Are You) Now That I Need You?* So, here goes – "*Buddy, where are you...now that I need you...?*"

In October of 1947, the press got hold of a story that Paramount and I were fighting. The studio wanted me for a movie called, *Sainted Sisters*, but I told them I couldn't do it because I was pregnant. After I did that, my salary stopped cold. I did argue with the studio, because when I told them I was available for it, the script wasn't ready. Then, when they were ready, I wasn't. We came to an agreement, and I was paid for several months, but not my full salary. I downplayed the feud when Louella Parsons cornered me, and I was forced to tell her about the incident. I confessed, there had been a bit of a misunderstanding, but it was fully resolved through friendly dialogue. That was not the whole truth, but I wasn't going to let her know it. Louella reported in her column, "You can bet Paramount won't do anything to hurt Betty. She's too valuable at the box office." Veronica Lake ended up as my replacement in the picture. The film also starred, Joan Caulfield, Barry Fitzgerald and William Demarest, and opened at the end of April 1948.

From that time on, Paramount and I never again saw completely eye to eye. I was taking too much control over what was going on at the studio concerning my career, and the big shots didn't like it. One report even surfaced that suggested I wouldn't be returning to Paramount after the birth of my second child. I have no clue where that rumor originated. It just showed that the friction that existed between us was being talked about. When trouble brewed at the studio, the word got around quickly. I'm not suggesting I wasn't to blame, because in part, I was. Even so, I made Paramount a lot of money over the time I had been with them, and I refused to allow them to control me completely.

On April 14, 1948, our second child, Candy, was born; another beautiful baby girl. Lindsay was happy to have a baby sister, and naturally their daddy was delighted with his precious little bundle. After our household returned to normal, I was anxious to get back to the studio. As it turned out, suddenly there were no properties for me to work on. It seemed to me, Paramount was silently flexing their muscle. By almost the middle of 1948, almost a year after making my last film, I was still without a new project. *Dream Girl* was out in the theaters by July, but that mess was worse than not having anything out to assist my public persona.

Finally in June, I was contacted by Paramount about their plans to star me in a movie called, *Lady from Lariat Loop*. It was to be a remake of an earlier film called, *Ruggles of Red Gap*, but rewritten for me to play the leading part Charles Laughton had played. The script just didn't work; they hadn't managed to completely convert the role from a man's part to one for a woman. In short, the script needed a lot of work. After I read it, I declined the movie. The studio scrambled to borrow Jane Russell from Howard Hughes at RKO to co-star with Bob Hope, but the deal fell through. The production was shelved for a time, but eventually it was revived in 1949 when they teamed Lucille Ball with Hope. The movie was finally released as *Fancy Pants* in September of 1950.

I announced to the press the reason for declining the role. "You have to be very careful these days. The public is shopping. One bad picture and you're cooked." I even went so far to say, "Movie audiences are getting tougher. They want their money's worth from a theater ticket, and when they get stung on a flop, they blame it on the star of the film. That's why many top stars are quaking in their golden slippers these days. There have been too many bum pictures with big names in them."

I received some criticism for being so bluntly honest with the press. I was beginning to lose my patience with the bad scripts, and becoming very nervous about the fate of my career if I continued to star in lousy movies. Playing the Hollywood movie game no longer seemed all important. It wasn't as if I would have the inner strength to call it quits any time soon; I simply no longer had that burning hunger.

So by early summer, I had a vaudeville show put together that I took to San Francisco for a short stint at The Golden Gate Theater. I told the press, "Working is better than chewing your fingernails beside a swimming pool in Hollywood." It was so wonderful to be back in front of a live audience again, there just isn't any substitute for it. It had been my bread and butter in the early days of my career, and I forgot not only how rewarding it was, but also how much I missed it. I was happy to find they still liked songs like, *Rocking Horse* and *Murder, He Says*, as well as the new numbers I performed. I knew then, if my movie career ever ceased to be, I would return to my first love, the stage.

I took, Ziggy Elman, and his eighteen-piece orchestra along to San Francisco. Ziggy was a jazz trumpeter who had been with Benny Goodman in 1936, but now had his own orchestra. His 1939 composition, *And the Angels Sing*, with lyrics by Johnny Mercer, became the number one song in the nation that year. I had been in the movie, *And The Angels Sing*, but this song was not part of the movie. I also took along four child acrobats, a singing team, and a dog act for my show. It felt just like the good old days.

About this same time, I threw an iron in the fire by announcing to Paramount that I wanted to do the outside movie my contract permitted for Buddy DeSylva. Buddy had what he considered the perfect picture for me about the life of *Eva Tanguay*, a brassy, self-confident singer and entertainer, who billed herself as "the girl who made vaudeville famous." Now that he was well enough to be up and about after his long illness, Buddy was right back at wanting to make a movie. The Tanguay movie he entitled, *I Don't Care,* was named after her most famous song, but was never ever made. Not until 1953, did George Jessel make the movie, *The I Don't Care Girl,* starring Mitzi Gaynor. At the time, when I said yes to Buddy, it had been my sole intention to take a stab at Paramount. I wanted them to see the love and loyalty I had for my friend and mentor. He was the one to whom I owed everything. Without Buddy, I wouldn't be where I was. Making the film was inconsequential. Little did I know, or anyone else for that matter, within a year Buddy DeSylva would be dead.

It had felt so good doing my live show in San Francisco, I decided to go to Europe and try my luck over there. I was booked for an engagement at the London Palladium for two weeks, with two shows a day. Teddy and I, along with my mother, set sail on the Queen Mary on August 31st. Before I accepted the engagement, my husband Teddy sent a telegram of inquiry to the Palladium, asking if the British people were ready for my overbearing style. Their response was simple and straightforward. They said they had managed buzz bombs during the war, and they were more than ready for Betty Hutton to bombard their stage.

My engagement started on September 15th. I was a big hit in London. All the people throughout the United Kingdom were so warm and responsive to my performances, I shall always remember them for their kindness. After my two weeks in London were complete, we went on to Scotland and to Paris, before heading home. I had received word from the studio while in Europe; they finally wanted me for a new film called, *Red, Hot and Blue*. I was to report to the studio in mid October to be briefed. Quite possibly my absence had made their hearts grow somewhat fonder.

When I returned from Europe, Buddy called with another project. This one was the Theda Bara story, and I committed to doing it for him. He said he offered Bara one-hundred thousand dollars for her life story, but was unsure if she would accept. He was sure Paramount would want the Bara story. Naturally, he felt a loyalty to the studio to approach them first, if they did. It was wonderful, after his long illness, to see Buddy back at what he loved best. Not until many years later did any movies get made about Theda Bara's life, and then they were mere biographies. Nothing was ever done like Buddy would have wanted.

A piece of me died the day I found out Buddy DeSylva was cut down in the prime of his life. He died from a heart attack at the age of fifty-five, on July 11, 1950. No one will ever be able to understand the personal loss I felt. He was a wonderful man who had a belief in my talent beyond any other. For now, rest peacefully my dear friend. I'll fill you in on everything when we meet up on the other side...

Red, Hot and Blue had been a lively musical comedy by Cole Porter. When it originally opened on Broadway in 1936, it starred Ethel Merman, Jimmy Durante, and Bob Hope. It was very loosely adapted into a film starring, Victor Mature, June Havoc, William Demarest, and me. It was so loosely adapted in fact, after Paramount purchased the screen rights, about the only thing taken from the stage version was the name. What the name had to do with the dreary storyline is anyone's guess. As always, it comes as no real surprise, Cole Porter's music and songs were unbefitting a film adaptation. All new music and lyrics were written and substituted by Frank Loesser.

Frank became so involved; he even made his acting debut in a small role in the film as one of the gangsters.

I play an ambitious chorus girl by the name of Eleanor Collier. I land a part in a musical comedy, which just happens to be bankrolled by gangsters. When one of the show's backers is bumped off, I end up being the wrong girl in the wrong place. Eleanor is arrested for suspicion of murder, and is then kidnapped by the villains to keep her from pointing the finger. My God, what was happening to films in Hollywood?

Production on the film ran into the early months of 1949. The movie was released on November 25th of that same year. My Frank Loesser numbers in the movie were fun to perform, simply because I was always partial to his tunes. *Now That I Need You* was the stand out song from the show. However, my rendition of *Hamlet* had the press telling folks to hold on to their hats before going to see the picture. *That's Loyalty* and *I Wake Up* were the other two numbers that I performed, both catchy and upbeat.

Response to the film was lukewarm. *The New York Times* reporter covering the opening of the film in New York stated, "Betty Hutton's particular brand of comical T.N.T., which has been known, on certain occasions, to blast people out of theatre seats, explodes with but mild detonation in Paramount's *Red, Hot and Blue,* a moist charge of romantic slapstick that came to the Paramount yesterday. That is not due to her shortcoming. No one can say she doesn't try to do her accustomed job of blasting with the material she has at hand. Playing a dizzy little show-girl who is scrabbling for a job on the stage, she attempts to ignite an explosion every time she gets hold of a straw. But, unfortunately, said material is conspicuously flimsy and damp, and Miss Hutton gets bogged down in it more often than she sets a modest glow. Between the songs of Frankie Loesser and the script by

John Farrow and Hagar Wilde, she finds it pretty tough going, since nothing is of much avail."

This is exactly the sort of thing that was getting me angry and discontented at the studio. Since Buddy's departure, I had been treading softly when attempting to hint at the fact my scripts suddenly weren't any good. Still, no one was listening. I didn't care so much if the studio went belly-up from the bad movies it was suddenly turning out, I just didn't want to take the rap for it. I always made the effort, no matter how good I was in one film, to be even better in the next. I felt I always needed to top myself, or ultimately I could kiss my career goodbye.

The critics were usually intelligent enough to see their way around a flimsy script, so I wasn't all that concerned with what they had to say. I was more concerned with my public perception. It's the public who shell out good money for tickets to sit and watch the damned film. After the movie has ended, and if you haven't enjoyed it, there just isn't much you can do. There aren't a whole lot of people to complain to. Your only real recourse is to avoid a Betty Hutton film the next time one comes to a theater in your neighborhood. Unavoidably, the public are the ones who end up passing final judgment. You just might say to yourself, "Oh that's right, I remember, her last film wasn't so great. I think I'll go ahead and skip her new one this time, just to be safe." So you see, it's ultimately the star of the film who gets blamed for a bad movie, regardless of the cause.

With John Lund in *The Perils of Pauline*, 1947.
Photo: Paramount, Betty's private collection

Returning home from my first
engagement at *The London Palladium*, 1948.
Photo: Betty's private collection, The Betty Hutton Estate

In one of my fancy "get-ups" from *Dream Girl*, 1948.
Photo: Paramount, Betty's private collection

Chapter Twelve

What I needed now was a really great property to bolster my career, especially at a time when it seemed Paramount was sending only weak scripts my way. I had talked with the big shots on several occasions about the projected film version of *Annie Get Your Gun*. I knew deep in my heart I would be perfect for the role, so I pleaded, prayed, and plotted with them to procure the film rights. They didn't listen, they never listened.

The stage musical of *Annie Get Your Gun* was written originally as a vehicle for Ethel Merman. On stage she was strong enough in the lead role to keep the show running for more than three years, but there was little chance of her reprising the role on film. Her larger-than-life personality was too overwhelming on camera. Initially, songwriter Irving Berlin shied away from selling the film rights while the musical was still running on Broadway, but he changed his mind when the 1946 film on which he'd worked called *Blue Skies* was receiving only mixed reviews. In an attempt to pump up his Hollywood career,

Berlin finally yielded to MGM producer Arthur Freed, who paid the then record sum of $650,000 for screen rights to the property. Although I had begged with Paramount to acquire it, Freed ultimately purchased it for top MGM star, Judy Garland. I was heartbroken at the loss.

Dorothy Fields and her brother, Herbert Fields, wrote the original story for Broadway. Our script for the film was one adapted by Sidney Sheldon. The result was a musical comedy that is a fictionalized account of the romance and rivalry between real-life Annie Oakley and Frank Butler. Annie, who can't miss anything she shoots at, eventually learns a valuable lesson, *You Can't Get a Man with a Gun*. In the end she gets Frank by learning how to shoot and miss.

In the purchase of the film rights, it was stipulated MGM couldn't release a film version of *Annie Get Your Gun* until the musical had completed its Broadway run. Production was therefore delayed until 1949. By that time, Judy Garland's personal problems had grown more than just serious. Her dependency and addiction to pills kept her from being reliable at the studio and consistent in her performances. At the beginning of shooting the film, Judy made a valiant attempt, and remained on her best behavior. Freed had assigned Busby Berkeley to direct the film, but due to earlier ill feelings between her and director Berkeley, Judy delved deeper into her emotional downslide. To complicate matters, co-star Howard Keel broke his ankle on the second day of shooting when a horse fell on him. The accident was caused in part by Berkeley's insistence that Keel ride his horse faster over a glossy studio floor. With Keel home recovering, Judy was under additional pressure as the only major character available to continue the filming. When she viewed the daily rushes, Judy was getting the feeling she wasn't right for the role.

In due course, Freed fired Berkeley, and replaced him with the man who had directed Judy successfully in *Easter Parade*, Charles Walters. By that time, it was already too late. On May 19, 1949, Judy Garland was fired from her starring role in *Annie Get Your Gun*, after a ten day suspension for not showing up to the studio on time and for storming off the set in a huff. She was accused of slowing up the production. Garland went into a hospital, and the production was put on hold until MGM could find a suitable replacement.

Several different actresses were considered as replacements. MGM's *Louis B. Mayer* was reported saying, "We'd be silly to give the part to somebody on another lot." With that in mind, it seemed the studio's first choice was *Betty Garrett,* from within the ranks of their own acting roster. Garrett had performed as a comic second lead in MGM musicals, but her contract had expired and her agent reportedly fouled the negotiations by greedily asking for too much money. *Ginger Rogers* wrote in her 1991 autobiography that she told her agent, Leland Hayward, to vigorously pursue the film on her behalf. She wrote that she would have accepted a single dollar just to seal the contract. Louis B. Mayer responded to her agent, "Tell Ginger to stay in her high-heel shoes and silk stockings, she could never be as rambunctious as Annie Oakley has to be."

Since I had campaigned from the very beginning, MGM was aware of my desire for the role. When I heard Paramount was talking with MGM executives about me, I was already shooting *Let's Dance* with Fred Astaire. It was said that Paramount wanted Metro to foot the bill for delaying the picture if they let me make *Annie Get Your Gun* first. When Metro was prepared to walk, I threatened Paramount by refusing to finish *Let's Dance* unless they allowed me to do *Annie* for MGM. That tactic worked, but Paramount never forgot I had used it. For several days there was no word from Metro, one way or the other. Then suddenly, word arrived saying they would hold the part for me until I finished up the picture with Fred Astaire.

Metro reached a deal to borrow me from Paramount for $100,000 and a stipulation they had the option to use me in two additional films. I was happier than I had been in a long while. In my excitement, I made the mistake of over-emphasizing to the press how I never gave up hope for the role even after the picture began shooting. I had even learned all the Irving Berlin songs just in case, something that did little to endear me to the film's crew when I reported for service. Their loyalty remained within their own studio, and particularly with the ousted and ill-fated Judy. I told Bob Thomas from The Associated Press, "I'm so excited I can't sleep. For four years I've been trying to do *Annie*. I haven't been happy with the pictures I've had since Buddy DeSylva left Paramount and I pleaded with them to buy it for me. I really bawled them out when they let MGM get it." That statement was an additional slap in the face of Paramount execs. Toward the end of our filming in November of 1949, syndicated columnist, Harrison Carroll, reported there was plenty of talk about MGM trying to woo me away from Paramount when my contract expired. He stated, "Betty, I hear, is willing. Metro has promised her everything except L.B. Mayer's bank account."

I wasn't at all as uncaring as my statements to the press about acquiring the role made me sound, I was merely excited. Things you say to the press are always misconstrued, especially when the fate of a fellow actor is involved. Before accepting the part, I made damned sure the studio wasn't just trying to punish Judy. I found out she wasn't exactly happy with the role from the start. *Annie Get Your Gun* really called for a star with high-voltage showmanship and an earthy essence, Judy was way too sophisticated for it. *Annie* called more for the loud kind of nonsense I can do. I hoped the crew on the film would be able to see it the same way, and accept me as one of their own. Years later, while we were both working Las Vegas, Judy and I became very good friends. She told me then she had never wanted the picture, that it wasn't right for her. She admitted the part was right for me, and after all was said and done, she was happy I got it.

I played Annie Oakley, along with Howard Keel making his movie debut as Frank Butler. Only two production numbers had been fully completed for the film with Judy in them, *Doin' What Comes Naturally* and *I'm an Indian Too*. Of course, we started everything over from scratch. Frank Morgan was to play Colonel Buffalo Bill, and my old friend Benay Venuta as Dolly Tate. I was overjoyed to pay off a long overdue debt to Benay by getting her the part of Dolly. I met her when she was headlining back in the days when I was just breaking into the business with Lopez's band. Benay did something wonderful for me before I got my very first paycheck that I'll always remember. We were in Philadelphia, and I was feeling pretty low about myself and the way I was being accepted by the band and our audiences. Benay took me shopping and bought me a new dress and a pair of flat heels, something I desperately needed. Then she chose a string of beads for me and a bottle of gardenia perfume for good measure! I never forgot her kindness. After all, a new dress meant a lot to a girl who never owned more than one at a time in her entire life!

By the time shooting resumed, with me in the lead role, other changes had also been made to the plagued production. For a reason which probably involved some sort of studio politics over the renewal of his expired contract, George Sidney had replaced Charles Walters as the director. Walters found out he had been cut by reading about it in Hedda Hopper's gossip column. Also, Frank Morgan, the original choice for Buffalo Bill Cody, unexpectedly died in his sleep. The new replacement for the role was Louis Calhern.

Since I was already busy making the film *Let's Dance* with Fred Astaire, accepting the *Annie* role meant night work learning dance routines and costume fittings. I didn't mind, I knew I had been handed the chance of a lifetime to star in this film. Not until we actually began shooting scenes did I find out how different MGM was from what I had become accustomed to at Paramount.

I arrived on set to save the day, something I did with my typical unrestrained enthusiasm. I was determined to work hard in this role, so I dove in with everything I had right from the start. I was sure my own passion would rub off on the rest of the crew. It would make for one hell of a fun set and an exciting film to be in. I guess I must have hit them like a cyclone. In hindsight, it was probably too much Hutton, too fast. Director George Sidney advised me, "You have to be directed on this picture; you are playing a character. You are not playing the girl from Vincent Lopez's band." I think it was more of a warning than it was any type of friendly advice.

On the very first day I reported for a shoot, I couldn't believe how somber the atmosphere was on the set. Everywhere I turned; people were calling me Miss Hutton instead of Betty, like I was some sort of visiting dignitary. In the same breath, imagine how I felt when they had the nerve, not to mention the poor taste, to send a messenger from the commissary all the way over to our set to collect a $3.25 bill I owed them. I knew I had become spoiled by the casual and friendly sets at Paramount, but this seemed almost unnatural. I was also used to the crew offering their applause as a genuine show of support after a successful scene. At MGM the crew said and did nothing.

Because of their lack of enthusiasm, the second day I hollered out a word of warning before I reported to makeup and wardrobe. I told everyone within earshot I wanted to hear some noise after I did something good. I returned to the set a short time later, all decked out for the part of a young *Annie*. My face was stained with walnut juice to make my skin appear weather-beaten. My hair was in pigtails that stuck out from underneath a tattered felt hat, and my own natural freckles had been accentuated by being enlarged and darkened. Covering the rest of me was a brown flannel dress, black cotton stockings, and funny looking little moccasins. From the way I looked, I'm sure it was difficult for anyone to take my request seriously. Nevertheless, after I finished up the *Doin' What Comes Naturally* number, energetic applause filled the set; despite a somewhat disingenuous and forced feeling. I was beginning to wonder if it was me or my acting they didn't like. I became rather worried when I realized that it quite possibly was both.

Just as I had always done at Paramount, I insisted upon air conditioning on the set when I was in front of the camera. Sets at my home studio always had a sign posted that referred to them as "Hutton's Polar Palace" when I was working. One morning, I was greeted on the set of *Annie* by three electricians huddled under blankets beside a steam radiator. Naturally, it had been set up as a gag, and I truly appreciated the gesture as a show of camaraderie. On another occasion, our Sitting Bull, J. Carroll Naish, told reporters when interviewed, "I've seen them all in the part, but Betty *is* Annie. I just don't know what keeps her from falling apart from all that energy she puts into it." These were two instances when I was actually made to feel at home on the set of *Annie Get Your Gun*. Still, compliments were few and far between.

The longer I was there, the more I came to the realization many didn't like me because of what had happened to Judy. Of course, it had not been my fault she had been removed from the film, but as an outsider, my presence must have been a constant reminder of the fate that befell one of the studio's biggest stars. I remember seeing Judy later when she was married to Sid Luft, and she was performing at the Copa in New York. When we got talking after her performance, Judy told me she was there doing it only for the money. She said, "Betty, I just hate it." That was so difficult for me to hear. She had always been so fabulous. There has never been a talent like Judy's, and there never will be again. They used her up so badly, there was nothing much left. She was pumped full of "medicine" if she got heavy, if she was nervous, or if she couldn't sleep. It was so cruel what they did to her. Judy was a sick girl, but they wouldn't listen or believe it for a minute. At least I had the satisfaction of working for the love of performing. Toward the end, poor Judy worked simply for the money.

On a day-to-day basis, my experience at MGM was pretty awful. Howard Keel thought I was always trying to upstage him in our scenes together. I never could understand it. Here he was in his very first movie role. Was this greenhorn attempting to call all the shots? *Annie Get Your Gun* is Annie's story, not that of Howard Keel's character, Frank Butler. If the story had been reversed, I would have gladly handed Howard the burdensome responsibility of carrying the film as I had. Keel proved to be my primary adversary during shooting of the film. There was much bad blood between us.

In spite of everything, I never once allowed what was happening on the set to show up in my performance. If you are professional about your work, you simply can't. Of course, the film ended up a roaring success which the public still adores, but for me it had been the heartbreak of my film career. From the very beginning, I had wanted that film so badly, and I had such high expectations for my success in it. After all was said and done, I was crushed with disappointment by my unpleasant experience of making the picture. I felt I needed to be tough in order to protect myself on the set of *Annie*. If that was what I needed to do to survive on set, and if I constantly had to be on my guard, then I couldn't possibly continue to be my very best on camera. Always being able to focus, so as to be my best on camera, was all important to me. That's pretty much how *Annie Get Your Gun* caused me to lose much of my drive to continue making films; I just didn't want to be tough in order to survive in the business. I only had the desire to make great movies. To this day, I have never watched *Annie Get Your Gun*. To do so would cause me to recollect bad memories from my one experience at MGM.

Annie Get Your Gun debuted at New York City's Loew's State Theater on May 17, 1950, brimming with its colorful costumes and extravagant Hollywood versions of Buffalo Bill's Wild West show. I flew myself to New York with my two children for the premiere. I really felt I needed and deserved to be there, although MGM execs failed to invite me for the festivities. I let them know I was there, but I mostly sat in my hotel room and cried. I snapped out of it for the sake of my kids. If I wasn't in New York to celebrate the opening of *Annie Get Your Gun*, then I was damned sure going to spend time with my children and enjoy the city. That night we got all dolled up before I took only Lindsay out to the *Stork Club* for dinner. Afterwards, we took a leisurely cab ride down Broadway, through the theater district, and back up again. I wanted my daughter to experience all the brilliant lights and buzz of activity emanating from the wonderful place where her mommy got her start. We made a stop in front of the theater where the larger-than-life picture of me as Annie Oakley towered out front for the entire world to see. People were lined up waiting to get in. Lindsay was in awe at the sight.

Despite the production problems, the film became popular in its own right. In its initial release it grossed more than $8 million, easily earning back its $3.7 million production costs. Almost half of the production costs had already been spent by the time Judy was fired. I was disappointed to receive only mixed reviews, but critics were forever comparing my performance unfavorably to native New Yorker, Ethel Merman's, from the original Broadway production.

The picture proved to be producer Freed's most successful. The lavish result of all his efforts went on to win an Oscar for best score in a musical, as well as nominations for cinematography, art direction, and editing. I was chosen the most popular female star of 1950 by *Photoplay* magazine, and received a nomination for a *Golden Globe* for best motion picture actress in a musical or comedy. *Time* magazine put me on the cover of their April 24, 1950 issue. I was decked out in all my *Annie* finery for the color cover photo. Sidney Sheldon won the *Writers Guild of America* award for best written American musical. After the great success of this film, Arthur Freed planned to team Keel and I up again in *Billy Rose's Jumbo* in 1962, a stage musical the studio had acquired in the 1930s. By the time I was available and the studio was ready to begin production, my career in film was already a thing of the past.

In 1973, *Annie Get Your Gun* was withdrawn from distribution due to a dispute between Irving Berlin and MGM over music rights. That decision prevented the public from viewing the film for almost 30 years. It was not until after Berlin's death, at the age of 101 in 1989, that his estate managed to settle the dispute. On the film's 50th Anniversary in 2000, the movie was finally seen once again in its entirety.

During the production of *Annie Get Your Gun*, Teddy and I split for a short time, but we patched things up the best we could and stayed together. At the time, I spoke candidly with Hollywood columnist, Erskine Johnson, when he asked me about our publicly aired marital problems. I blamed our brief separation entirely on myself, saying, "When I'm working, it's difficult for me to be a wife. Ted and I had fun when I didn't make a picture for a year. Then, I started getting up at 5:00 in the morning in time to make it to the studio and came home dead tired at 7:00 pm. Teddy suddenly discovered he was married to a factory instead of to a girl. We had a big fight, but now things are okay. He understands. Really, I think when I'm working on a picture, I should live by myself."

By the time production wrapped on *Annie Get Your Gun*, it was only a week before Christmas. Immediately, we gathered up the kids and headed for a two-week vacation at Sun Valley in Idaho. The girls got red snow suits for Christmas and were anxious to see the real snow they had only heard about from their Midwestern parents. I hadn't gotten to see or spend much time with them for the better part of a year, except on Sundays. A little more than three months had been spent on shooting *Red, Hot and Blue*, with a week or so in-between time where I nearly managed to get accustomed to having a husband and two children again. Then four months were spent on *Let's Dance* with Fred Astaire. The rest of the year was spent on *Annie Get Your Gun*. I did manage a little time out when I accidentally cracked two vertebrae while doing the wild Indian routine in the film. So, no wonder my marriage was in trouble, I had been out of commission for my family for the better part of a year. We were all happy to finally get away and enjoy some family time together. Enjoy it I must, because a little more than a year later, our marriage would end for good.

Annie Get Your Gun, 1950. I look troubled in this photo,
probably due to the stress on the MGM set..

Photo: MGM, Betty's private collection

Annie Get Your Gun, 1950.
Photo: MGM, The Betty Hutton Estate

The Ted Briskin Family, 1949.
Photo: Betty's private collection, The Betty Hutton Estate

Chapter Thirteen

In July of 1949, we officially started shooting the film *Let's Dance*, although many of the musical numbers were worked on prior to that time. We rushed the production of the movie, so I was free to go off and do *Annie Get Your Gun*. *Let's Dance* was finished before *Annie*, but it was released almost six months after, around the time of Thanksgiving in 1950.

I play a more tranquil role than usual as war widow Kitty McNeil. Not wanting to have my young son grow up surrounded by his overly prim and proper Bostonian grandparents, I sneak off with the child and resume my pre-war show-business career. My character is reunited with her USO dancing partner, Fred Astaire, who, nonetheless, hopes to give up performing in favor of the business world. Inevitably, Kitty and Astaire end up resuming their old act. At the same time, Kitty's Boston in-laws predictably attempt to gain custody of their grandson. With the help of her dance partner, Kitty fights the legal battle to maintain custody of her son. Naturally, there are dance and song throughout to lighten the heavy mood. Two of the Frank Loesser numbers I performed in the picture were really memorable, *Can't Stop Talking about Him* and *Why Fight the Feeling*.

In 1946, Fred Astaire announced his retirement from motion pictures, and the following year he launched a successful string of dance schools, a business venture that proved to be quite successful for him. However, in 1947, he returned to movies by stepping in for Gene Kelly in *Easter Parade* after Kelly was injured. *Easter Parade* was a huge success, thanks to solid dancing from both Fred and Ann Miller, and last but certainly not least, by Judy Garland's wonderful renditions of some really fine Irving Berlin numbers.

Astaire went on to make *Let's Dance* with me in 1950. Many people were very upset at Astaire receiving second billing to me in the film. I loved the man dearly, and would never have wanted to hurt him in any way. Yet, the studio saw him as a retiree returning for a limited engagement, hence the billing. Fred went on to star in eight other musicals after making *Let's Dance*. His partners in those films included Ginger Rogers in one picture, as well as Vera-Ellen, Cyd Charisse, Leslie Caron, Jane Powell, and Audrey Hepburn.

Fred and I made a surprisingly good screen team in *Let's Dance*. He managed to match my signature roughness during the cowboy musical number, *Oh, Them Dudes*, and yet, when he was given the opportunity to do the sort of dancing he did best, he shined in the brilliant routine he did atop and around a piano.

Fred Astaire was a dear and wonderful man. He was down to earth, and immediately made everyone around him comfortably at ease. In the movie, I wear my hair braided back with pink yarn tied on the ends. One afternoon, Fred came into my dressing room to visit. Just before sitting down, he took off his hat, and there without his standard toupee in place, he had the few strands of what was left of his own natural hair tied up in pink yarn bows. There must have been about five or six of them standing straight up on the top of his head. He was forever pulling small pranks. It was his way of showing you he was your friend, and I adored him.

He said I was the only one who ever managed to do a take of a dance number without stopping. Fred was a perfectionist, but then, so was I. We had this five minute dance number to do on camera, and I said to Fred, "Please, if we do it, let's not do it again. I don't think I can do it twice." Sure enough, after that first take, Fred motioned to cut, and that was the end of it. We had done the entire number in one take without stopping. That was my proudest moment in the making of *Let's Dance*.

Paramount really wanted to make a big bang with *Let's Dance*, and to do so, they knew they needed a good promotional gimmick. They finally found just what they were looking for when the city of Lansing, Michigan invited us to have the premiere of the film there. The reason they wanted me back was because it had been highly publicized I was from there, and they were proud to call me and my mother hometown girls.

The publicity department at Paramount became highly involved; they saw this as an ideal opportunity to cash in on me and the film. Plans were laid out to the smallest detail. Our first stop was to be in Detroit, the sight of our extreme poverty, but also the place where my mother had worked in the Chrysler plant for twenty-two cents an hour spitting upholstery tacks. Paramount thought the city would be at my feet, but neither I nor the studio could foresee the true star of the day was going to be my mother. The publicity department was shocked when the very head of Chrysler invited my mother and me to a luncheon with them. When we received the news, my mother looked at me in the way she always did when things were suddenly going our way. Before this time, my mother never had the ability to express her gratitude in words; she only did it with that look she gave me. The love she had on her face at that moment was worth everything I had been through to get to where I was. I was so happy for mama to get her just reward. Anyway, I had a lot of guilt feelings about not being able to spend the amount of time with my mother I had spent with her before my marriage to Ted. Our marriage was now on very shaky ground. Less than a month later, I would file for divorce for a second and final time from Ted Briskin. I was already back depending upon mother for my moral support, and we were once again becoming inseparable. It felt pretty much like old times between us.

My mother told the publicity department she would be delighted to accompany her daughter as the guest of honor at the Chrysler luncheon. She requested, actually she pretty much insisted, we first be given the opportunity to walk through the plant where many of the employees with whom she had worked still were. Mama's very dearest friend, the one I referred to as my Aunt Merna, still worked the line.

When we arrived in Detroit, the standard local dignitaries were on hand to welcome us, along with a handful of Chrysler big-wigs. We were escorted to our lavish hotel suites, where upon arrival, Mama called absolutely everyone she had known, or thought she had known, in Michigan. Naturally, the word spread like wild fire that we were in town. Everyone remotely interested was suddenly made aware of the fact we would be arriving at the plant the next day for a tour. When the moment came, I stayed pretty much in the background. Down on the assembly line where mama had worked, you could not believe the rousing cheers that came from the workers. Most of them knew my mother, and were undoubtedly amazed at the triumphant return of a sober and happy looking Mabel standing directly in front of them. Tears of joy ran down mama's face as folks yelled out, "Mabel, you're back!" The crowd surrounded my mother and spontaneously hoisted her to their shoulders, parading her throughout the plant. Still on their shoulders, the workers crossed the street to the executive offices where she was reluctantly released by the workers to a seat of honor in the dining room.

Mama insisted my Aunt Merna be allowed to remain for the luncheon. At first, Merna attempted to beg off; I don't think she felt exactly comfortable being around the company executives, never mind her greasy working uniform. Mama piped up, "What the hell difference does a bit of grease make between you and me? I haven't changed a bit, Merna. The grease and dirt are all still inside, even though the outside may not look the same. I will never forget the love and friendship you showed to Betty and me. Your help pulled us through."

Merna proudly sat with mama and me up at the head table. They both appeared quite comfortable as the *Detroit Free Press* and the other newspapers in attendance continued snapping pictures; a myriad of flashbulbs blinding their eyes every few seconds. There wasn't a dry eye in the place, everyone beamed with pride realizing this humble woman was really one of them.

I was taken back when my mother was asked to make a speech. Through all the planning stages, this was something we were unprepared for. I was horrified mama would somehow manage to spoil the perfect day with her somewhat crude language. Mother's English had always been on the rough side, something else which had not changed. I was fearful she might say something like, "I seen 'um when they done it." But to my relief, mama made an eloquent speech. Looking directly into the face of the head of Chrysler Corporation, mama commented, "If the workers are only allowed to know you, the executives, on the same level I am relating to you today, there will never again be a strike in this plant." She also sincerely thanked them for the love she felt surrounding her that day. Before she finished, mama suddenly turned to me and said, "Betty, and I thank you from the bottom of my heart." I was instantly overwhelmed with emotion.

At the end of mama's speech, everyone rose to their feet and cheered her. I was so proud of my mother at that moment, I was trembling. The top executive came over to mother and said, "Mrs. Hutton, would you please follow me?" I instantly wondered to myself, what now?

Our procession returned us across the street and back into the plant. We followed the assembly line all the way to the very end, where the cars rolled off completed. Suddenly, I knew what was about to happen. The company exec turned to my mother, and with an intense look of pride on his face said, "Mrs. Hutton, it is our pleasure to extent this gift as a show of our love and friendship to you, a woman who worked beside us in this plant, and who has gone on to even greater successes." The Chrysler chief pointed to the last car in the line, a gorgeous green 4-door, all shiny and new, like out of the pages of a sleek magazine. I'm not exactly sure how mama was feeling at that moment, but I knew it was surely a feeling she would remember for the rest of her life.

Mama managed to thank everyone profusely before the press moved in to take more pictures. Prior to leaving the plant, mama was assured her car would be delivered to her front door in California. We were escorted out to our limousine waiting to take us to the airport for our short flight to Lansing. Hugs and kisses were exchanged by all, and as we drove off down Jefferson Boulevard, the necks of company employees craned from plant windows to gain a final glimpse at our departure.

Once in the car, mama had different ideas about our intended schedule. "I want to stop at a few of my old haunts, Betty, just for old time sake." The guys with us in the car from the press got a real kick from the idea. I guess they were thinking along the lines of some additional good photo opportunities.

First we stopped at The Green Tree, a real dive where mama used to get so drunk; some of the other patrons would spit on her. Having that image in my head, I walked bravely behind mama as she headed inside. It looked absolutely the same. Even the guys standing up at the bar looked the same, although I'm sure this was a fresh batch of drunks. As mama sat casually on one of the stools at the bar, the press hung in the background by the door. I walked over to the beat-up old bandstand; it hadn't changed one damned bit. I turned on the microphone and gave it a few taps to make sure it worked. I turned toward the crowd and said, "You no longer have to throw pennies at me." With that, I started in on a song that I used to sing before I helped my mother off of the floor to lead her home in her drunken stupor. As I sang *Black Bottom*, my eyes scanned the entire room. I suddenly recognized the bartender; he was the same one from all those many years before. There was thunderous applause from everyone after I finished my song. I walked back to mother and noticed tears glistening in her eyes. She looked right at me and said proudly, "Betty, you don't have to help me out of here this time." The press was not privy to any of the background information needed to piece the story together, but somehow they knew it went way beyond what they were witnessing. Therefore, they managed to remain respectful the entire while.

If that experience hadn't been enough, our next stop was a place called The Cave. We walked down the same flight of stairs where at seven years of age, I punched a man who called my mother a drunk and told her to get out of his way. This time my mother held her head up proudly as she kissed each and every person who remembered her.

They called her Mabel and slapped her on the back, as if she were one of the guys. In a strange way, I think they all appreciated the fact mama came to see them. Quite possibly, they were even honored to see she had not forgotten them.

We arrived at the airport for our flight to Lansing. We had no sooner taken off, when we were already descending for our landing. As we taxied in, we peered out the window to see about fifty policemen assembled on motorcycles, it was obvious we were going to be escorted into town by a motorcade. The mayor was right out front, his arms laden with beautiful roses. The scenario was too unreal for us both to comprehend. As childhood memories rushed into my head of our unfortunate life in Michigan, I couldn't suppress the laughter. Everyone in the limousine looked at me, as if to say they wanted in on the joke. Only my dear mother knew the reason for my outburst, and the quick wink she gave me told me she agreed.

After we deplaned, the mayor came forward and welcomed us to Lansing. He placed huge bundles of roses in first my mother's arms and then mine. Before members of the press were allowed to descend upon us for photographs, the mayor asked our permission to take us to the house where we had lived. He said he had a big surprise to show us. When I managed a second alone with mother, I whispered into her ear, "If they want to give you that beat-up old house, please mother, be very polite, but say, no thanks!"

As we departed the airport, sirens on the motorcycles blared loudly. We entered Lansing proper, the town we had been thrown out of all those many years before. I had mixed emotions when we pulled up in front of the humble little house where my story all began. Approaching the front door on foot, the mayor pointed out our surprise, a shiny brass plaque attached near the entry that stated, *Betty Hutton Lived Here*. The neighbors were out in full force to welcome us back. It was a nice tribute to us by some wonderful people.

My mother turned to the mayor and asked if it would be possible for us to make an additional stop. He responded by saying, "Mrs. Hutton, the city belongs to you this day, anything your heart desires." I knew what mama was up to, and my hunch was correct when we pulled up in front of my Aunt Ida's house.

Our reunion with Aunt Ida was amazing. She came out of her house and grabbed both mama and I, as tears rolled down all our faces. We all hugged until I thought we would suffocate. We went inside for what I thought was a brief time, to exchange old stories and to catch up on new ones. Not until a person from the Paramount press department came forward to alert us of the need to depart for the theater and the film premiere, did we realize how much time had actually passed.

Mama turned to Aunt Ida, and in a manner that was more of an assumption than a question, asked, "You are going to the movie, aren't you?" Ida said she had made an attempt to get tickets, but they had been sold out. My high-stepping mother went to the front door of the house and with a single index finger managed to summons the good mayor of Lansing. "My friend, Ida, is coming along with us to the theater. There isn't any problem, is there?" The mayor indicated with an agreeable gesture of both hands that my mother's wish was his command.

The ride to the theater was interesting, to say the least. The fact that we were being chauffeured around in a fancy limousine made not the slightest bit of difference. It might as well have been an old school bus full of family and friends going off to a Sunday church social. If there had been time, I'm quite sure my Aunt Ida would have made a batch of fried chicken for everyone to enjoy on the way.

We arrived at the theater on time. The mayor escorted my Aunt and our other guests into the theater. Mama and

I headed backstage, as we needed time to make ourselves presentable for the show that followed. While the movie was on, my hairdresser was getting me ready to go onstage. My mother took it upon herself to sneak out the side door of the theater and invite all the police who had escorted us to come backstage and enjoy the show. Raising her fist to them in jest, mama said, "If you don't come backstage, I'll plant one on ya!"

The audience is what made this such a thrilling experience for us both. After the film was over, I went out onto the stage. I sang a few songs to get the crowd warmed up even more before I called for mama to come out. I can't remember a grander ovation than the one reserved for my mother. Everyone was on their feet, screaming out things like, "Hey Mabel, remember when I used to come to your gin joint?" The laughter and joy mama and I shared with the audience as we stood holding hands on stage will forever remain in my mind and heart.

Finally, mama and I sang a song we had rehearsed together for the occasion, *Some of These Days*. After we finished singing, I didn't think the audience would ever settle down. Mother decided to take control of the situation by raising her arms and appealing for quiet. When the crowd was silenced, mama thanked everyone for making this the most wonderful time she had ever known. She called me forward, and after kissing me tenderly, she said to the audience, "I need to tell you, without my beloved daughter's faith that all of this would one day come to pass, it could never have happened. She told me one day she would be a star. When I had no belief, Betty had it all, because she loved me. Believe me, it can happen, and it can happen to you. God bless you all, and good night."

So much happened after that, it's difficult to recall. I knew we had to catch a plane back to the coast, but the press was frantic for interviews and photographs. We bid our farewells and hurried through the crowd of reporters as graciously as possible, eventually making our way to the waiting limousine. As the police motorcade led the way, we sped our way from the front of the mobbed theater, sirens once again blasting away. Laughter of pure joy came over my mother. She was remembering the last time we left Lansing with the police hot on our trail. She leaned toward me, and in a sarcastic but joyful manner said, "Well honey, at least this time the cops are in front of us!"

Together with Fred Astaire in *Let's Dance*, 1950.
Photo: Paramount, Betty's private collection

Our triumphant return to Lansing, Michigan
for the premier of *Let's Dance*, 1950.
Photo: Betty's private collection, The Betty Hutton Estate

Oh, my mother. How I adored her!
Photo: Betty's private collection, The Betty Hutton Estate

Chapter Fourteen

After my success in *Annie Get Your Gun*, no one believed I could ever top my performance from that movie. I guess I had my own self-doubts, not so much in my ability, but rather in finding another role that could measure up to the one of Annie Oakley. To get a great part at the studio following the departure of Buddy, it was necessary for me to seek one out, not wait around for one. Because of tensions between me and the studio, I knew the great roles weren't going to come looking for me any more. So, I was always on the lookout, and hopeful that when the perfect role came along; I would be in the right place at the right time.

As soon as Cecil B. DeMille announced his intention to make a colossal tribute movie based more or less upon the Ringling Bros. and Barnum & Bailey's Circus show, I began to formulate a plan how to get a part in it. I knew there would be a leading role for a risk-taking female circus queen. After asking around, I found out there were two major female parts, but which one happened to be the lead, I hadn't any clue. I assumed, or probably just made a lucky guess, that it was the trapeze artist. It sounded more glamorous and significant a part than the elephant girl. Immediately, I found some trainers and took it upon myself to learn some basic trapeze skills on the still bar behind closed doors in one of the studio's empty sound stages.

I let it be known throughout the studio I wanted such a part, and busied myself sending notes and making calls to DeMille's studio office. After a few weeks without hearing a word, I decided it was high time I marched over to DeMille's office for a little visit. Because of my clout at the studio, it wasn't that difficult to get in to see *the man.* He kept me waiting in the reception area just long enough for me to recollect who was actually in charge. Thankfully, I was friendly with Gladys Rosson, his long-time secretary, and therefore relied heavily upon her association with DeMille and her best judgment when I got around to asking the rather blunt question, "Gladys, what should I do in there?" Her response was equally straight forward, "Don't worry Betty, you won't get the part anyway, Mr. DeMille wants a professional circus performer for the trapeze artist."

I shot back, "Oh, I already know how to do all that stuff." I hadn't quite gotten the answer I had expected out of Gladys, but at least now I was sure I was in pursuit of the lead role. I was happy to know it was the part of the trapeze artist I was after, it would help me to sound as assertive as possible when I went in to meet with DeMille.

"Then go in and tell him so, Betty." Gladys insisted.

Mr. DeMille listened as I spoke candidly of my desire to be in his picture. I wanted to be persuasive without sounding desperate. I gave him a complete rundown of my movie credits. He seemed impressed by the recent success in my *Annie Get Your Gun* performance, but I could see he still wasn't convinced.

"No, Betty, I'm going to hire someone who knows how."

"Oh, Please, Mr. DeMille," I pleaded. "Won't you please reconsider and to give me at least a chance?"

DeMille rose and pushed back his chair before coming around the front of his desk to get an up-close look at me. "Let me see your feet, Betty," he said with much conviction. His eyes traveled down from my legs to my feet.

"Mr. DeMille! What?" I had no idea where this sudden switch in the conversation was headed.

"Betty, a trapeze artist has to have perfect feet. You must point them at all times during a performance, so they look beautiful and the performer appears poised." His explanation had put me at ease. I took off my shoes and stockings, so he could get a good look.

"They're perfect, Betty! Alright, let's talk. How much do you think you can do physically? You know, Betty, I need realism. My actors are going to need to do a lot of their own stunts."

"Mr. DeMille, I'll call your secretary to make the necessary arrangements tomorrow. Won't you please come over to the stage where I'm working in a week or so? There I'll be happy to show you exactly what I'm capable of." DeMille agreed to give me a chance. I didn't tell him I had already been practicing for quite awhile.

After leaving his office, I immediately went to a florist and had a massive flower arrangement created that looked like a circus ring with a blonde female doll going through her routines on a trapeze. My card accompanying the floral arrangement simply said, "Mr. DeMille, my fate rests in your hands." I wanted him to think about me, and only me, each and every time he sat in his office and glanced at that arrangement. It was large enough that he couldn't miss it. When Mr. DeMille finally made it over to the sound stage where I was taking trapeze lessons, he almost burst with pride when he saw how much I could do. I had accomplished the impossible, the part was finally mine.

Unlike most of DeMille's films, *The Greatest Show on Earth* would be based on an original screenplay, and it would take over a year to produce an acceptable one. In the process of coming up with a script, DeMille's behavior was not the kind to endear him whatsoever to his writers. DeMille verbally bashed them again and again in conference for their failure to produce something that pleased him. At times, he seemed close to panic. Five writers were assigned to the story, and the cost of salaries to pay them was piling up. All there was to show for the expense was stacks and stacks of notes and jotted down ideas, but nothing actually concrete enough to put together in script form.

As the time swiftly passed, DeMille finally decided to take matters into his own hands. An idea suddenly came to him while sitting and watching movies with his eight-year-old grandson. DeMille knew full well when his grandson would say, "That's the bad guy grandpa," or "That's the good guy," the story was clear and concise. So one day at lunch, he told one of his staff writers to bring him an outline of a circus story that his grandson would be able to understand. The writer came back a few days later with seventeen typewritten pages that began:

Once upon a time there was a circus and the boss of this circus is a strong, tough young fellow named Brad Gable. Brad lives and breathes circus. Brad is in love with Holly the flyer, but Brad could never tell Holly that he loves her. In fact, he hardly admits it to himself. He knows it isn't good for the boss of a circus to be in love with a performer. When this happens he gets to worrying about her because she might fall and be hurt. She becomes more important to him than the circus...

DeMille was thrilled with the simplistic results, and was ready to move forward. He purchased the rights to use the title motto, *The Greatest Show On Earth*, and the Ringling Bros. & Barnum & Bailey's facilities and performances for $250,000. Finally, with an approved storyline, DeMille and a small crew met up with the Ringling Brothers Circus in September of 1950 in Milwaukee, Wisconsin. There they started a two-month tour of the Midwest with the circus.

DeMille was eager to absorb the feeling and language of the circus, and to collect anecdotes and ideas. He was hell-bent to get an idea of how everything would look on camera. At nearly seventy years of age, DeMille was pushing himself to the limit. One night at dinner, Mr. DeMille slipped into a sort of semi-consciousness. His secretary, Gladys Rosson, held up his head to keep it from falling into his food. When he snapped out of it, he resumed his meal as if nothing at all had happened.

For his leading man, DeMille originally had interest in Kirk Douglas or Burt Lancaster, but settled on Charlton Heston. It was rumored Heston was driving through Paramount Studios when he spotted DeMille. Heston had never met DeMille, but waved in a strong, friendly manner. Supposedly, DeMille was so impressed by Heston's wave, he made inquires that in the end led to Heston being cast in the film. One fan actually wrote a letter to DeMille, telling him how much she enjoyed the movie. She also commented how well the circus manager, played by Heston, worked with the real actors. Heston thought it was one of the finest reviews he had ever received.

For the female aerialist, DeMille chose me over his first choice, Hedy Lamarr. The fact that I could perform on the trapeze, as well as sing, probably cemented the deal. I studied with, and learned many aerial tricks from Antoinette Concello and Bill Snyder, both of whom were billed with the circus as the act, The Flying Concellos.

Antoinette became known as the "greatest woman flyer of all time" because she was the only woman to complete the fabled triple. We started out with the trapeze eight feet from the floor, but before we left for filming in Florida, it was close to the top of the sound stage at about forty feet. DeMille warned all of us we would have to get our screen roles down pat before we took off for the Ringing Brothers winter quarters in Sarasota to begin the picture. I took the demanding DeMille at his word when he said that he wanted nothing but realism in *The Greatest Show on Earth*. After the campaign I put on to get the part in the film, I had better make damned sure I was good.

Cornel Wilde was chosen as the handsome male aerialist, Lyle Bettger as the elephant trainer and Gloria Grahame as his elephant girl, Angel. Dorothy Lamour, who played the "Iron Jaw Girl," was taught to spin forty feet in the air while biting a leather strap. Lamour joined me in doing many of her own stunts. Jimmy Stewart, at the height of his career, took the role of a doctor on the run from the FBI who hides out as a clown in the circus. During the entire film, Stewart never appears out of his full clown makeup, a risky thing for any other actor but Stewart to do.

The actors learned their respective circus roles and participated in the acts. Many of the stars were coached by circus performers and executed their own stunts. In addition to the actors, the real Ringling Bros. and Barnum & Bailey's Circus ensemble appeared in the film, along with its complement of 1400 people, hundreds of animals, and 60 carloads of equipment and tents.

Principal filming began in Sarasota on a massive scale in mid-January 1951, the same time my divorce from Ted Briskin became final. I was a free woman. Lucky for me, I was involved in the circus movie project, something that helped divert my attention away from my personal problems. A special train carrying three hundred cast and crew, including two writers, arrived in Sarasota from Hollywood. DeMille wrote, "There must have been more than 50,000 people on the streets of Sarasota when we let it be known that we were going to film the circus parade there and ultimately photograph the crowd as well."

We had quite a time in filming the picture under the big top at winter quarters in Sarasota. My mother was there to comfort me, having just arrived in town from California. She came on set and immediately saw me sixty feet up in the air, about ready to fly. By this time, I had been practicing seven months to get enough strength in my arms and get my timing straight. I was the only one in the picture who didn't need a double for those trapeze stunts because I actually learned to do them. Now I was ready to do the act in front of circus people who were waiting to see what I was capable of, not to mention a full audience.

My mother rushed out to the center ring and yelled up, "Betty, you come down from there this minute!"

I hollered down to her in embarrassment, "Mother, we're ready to shoot a scene here!"

"Betty, are you insane? She insisted, "Come down this minute!"

De Mille was standing patiently silent next to the camera, no doubt wondering when he would be able to resume shooting his movie, something which was costing him umpteen thousands of dollars every single hour. I tried to tell my mother I had rehearsed the flying act many times before. Eventually, Mr. DeMille came over and reassured her that I was up to the occasion. He asked her if she would feel more comfortable by leaving the tent, but mother said she preferred to remain and suffer.

In addition to six weeks of shooting in Sarasota, the production accompanied the circus for its dates in Philadelphia and Washington, D.C., filming actual live performances under the big top. In April 1951, production was halted for ten days so that DeMille and his technical staff could observe the circus while opening in New York's Madison Square Garden. The remainder of the film that didn't necessitate being shot in front of a live audience was shot back in Paramount's Hollywood studios.

While filming *The Greatest Show On Earth*, Cecil B. DeMille presented me with the *Photoplay* award for favorite actress of 1950 for my role in *Annie Get Your Gun*. The presentation was filmed with DeMille rising to meet me at the top of the trapeze, some 60 feet above the ground. When he first told me of the award, I screamed out and scared poor Mr. DeMille out of his wits. He was always so nervous I was going to make a mistake and fall to my death. The entire award ceremony with DeMille and me high atop the circus tent was taped and shown on a newsreel, something which survives to this day.

For the train wreck scene, DeMille purchased a number of salvaged cars. With the aid of steel wrecking balls, he managed to give the cars the proper amount of distressed realism. Six cameras recorded the scene for added effect. No expense was spared. Likewise, the big top used in the picture cost $100,000 to construct. The circus costumes, especially designed for the picture by Miles White, cost $200,000. DeMille wanted his circus spectacle to be the best. Since the circus is basically a visual event, full of color and life, it was the ideal subject matter for a DeMille production. Wonderful camera work was the hallmark of the film, both of the circus acts and of reaction shots from the throngs of spectators in the audience.

Mr. DeMille was a wonderful man. We became very good friends during our time together on the film. One day we were shooting a scene, and I noticed something strange in his face. I moved toward him to get a better look, and just as I did, it seemed as if he were about to collapse into his chair beside the main camera. I quickly slipped beneath him in the chair, more or less allowing him to fall onto me. It was my spontaneous attempt to soften his fall. When his mouth was within range of my ear, he softly whispered, "Betty, I'm having a heart attack, but please don't let them know."

I turned to the girl assistant by the camera and demanded, "Get the man a brandy."

She stared at me blankly for a brief moment, but finally managed to utter, "Mr. DeMille doesn't drink."

"I *said*, get the man a brandy!" My more forceful approach obviously warranted action. One of the fellas on the crew ran up within moments with a drink. I grabbed it from his hand and poured it down Mr. DeMille's throat. Within a few minutes, DeMille stood up and resumed his direction of the cast for the rest of the day. The man was from the old school. He was driven in his movie work, and rarely, if ever, took a day off. During on-location filming in Egypt of the Exodus sequence for *The Ten Commandments* in 1956, the then 73-year-old DeMille climbed a 107 foot ladder to the top of the enormous Per-Rameses set and suffered a near fatal heart attack. Against his doctor's orders, he was back directing the film within a week. Cecil B. DeMille eventually died from heart failure in January of 1959. His passing was a major loss to the industry.

The Greatest Show on Earth premiered at New York City's *Radio City Music Hall* on January 10, 1952. It was produced, directed, and narrated by Cecil B. DeMille. The film's storyline was supported by lavish production values, actual circus acts, documentary, and behind the scenes looks at the colossal logistics effort which made *big top* circuses possible.

According to an October 1952 *Hollywood Reporter* article, the film was a box-office hit, earning $10,000,000 in its first six months. Not a bad take for a film whose original budget was approximately $4,000,000. A May 4, 1953 *Daily Variety* item reported that it had earned $18,350,000 in worldwide rentals. By the end of the

1950s, *The Greatest Show On Earth* ranked fifth among the all-time dramatic film money makers.

In addition to its financial success, *The Greatest Show on Earth* won many accolades and awards. Prior to 1952, DeMille had never won an Academy Award. During the filming of the movie, he asked me why I thought he had never won an Oscar for any of his films, and for my suggestions on how he might do so. Never one to hold back, I told him that his movies were basically corny, hence the reason for the absence of awards. Mr. DeMille was suddenly taken back; I knew he wasn't enjoying much of what I had to say. In defense, he insisted his films always did well at the box office. I reiterated, "Of course they do, Mr. DeMille, because they're corny, and people love corn." I recommended that since the circus already was corny; to just leave it alone, and don't add to it. I guess it's quite possible that Mr. DeMille listened to my recommendations.

The Greatest Show On Earth won Academy Awards for best picture and best writing of a motion picture story. It was nominated for best director, best film editing and best costume design (color). When actress *Mary Pickford* presented Cecil B. DeMille with the Oscar for best picture on March 19, 1953, it the first time the Academy Awards ceremonies had ever been televised. Although DeMille did not win the directing Oscar, he was honored with the 1952 Irving G. Thalberg Memorial Award. The film won a Golden Globe for best motion picture drama, best director, and best cinematography (color). DeMille was also nominated for the Directors Guild of America award for outstanding directorial achievement in motion pictures. *The Greatest Show on Earth* was also honored by the Foreign Press Association and several other organizations.

The New York Times said of the film, "The story told is shaped by glamour and sentiment, romance and razzle-dazzle, excitement and dare-deviltry. It isn't penetrating. It certainly is not profound. It is simply a romance of the circus. The captivation of this picture is in the brilliance with which it portrays the circus and all its movement, not as a mere performing thing but, as Mr. DeMille says in the narration, as a restless and mobile giant. All of the wonderful excitement of this mammoth caravan pulling out of winter quarters in Florida, with the animals and wagons loaded on the trains, the bells clanging, the people rushing and that old Coast Line engine whistling *all aboard!* has been captured in fine pictorial crispness. And then the imagery of arriving in a town, rolling to the lot, spreading the canvas, raising the tents and getting ready for the show have the authority and the impact of a top documentary film. To Mr. DeMille's credit, the montage effects in this picture are dynamically superb." *Time* magazine called it, "A mammoth merger of two masters of malarkey for the masses, P. T. Barnum and Cecil B. de Mille."

In retrospect, it is nearly unbelievable that *The Greatest Show on Earth* won the Oscar over such classics as *High Noon* and *The Quiet Man*. I think this epic look at circus life succeeded because of its melodramatic approach. Its use of stereotyped characters, exaggerated emotions and language, and constant conflict all perfectly fit with the public perception of what the circus actually is, or is supposed to be. Add in DeMille's creative camera work, and everything combines to create a genuine sense of the spectacular.

It was somewhere around the time we were shooting the film in Florida, that I took my first pill. I remember it distinctly because my friend, Sophie Tucker, was playing at the *Fontainebleau* in Miami, and I went down to help her out and visit for a couple of days. I had just dissolved my marriage with Teddy. That, coupled with the stress of working on the movie, was getting to me. In addition, I was not at the weight I wished I had been for the film. The skimpy circus costumes revealed everything, and I wasn't happy about it. I don't even remember how I came upon my first Dexamil, but it was in Miami, and I took it to increase my energy level and reduce my desire to eat. It sounded like the perfect combination for what ailed me. I never liked alcohol; it just got me depressed, plus it added on all those extra pounds.

Dexamil was an amphetamine, later known as *street speed*. In those days, the pills were given out freely. After I tried it, I rushed to a doctor who prescribed it for me as a simple pep-me-up and to control my weight. No one knew the harmful effects these synthetic substances had on the mind or body. Doctors understood this medication helped people, and that was about the extent of it. I could take the prescription from town-to-town and easily get it filled as often as I wished. I believe it was widely known and used casually throughout our industry at the time.

Amphetamines reduce the awareness of hunger. They do not diminish the bodies need for food; they simply suppress the perception of that need. They also stimulate mental activity, at the same time, rendering sleep impossible. Lack of sleep is a side effect I didn't realize until much later, and I have always had the worst trouble with sleeping. The other complication I failed to understand, or possibly chose to overlook, is that they are dangerously habit forming. When I started taking them, I experienced increased energy, with better self-esteem; I was more sociable, and quite self-confident. That, in itself, was a big shot in the arm in helping me to overcome my fears when performing. This substance gave me the pep I needed to do the impossible. I began relying on the substance, not once thinking I was abusing it. The other negative aspects were increased excitability and constipation, the latter being one additional problem I had to carry throughout my lifetime. The pills only increased the length and discomfort I experienced with that problem.

From there I moved on to Dexadrine. It was pretty much the same thing as Dexamil. I found out from someone the U.S. Air Force gave Dexadrine to pilots on long missions to help them remain focused and alert. If it was good for our men in uniform, it had to be right for me! Naturally, I began counteracting the side effect of sleeplessness by upping my typical dosage of sleeping pills. It was a dangerous combination. I wasn't aware of it then, certainly I had no clue, but the pills were to become a major vice, and led to my eventual and complete downfall. For the remainder of my life, they were instrumental in the end of my family relationships, and continued career decline.

We finished up production of the *The Greatest Show On Earth* in July of 1951. It was just in time, as my voice was starting to give out. All the years of screaming and shouting had taken a real toll on my vocal cords. I was amazed my voice had lasted that long. Back in the Lopez days, I did my act every single night without a microphone! The result after all those years of abuse was that my voice was becoming breathy and hoarse. I got to the point where I couldn't even talk, let alone sing.

On the parade route in Sarasota, Florida during
filming of *The Greatest Show On Earth*, 1952.
Photo: Paramount, Betty's private collection

With the "Ring Master", C. B. DeMille.
Photo: Paramount, Betty's private collection

I love this photo of me with Chuck Heston. I'm glad
that he was a strong man, I look a bit hefty here.
Photo: Paramount, Betty's private collection

Chapter Fifteen

The doctors said I had growths on my vocal cords that had a structural resemblance to a corn on a toe or a callus on the hand. The nodules had to be removed or my voice would continue to deteriorate. I was told the operation was minor enough, but I couldn't be promised about the fate of my singing voice.

Following the operation, I was silenced for about three weeks, until the beginning of August 1951. I was forced into to putting anything I wanted to say down on paper. It was the first time I came to the realization, I talk too much. The doctors were reasonably sure the surgery wouldn't damage my loud style of singing permanently; I was given a voice test just to be sure. I decided to try out my voice out on *Way Down Yonder in New Orleans*, one of the songs I was working on for my next movie. Everything came out fine. I had been lucky. Production of the film, *Somebody Loves Me*, was to begin in earnest immediately.

In my first interview in which I discussed the surgery, I told Hollywood columnist, Erskine Johnson, "I sing much better and smoother now. I can hit those lower and higher notes right on the button without screaming for them. It's marvelous, I sing, and I don't blow out any fuses. The lights don't even flicker." Actually, my role in *Somebody Loves Me* was a quieter, more mature part for me. I wasn't required to mistreat my singing voice in the manner typical of most of my earlier comedy films.

Somebody Loves Me was written and directed by Irving Brecher, better known for his weekly TV series, *The Life of Riley*. The film is the fictionalized life story of vaudeville and Broadway star, Blossom Seeley, played by me, and Benny Fields, her husband-partner. Fields is depicted unfavorably in the movie, somewhat as an opportunist, who maneuvers Blossom into marriage for the benefit of his own career.

Paramount borrowed Ralph Meeker from MGM to play the role of Benny Fields. Originally, the studio tried to get Robert Alda, who was hot as a pistol at the time doing *Guys and Dolls* on Broadway, but the producers of that show wouldn't release him long enough to make the picture. In my estimation, Meeker was the wrong choice. My biggest complaint is that he didn't even do his own singing; his songs were dubbed. Concerning Meeker's part in the movie, one critic wrote, "Things would be better if Betty Hutton had support from her co-star, but Ralph Meeker is dull and uncomfortable in the part. The supporting cast helps, but they can't overcome the trite, clichéd script."

I had asked for Frank Sinatra in the role of Benny Fields. At the time, he was suffering with throat problems, and the producers of the movie, William Pearlberg and George Seaton, said no. After the film failed to make money at the box office, Pearlberg and Seaton sent me flowers and a note of apology for not heeding my warning about Meeker. Sinatra was *the* song and dance man of all time. If he had been allowed to star in the movie, today we would be watching it on television every ten minutes.

Ralph Meeker got his start by replacing Marlon Brando in *A Streetcar Named Desire* when Brando left the original production in 1949. That success led Meeker to a new career in the movies. In the early 1950s he starred in a few good, but minor films. In 1953, he starred in the Broadway production of *Picnic*. Meeker was awarded the New York Critic's Circle Award in 1954 for his performance in that show. *Picnic* was made into a film in 1956, with William Holden and Kim Novak starring in the roles originated by Meeker and Janice Rule on Broadway. In an interview, Meeker once stated he was offered the starring role in the film version, but didn't want to sign a long-term contract with Columbia Pictures, instead opting to sign on for a minor career with MGM. He continued in a string of Broadway shows in the 1960s. Meeker was kept extremely busy in television well into the late 1970s, after finally hitting his stride by playing the typical tough guy.

At the same time I was working on *Somebody Loves Me*, I appeared in a cameo walk-on, walk-off role in a film called, *Sailor Beware*, starring the comedy team of Dean Martin and Jerry Lewis. It was basically a remake of my very first film, *The Fleet's In*. I played Dean Martin's hometown girlfriend by the name of Heddy Button. The film was in production for one month between September and October of 1951, and opened on February 9, 1952. The last scene at the end of the film where I appear for a second time was actually shot independently at the studio and then merged into the film. I was too busy to take the time to appear on the actual set of the film. The girl who runs after Martin in the final shot was supposed to be me, but was actually a stand-in.

Production on *Somebody Loves Me* wrapped in October of 1951. The release of the film was held up until September 24, 1952, nearly a year later. When it finally was released, reviews of the film were generally mixed. I felt production had been rushed. I suppose I was responsible, in part. My throat surgery had set the schedule back by weeks. One report stated, "Even the most dedicated fans of the screen's most energetic performer may find this biopic to be lacking. Hutton is not to blame; as always, she gives 110% of herself. Her rendition of the title song is lovely. Indeed, she makes all her numbers shine, but she can't do much with a script that is tired." Maybe another good reason the movie didn't do so well at the box office is because I was playing an almost completely dramatic role here. Over the years, my fans came to expect, and loved me for my comedic talent.

Irving Brecher, the director of *Somebody Loves Me* said, "Betty is still the essence of show business, a mixture of Eva Tanguay, Clara Bow, Bette Davis and a six-alarm fire. Put her on the stage and she'll wow an audience. Put her in pictures and she exhibits an amazing emotional appeal. Put her in the middle of the Sahara and she'd draw a crowd."

With almost twenty musical numbers in the film, there was more than likely something for everyone. Many songs were written in a style appropriate to the turn of the century and, therefore, pretty much had appeal only to the movie. The one song that did have popular commercial appeal was the title song. The music to the song, *Somebody Loves Me*, was written by *George Gershwin*, with lyrics by my wonderful *Buddy De Sylva* and a New York City Tin Pan Alley lyricist by the name of *Ballard MacDonald*. The song was first published in 1924. I also loved the song, *Way Down Yonder in New Orleans*, written in 1922. Both of these really great numbers from the film weren't even written originally for it.

I met Charles O'Curran on the set of *Somebody Loves Me*. We seemed to hit it off pretty well. Charlie was the film's choreographer and he also staged the musical numbers. He was originally from Atlantic City, New Jersey. He had a long history in the entertainment field. When he arrived in Hollywood in 1944, he turned to the production side of film making.

Charlie and I spent a lot of time together. I wasn't fond of not being married. I guess along with a successful career, I also felt entitled to a successful home life. I was taking things slow with Charles, it least that's what I thought. I really enjoyed his company, but had no idea where our friendship would lead.

When the picture was finished, I vowed I was going to take at least four months off from Hollywood. I decided to rent a house in Honolulu for me and the kids, and really have a chance to rest up. I needed the time to regroup. It had been a miserable year for my personal life, but a rather good one for my career. Regardless, I was tired and needed a well deserved break.

My vacation was cut in half. I never could get as much time to myself as I would have liked. The time I did spend in Hawaii with the kids was wonderful. I didn't know how exhausted I really was. I slept long hours each night and even managed afternoon naps. I returned home in time to celebrate Christmas and the New Year holidays with mother and the children. When I arrived home in Los Angeles, Charlie was waiting for us at the airport.

On February 21, 1952, I left California for three weeks to entertain our troops in Japan and Korea. I was accompanied by The Skylark vocal quintet, two musicians, and Charlie. Details of our itinerary were arranged by the Hollywood Coordinating Committee, which handled the volunteer entertainment program for GIs overseas. After we visited hospitals in Tokyo, we were transported to Korea by airplanes, helicopters, and jeeps. We packed a real punch that warmed the hearts of soldiers in a makeshift arena that had snowcapped hills for a backdrop. I appeared in costumes not designed for winter warmth. I got a terrible case of laryngitis from the biting winter wind in Korea. Still, I and the fives Skylarks wowed the boys with musical numbers and dance routines. It was a satisfying tour that gave me some well needed practice in front of a live audience, before returning home to a planned engagement at New York's *Palace Theatre* in April.

After returning to the States, one evening over dinner in Los Angeles, Charlie proposed marriage. God only knows what I was thinking, or better yet, what kind of pill I had taken before going out. It was 10:00 in the evening by the time we made the reckless decision to charter a plane and elope. We arrived in Las Vegas at 12:30 in the morning and were married 30 minutes later, on March 18, 1952, in the Church of the West at the Hotel Last Frontier.

I wore a navy blue wool suit and a little hat with a turned-up brim. I look at pictures from our wedding day now, and am surprised to see I actually looked happy. I can't say if I ever truly loved Charles O'Curran. I do know one thing for sure; I was in desperate need to have someone there watching over me and guiding my career. I hadn't had that since Buddy. Teddy never provided it for me. I hoped with all my heart Charles would offer me that protection and stability. Charlie was 37 at the time. He certainly appeared much older in the photographs. My childhood needs and insecurities were coming back to haunt me, since I admittedly saw Charles as more of a father figure than a husband. I was all of 31, and already moving on to marriage number two. I don't know if I looked older in person than I did in my wedding photos, but I sure as hell felt it.

We decided to delay any form of a honeymoon, I needed to return to Hollywood and practice my routines for my upcoming show at the *Palace* in less than one month's time. Little did I realize, my hope for matrimonial bliss wouldn't last very long. This time around, when the marriage eventually failed, my movie career would already be a thing of the past.

I confided in columnist, Sheilah Graham, "You know, when I married Ted Briskin, I had two lives. I felt my career and my home life should be distinct and separate from one another, but it didn't work. I believe that it takes one actor to understand another's emotional strain. While Charlie isn't an actor, he was a performer for many years, and he's in the business as deeply as I am. What's more, we're both interested in the same type of entertainment. You know, when actors get together all they talk about is themselves. This gets a bit tiresome for an outsider like Ted, but Charlie's part of it all. We have a wondrous rapport." At first, I felt comfortable in my new marriage because we had something in common, but even that changed over time.

On Saturday April 12, 1952, I opened at the *Palace Theatre* in New York. I was following Judy Garland. No one, not even I believed I could break her record there, but I did. My entire four-week stint with two grueling shows a day was a complete sell out, something it was said could never be done. I played the entire second half of the show, some fifty minutes. My costumes and gowns were all designed by my studio friend, Edith Head. I wanted everything first class all the way. My mother was along for my moral support and to help with the costume changes.

My act was staged and produced by my new husband, Charlie O'Curran. In retrospect, not the best decision I could have made. I pretty much allowed Charlie to move in and take over my life and career. After all, I needed that moral boost, not to mention someone standing behind me to call the shots I didn't feel comfortable calling, or just didn't have the time to call. It did manage to take a lot of the pressure off of me. Nevertheless, I should have been able to foresee it was one of the worst decisions of my life. After all my years of hard work to get to where I was, I basically handed the decision making concerning my career over to someone else. For sure, Charles O'Curran was no Buddy DeSylva. I just could not have realized my decision would soon have such devastating effects on my career and life.

Along with the assistance of the *Skylarks,* I paid musical tribute to Buddy DeSylva and the singing style of Blossom Seeley. At the end, I wound up doing tricks on a trapeze flying out over the heads of the audience. I had to do something crazy in order to pack them in. It's amazing; you can get away with murder on stage. A live audience is forgiving, as long as you establish a rapport with them right from the start. On the screen, forget it; you've got only one chance.

Lewis Funke, a reporter covering my show for *The New York Times,* said, "This, of course, is exactly the kind of performance Miss Hutton's legion of movie admirers have been educated to expect. She sings, naturally, but she also screams, shouts, giggles, wriggles, struts, waves her arms, clenches and unclenches her hands until it seems that if she doesn't wear herself out she is, at least, bent on wearing out the less sturdy members of the audience."

New York's own *Brooks Atkinson* stated, "Anyone who is not entertained by Miss Hutton's explosion of energy is likely to find themselves uncomfortably conspicuous. The quality that conquers the audience is Miss Hutton's wild, wholesome nature."

It appeared I still had what I needed to wow them on stage. That's because everything in a stage show that an audience sees is really up to the performer. Not so in a movie, you have to depend on a host of others who are capable of messing the thing up for you, regardless of your efforts or intentions.

The audience could understand I was working from my heart. I wasn't always the best singer or dancer, but put them all together, don't look too closely, and we'll make it.

I told syndicated columnist, Sheilah Graham, "Blossom Seeley opened up a brand-new career for me. She taught me to do more with a shrug of the hip than I used to accomplish with three hours of shouting. She taught me how to sing so that every man in the audience will feel I'm singing to him alone. She showed me how to put sex into a song." That's how I played it, like there was only one person out there who I was performing to. If I showed an audience I loved them with all my heart, they were sure to feel it. There aren't many people who still work by pouring out their hearts over and over again like that; eventually, it will devour you.

The stint at the Palace in New York was a huge success. We returned to Hollywood and an offer to do a movie called *Topsy and Eva*, the story of the *Duncan Sisters*. The Duncan Sisters were a vaudeville duo who became popular in the 1920s with their act *Topsy and Eva*, a musical comedy adapted from Harriet Beecher Stowe's *Uncle Tom's Cabin*. I wasn't all that happy with the script, but then, I seldom was those days, considering the type of scripts the studio was coming up with. I marched into the studio big-wigs and loudly voiced my concerns.

The studio was run by Frank Freeman and Henry Ginsberg at that time. Freeman had little direct involvement with filmmaking operations, concentrating instead on the day-to-day management of Paramount's twenty-one-acre studio and its three thousand employees. The supervision of top features was handled by Henry Ginsberg, and, of course, Buddy De Sylva before he left the studio for good. Ginsberg had been the business manager at Paramount before taking over, so what he knew about film creativity couldn't have filled a thimble. Without the creative talents of Buddy, there wasn't much use in fighting, as nothing much could or would be done to fix a bad script anyway.

After being dismissed without receiving any consideration at all, I demanded my husband, Charles O'Curran, be allowed to direct the film. My reasoning was simple, together Charlie and I could work through the difficulties of the script, and in the end, make the movie our own success. The studio bosses vehemently refused to allow Charlie to direct the film. I was fuming mad when I told them to rip up the remainder of my contract. It was one last attempt on my part to get what I wanted. The bosses agreed to do exactly what I had asked, and I was sent packing. I had attempted to call the studio's bluff, but they called mine instead; a terrible miscalculation on my part. I didn't regret walking out that studio gate. What I regretted was not being able to ever get back in. After the friction between us, I knew damned well this sort of thing was bound to happen one day. The day just came sooner than I had expected.

On Saturday July 19, 1952, I walked out the gates of Paramount studios for the very last time. A press release attempted to downplay the event. Media reports stated, "Betty Hutton will leave Paramount after twelve years on the lot to go into independent film production with her husband, Charles O'Curran, and also to enter television." The announcement that I had obtained a release from my contract was made by my longtime friend and agent, Abe Lastfogel, president of the William Morris Agency. It was reported Charles would leave the studio as well.

So, that was that. The deed had been done. There was no turning back on this one. If it was a mistake, it was one I had to live with. The fortunate part was, I hadn't yet gotten to the point where I saw it as a mistake, I was still too mad. I tried to put it out of my mind, but a little voice in the back of my head told me there would be a day, or a time, quite possibly when I least expected, when what I had done would hit me like a ton of bricks. Then I would say to myself, "Betty, what the hell have you done?" I wasn't looking forward to acknowledging that moment.

The one saving grace that helped me maintain my sanity at this difficult time was my stage show. I loved performing for a live audience and I remembered telling myself if ever my movie career came to an abrupt end, that's where I would turn. I disclosed to James Bacon of The Associated Press, "The money doesn't bother me, because I can make as much in eight weeks with my stage show as I could in a year with the studio." Charlie and I immediately formed a new corporation in which my stage show would go on the road almost like a traveling circus. We would rent the theaters ourselves, and handle all the other details as well.

I was happy to get some of this out in the open. It was more or less damage control for what was left of my career. Anyway, talking to reporters could help clear the air. James Bacon asked if there was any truth to the reports that the Paramount hassle followed my insistence that O'Curran direct *Topsy and Eva*. Some columnists had even circulated rumors that co-star, Ginger Rogers, refused to be directed by Charlie O'Curran in the movie, possibly because it represented a conflict of interests of sorts. One female star's husband calling all the shots while directing another female star did seem a bit awkward. I can see how the rumor could have started. I responded with a rousing no. "Nothing to it," I answered, holding up my right hand as if swearing to it in a court of law. "The real trouble was over the script. I'll argue like hell when I know I'm right." Everyone who heard my explanation eventually believed it when learning the Duncan Sisters story was shelved at Paramount. I finished up by telling reporter Bacon the only fight I had at Paramount was trying to get Charlie's contract broken. I jokingly added, "They were glad to drop a hot potato like me, but they wanted to hang onto Charlie. He didn't need me, but I needed him to stage my road show."

I was a wonderful actress! When the shit hit the fan, I knew exactly where to stand. I was successfully accomplishing my damage control mission. Charlie kept his mouth shut, one of the few times he would manage to do so. I gave the reporter one more statement for good measure; after all, I was on a roll. I admitted, "Eventually, I want to concentrate on directing. If that doesn't work out, I could even be a character actress. Anyhow, I'll never quit. I can even follow Sophie Tucker's footsteps. All I need is some red-hot lyrics, and I'm set for the next thirty years! Cabarets are where I came from, and I can go back to them if I must. After all, Charles and I have formed a new corporation, and I'm nuts about corporations. I've been supporting my family since I was a kid, so I have a real business head on me. I'll bet you'll go away from here thinking I'm not a lame-brained blonde after all."

In August of 1952, I was interviewed at my home in Brentwood by *Los Angeles Times* reporter, Walter Ames. I wanted him in my home because I was sure he would report to his readers everything appeared peachy-keen in the Hutton household. As we sat around our swimming pool and casually chatted, Charlie was giving our five and three-year-old daughters Lindsay and Candice their swimming lessons. The purpose of his interview was to address the rumors floating around about the possibility of me moving into television. He wanted to hear the real story from the horse's mouth, now that I was free of my movie contract. It was true that just about every big show in television was after me to make guest appearances. I even had offers from virtually every network to start my own program any time I wished to put my signature on the dotted line. I told reporter Ames, "You can tell your readers that this little girl is going to get into television, but quick. And when I do, I'll have the greatest director in the world handling the show, my husband. He's the one looking over the scripts and story ideas for me. That's a great relief to have someone else do the worrying."

It had been one more attempt on my part to soothe my battered image. I was so frightened somebody somewhere might pass along some really hurtful information that could further complicate matters. So, I took it upon myself to lead the story where I wanted it to go by telling as much as possible, thereby attempting to set the record straight. Of course, what I was telling reporters was often far from the truth, but at least they had heard it from me. The fact of the matter is, at the time, I had no intention of going over to television, I wasn't ready. I guess I was too scared. Television was getting so big, and it was a facet of the entertainment industry I knew little to nothing about. As usual, I thought I would probably fail.

Also in that same month, being free for good from the entrapments of my movie career, we vacationed at Lake Tahoe for our belated honeymoon. It was relaxing to have a change of scenery, but my mind was still cluttered with thoughts of what was to come next. I was a planner, and as such, I couldn't stop my head from hashing things around and around, and over and over. I had a certain amount of remorse for walking out on my contract, but when I started feeling bad, I would stop and think about how difficult things had been at the studio after Buddy left. That was enough to immediately justify what I had done in my head, and I would calm down and start feeling better. After all that had happened within the past month, our trip to Tahoe as a honeymoon was anticlimactic, to say the very least.

While vacationing at Lake Tahoe, I received an offer by cable to play a top role in a movie called, *Mathew, the Matador*, from a man by the name of J. Arthur Rank, a big British film producer. Rank was casting his comedy film to be shot entirely in Spain the following year. My role was to be a high jinks part co-starring with British comedian Norman Wisdom. I was offered a straight salary or a part ownership deal; both of which I respectfully refused. Now that I was free from the bonds of my contract with Paramount, unusual offers were coming from every direction. I did appreciate being offered a part by an Englishman. They were quite fond of me and my talent in the UK. Likewise, I was fond of them. The offer gave me the terrific idea to return to the British Isles.

I was eager to return to the place where I had been accepted with open and loving arms by so many. We booked a three-week stint at the London *Palladium*. My show opened there on September 20, 1952. It was another roaring success, just as my previous engagement there had been. I was sad when my time there was over; it had been such an enjoyable run. After London, we took the act on tour to Ireland.

There was a particular woman who came night after night to see my show at the London Palladium. Nan, (I eventually learned her first name), always ended up waiting backstage for my autograph. When I inquired what she intended to do with them all, she said she planned to take the autographs back to her hometown of Douglas in Scotland. There she would distribute them among her friends who had been unable to come to London. I applauded her efforts, and took a genuine liking to this soft spoken and gentle woman. Impulsively, I promised to visit her at her home after my time in London.

When I arrived in Douglas, Nan was waiting out in the street for my arrival, and she was surrounded by several hundred Scottish miners. She had told everyone I was coming, and the miners in particular had been released from work just to welcome me. Nan ushered me into her cozy little house for tea. I thought that would be the extent of our visit together, but Nan had other plans. After tea, we were whisked off to the local hospital. Leaving her cottage, it was raining like crazy. Still, the streets leading to the hospital were lined with people who had come out to witness Nan entertaining her famous American guest.

At the hospital, I finally got to see where all the autographs Nan had collected from me had ended up. As we entered a communal ward, patients with wonderful smiling faces waved them above their heads like flags of welcome. With tears in my eyes, I glanced over at Nan. This simple woman had a great look of pride and contentment written across her entire face. Suddenly, I was delighted I had taken the extra time from my schedule to travel to Douglas. It's funny, I never did learn Nan's last name, but I know I'll never ever forget her or my visit to Scotland.

Back home, I opened my show with a four-week run at the *Curran Theater* in San Francisco on January 19, 1953. Charlie had staged, produced, and directed the show. Since my husband had been so involved, when we opened, I joked with reporters that we were thinking of changing the *Curran Theater* marquee to read, "The *O'Curran Theater*."

The show was a real family affair. Naturally, Charlie ran the whole thing, even going so far as to design the sets and scenery. Once again, Edith Head designed my costumes. My mother acted as my wardrobe lady, having responsibility over costumes for the entire cast. The show was another smash. We broke all kinds of box office records. After San Francisco, we continued on to do the same thing in Portland and Seattle. I was more than just happy with the way in which our audiences accepted us. Hollywood columnist, Erskine Johnson, met up with me along the way and asked me to compare movies with the stage. I admitted to him, "After twelve years in front of Hollywood cameras, I was out of touch with the people. You lose greatness on the screen by not appearing before live audiences. I needed those shows in San Francisco,

Portland, and Seattle because I was rusty and out of touch. Now I know why my first boss in Hollywood, Buddy DeSylva, made me break in all my songs at the Hollywood Canteen. Both I and the songs were great because they were audience tested. It's a show-biz lesson Hollywood seems to have forgotten."

On October 14, 1953, I returned to the *Palace* in New York for three weeks. Associated Press reporter, Mark Barron, was there to cover opening night. In his column he stated, "An H-bomb landed on the stage of the Palace Theatre last evening when blonde Betty Hutton departed from her Hollywood roles and brought her talents in person to a Manhattan audience. She is a terrific performer, and the audience demanded encore after encore. So, Miss Hutton, somewhat exhausted, had the piano pulled front stage, crawled atop it and continued to be "H-bomb" Hutton. Miss Hutton won over the Palace premier audience of professionals. She already has a $50,000 advance sale for her show. Her performance is not an act. It is strictly one of a show-woman, a personality, and she achieved it in this starring role at the Palace. For more than two hours Miss Hutton, with remarkable physical endurance, sang the songs of Blossom Seeley, imitated Benny Fields, and then sang the songs of *Sophie Tucker*. This was climaxed when Miss Tucker, now starring at the *Latin Quarter Night Club* on Broadway, walked up from the audience and threw her arms around Betty."

The story was totally different coming from Broadway's own Brooks Atkinson. He really let me have it in his column the day after my opening. "When Betty finally reaches the stage, she sings the Betty Hutton Story, which chronicles in the corny fashion of second-rate show business her step-by-step ascent to immortality. It is a tribute, not so much to her genius, but to her success, and she naturally plays the leading part in her own canonization. Let her entertain the folks with entertainment. That's what she used to do."

That last review really threw me for a loop. If that was really the case, then I was losing it. "It" being my ability to entertain even in front of a live audience, something I thought I was my very best at. It had always been said, just because you have it once, doesn't mean you keep it forever.

In the spring of 1954, I was ready for some change. I was kept busy on the lucrative nightclub circuit, but wasn't happy. Charles O'Curran and I separated over differences stemming mainly out of our working relationship. He was an out-of-control perfectionist, but along with it, he possessed a violent temper. When we were on the road doing our nightclub act, he made tremendous scenes in front of the cast and anyone else that might happen to be present. These arguments carried over into our home life, and made the marriage inevitably impossible. Also, I guess I always managed to justify in my mind blaming Charles for the end of my movie career. It wasn't really his fault, but I felt better being able to pass the buck.

Separating from Charles meant not having anyone to look after me on the road while doing my sometimes grueling nightclub act. Of course, my mother was still there for me, but I really needed more help than she was able to provide. My daughters were at home, and I couldn't do everything myself. I had been putting off the decision for a long while, but now I was convinced the crucial move was into television. It had been taking its toll on films and their box office earnings for a long while. If for instance, I could land my own show, I could work a normal schedule and be home for the children on a regular basis. Television seemed to be the eminent wave of the future, and I needed to make the transition.

It was with television in mind that I finally landed a gig with NBC. They were in the process of putting together a series of what they termed "spectaculars" to be presented in color every forth Sunday from 7:30 to 9:00pm. My planned original musical comedy was to be the very first, airing on September 12, 1954. I was extremely excited about the prospects, especially since television had the potential of being viewed by so many people. The part I wasn't so excited about is that it was to be a live performance. The likelihood for a complete disaster was an ominous threat. It had taken my entire career for me to even begin to understand my shortcomings. The one I was thoroughly familiar with was my unmitigated fear. Fear so huge that as I remember it now, it makes me fight back a feeling of nausea in the pit of my stomach. Sometimes I wonder how I managed to get as far as I did. I would have ended it but for the drive, something only a true performer has, and makes you regroup and carry on, again and again.

I was to do the show with a man by the name of *Max Liebman*. He was supposed to be great because of his reputation with *Sid Caesar*. He was a lovely man, but had absolutely no creative talent. When I arrived in New York for rehearsals, the first thing I wanted to get my hands on was a copy of the script. Liebman turned to me and apologetically said there wasn't one! A rough outline was all that was offered. I was supposed to make the rest up as I went along.

"But, Max," I screamed. "I can't. I'm no writer. All I brought along with me is Jay Livingston, Ray Evans, and their songs. The music is great, but it ends there. I need jokes and dialogue to piece it all together."

Max Liebman just looked at me and smiled. "Betty, the musical numbers will fill in the ninety-minute slot." That was all he was worried about, using up the ninety minutes. What came in between those ninety minutes was obviously my problem. To finish on time in television seemed to be a miracle in itself. That afternoon I called the only man left in the world I trusted to help me, Abe Lastfogel. I had loved him since my early days in New York, and I was sure he could fix the problem.

I affectionately called Mr. Lastfogel "pa" and in turn he called me "ma". When I finally got him on the phone I started in, "Pa, I've got a problem. There is no script, and without one, I'm afraid the show will be a terrible disaster."

"Ma," he replied. "Don't worry, Max is a great producer, and everything will be fine."

My tone changed slightly when I continued. "Abe, you haven't heard a word I've said. I *have no script.* God knows, I'm no *Sid Caesar* or *Imogene Coca.*" The two were masters at ad-libbing; they each knew the other's every move. Besides, they had one of the great actor-writers of all time working with them on their team, *Carl Reiner.*

I continued to argue until Abe finally divulged the real reason he was unable to intervene on my behalf. It seems the William Morris Agency also handled Max Liebman. His hands were tied, and I was on my own. It was this same kind of thing that ruined it for me in films. Now it was happening in television, and even before I did my very first show. Abe left me hanging with, "I'm sure you can pull it off, kid." It hurt like hell for me to have to do so, but I called Charlie O'Curran to come and help stage the dance numbers. I was desperate, and Charlie kindly agreed to help out.

The whole show, of course, was geared strictly as a romp for me. What I ended up with by way of a script, particularly after all my venomous complaints, cast me as a rodeo queen in the Annie Oakley tradition. She makes her way to New York where she becomes involved romantically with a *Life* photographer assigned to shoot a picture layout of the rodeo gal for the magazine. An unidentified New York Times reporter's review stated, "There is no question that Miss Hutton did her best trying to make a hit out of *Satins and Spurs*. She probably got more help from the music and lyrics from Jay Livingston and Ray Evans than she did from the book by William Friedberg and Max Liebman. This is not to say that all the music was great, for it wasn't. In fact, Miss Hutton's sheer personality probably put more in it than was there to begin with. Although no one expects any great story line in a musical comedy, the book by Mr. Friedberg and Mr. Liebman seemed to be unusually weak and short on comedy."

The other point that was highly criticized was the color. Of course, the "color" was supposed to be the reason for the spectacular in the first place. It was said the fidelity was not maintained throughout the show. I guess that means it wasn't uniform or reliable throughout the program. Big deal! The crazy part is that no one I knew even had a color set at the time. Color television was just on the verge of being released. For the time being, we were all quite happy with, and accustomed to, watching television in black and white. For the few people who did have a color set, it didn't work well half the time anyway. That added an additional blunder to the equation for Max Liebman and his NBC "spectacular". It was the worst way I could imagine for me to be introduced into television.

I was not only humiliated by the television flop, I was also devastated by the disastrous experience. About the same time, I committed to the NBC blunder; I had been approached to star in the movie version of *Oklahoma!* I actually turned down the role of Ado Annie, instead opting to do the TV spectacular, *Satins and Spurs*. I was so positive it would be a smash hit on television; I refused to pass it up. It is quite possible the role I turned down in *Oklahoma!* could well have revived my failed movie career.

All it takes is one good break. It was the last decent chance I was to be given, and I blew it.

Tone deaf, *Gloria Grahame*, who ended up playing the part I had been offered as Ado Annie, sang without being dubbed by anyone. The result required that her songs be edited together from recordings made almost literally note by note. Gloria Grahame appeared as my co-star in *The Greatest Show On Earth*, and I can attest to the fact she was incapable of singing a single decent musical note.

Director of the film, Fred Zinnemann, wanted the part of Ado Annie to be played comically, but Gloria Grahame kept putting too much sex into the part. Consequently, he told the two backup *Goon Girls* that he would be using them more extensively as comic relief to compensate for Ms. Grahame's improper interpretation. The *Goon Girls*, so called because they were always gooning or fooling around, were originally slated to be in only one number with Grahame. They appeared in every dance scene, and ended up having more screen time than some of the major co-stars.

Composer, Richard Rodgers, and lyricist, Oscar Hammerstein, wrote the original musical play in 1943. It was adapted into a musical film in 1955, but Rodgers and Hammerstein personally oversaw the film themselves to prevent the studio from making the changes that were then typical of musical adaptations from stage to film. These two brilliant men also maintained artistic control over the film. I felt particularly remorseful about refusing the part when I found out this information. It sounded to me like a movie was being made the correct way for once. I liked the fact Rogers and Hammerstein were smart enough not to allow Hollywood to mess this one up. I would have loved working with these two men, and I knew I would have been perfect in the film. The screen classic was released in October of 1955, and went on to win two Oscars.

Oklahoma! was produced by Magna Theatre Corporation and Rodgers & Hammerstein Productions. It was the first feature film photographed in the Todd-AO 70 mm widescreen process. It was simultaneously shot in the more established Cinemascope 35 mm format to allow presentation in theaters without 70 mm equipment. The reason I tell you all this seemingly insignificant and very technical information is because, in its original theatrical releases, the two versions of the film were released by different distributors. The Magna Corporation handled distribution of the Todd-AO 70mm version, while RKO Radio Pictures handled the 35mm Cinemascope version. It's interesting to note, making movies was no longer a simple process controlled in its entirety by one studio, as the majority of my films had been during my tenure at Paramount. I also want it to be known, just in case you didn't, *Oklahoma!* wasn't produced by Paramount. No, they hadn't promised me a cozier dressing room, and in the process lured me back into their fold. That was something I knew would never happen.

It was reported that Frank Sinatra had been offered the lead role of Curly (played in the film by Gordon MacRae), but when he heard that every scene of the film would be shot twice; once in Todd-AO and again in Cinemascope, he turned it down. Sinatra was accustomed to filming his scenes in any motion picture once only.

I was despondent after the television escapade. On September 28, 1954, a little over two weeks after the show aired, I announced my retirement from show business; I just couldn't take the heartbreak anymore. I said that after a Las Vegas nightclub engagement at the Desert Inn, I would quit performing and devote my entire time to being a mother.

I spoke candidly with Bob Thomas from the Associated Press of the disappointments of the past few years, and how I had been unable to find a movie that I really wanted to make. Above all, I emphasized the disappointment I felt after my first television engagement drew mixed reviews and failed to draw a substantial share of the ratings, despite its exorbitant costs. Bob Thomas reported, "Betty feels the television show was the crowning blow. Nevertheless, insiders believe part of Betty's unhappiness is due to the failure of her two marriages. Betty is now committed to a four-week stand at the Desert Inn in Las Vegas starting Oct. 12. She says that will be her farewell appearance. But Hollywood, where retirements are often announced but seldom take, couldn't work up much excitement. "She'll be back," was the verdict of insiders. One source, who has worked close to Betty for many years, said she has announced retirement, privately, more times than Fred Astaire, who has been retiring off and on since 1932."

I visit with Blossom Seeley and Benny Fields
on the set of *Somebody Loves Me..*
Photo: Paramount, Betty's private collection

With Ralph Meeker, *Somebody Loves Me*, 1952.
Photo: Paramount, Betty's private collection

Leaving to entertain the troops in Korea, 1952.
Photo: Betty's private collection, The Betty Hutton Estate

Entertaining the guys in Korea, along with the *Skylarks*.
Photo: Betty's private collection, The Betty Hutton Estate

I'm glad all the guys were dressed warmly, I sure wasn't.
Photo: Betty's private collection, The Betty Hutton Estate

Charlie O'Curran and I on our wedding day, March 18, 1952.
Photo: Betty's private collection, The Betty Hutton Estate

Mr. and Mrs. Charles O'Curran.
Photo; Betty's private collection, The Betty Hutton Estate

Sign announcing my *Palace Show* in New York.
Photo; Betty's private collection, The Betty Hutton Estate

Performing at the *Palace*, 1952.
Photo: Betty's private collection, The Betty Hutton Estate

Also at the *Palace*, 1952.
Photo: Betty's private collection, The Betty Hutton Estate

Max Liebman at the Brown Derby party in Hollywood I hosted
for the NBC spectacular, *Satins and Spurs*, 1954.
Photo: Photo Nat Dallinger, King Features Syndicate, Inc.

Chapter Sixteen

I opened my show at the *Desert Inn* in Las Vegas on October 12, 1954, to rave reviews. There was a lot of media attention surrounding the event, due to my earlier announcement that this was to be my final engagement prior to my retirement. I told Bob Thomas of the Associated Press, "I'm giving this show everything I've got. I want to bow out with nothing but the greatest." When asked about my future plans, I revealed, "I'm going to get married. This time I've found the right kind of man. We're going to live quietly. I'll be a den mother for Lindsay, who's eight and in the Brownies." I didn't name my third husband to be, but the word was already out around Hollywood, I had promised myself to Capitol Records executive, Alan Livingston.

Thomas asked me about a report that had surfaced, stating I was broke and would have to keep working. I shot back, "How could I retire if I was broke? I'm not loaded. But I've got enough to retire comfortably. I don't have to live the way I have. I can sell the Cadillac."

Naturally, no one believed for a minute I was going to give up show business for good at the age of thirty-three. I reiterated, "I don't care, this is the end, I'll never do another show." For good measure I added, "I can't wait for these four weeks to be over. Then I'll really start to live."

I was bound and determined to make my swan song the best show ever. I guess I went a little overboard. At one of my performances, I dropped over on stage, something I had never done before. Hollywood Columnist, Erskine Johnson, reported, "It wasn't until Betty opened at the Desert Inn in Las Vegas that she joined the Tuckers, the Jolsons and the Cantors with an act to remember in the show world's hall of fame. Wringing wet after an hour of singing, yelling, clowning and hoofing at the Desert Inn, the show ended to the greatest applause I've ever heard in a night club. The way Betty jams every ounce of her energy into her performance, it's no wonder she collapsed from a combination of the heat and physical exhaustion and is in the medico's hands. She really gives her all."

On November 9th, I was more than ready to call it quits after a tiresome four-week run. After my usual show on the final evening, I bade a tearful farewell to show business. I don't believe there was a dry eye anywhere. Even waitresses cried as the audience of nearly six hundred rose to their feet. Shouts of "No, no!" were heard from the crowd. The orchestra struck up *Auld Lang Syne* and everyone sang. I cried, as an executive of the hotel presented me with three dozen roses and a gift. After my final goodbye, I fled to my dressing room and the comfortable waiting arms of my mother. Alan hurriedly made an appearance from his front row table to congratulate me on my final performance. My divorce from Charles O'Curran would be final in February, and then I would be free to become his wife, Mrs. Alan Livingston. Betty Hutton would be a thing of the past, a buried relic. I was thankful this chapter of my life was coming to an end.

I couldn't stop thinking how happy I would be as a full-time wife and mother. The possibilities were limitless. At this point, it seemed far more important for me to be a woman than a star. At least so I thought.

I began 1955 with a renewed spirit and a fresh start. My divorce to Charles was final on February 21st. I moved to a new house, and at first, I was kept quite busy playing the happy homemaker. Once I got settled, I realized I had nothing much to do all day long. With the energy I had, sitting around without a specific purpose was difficult.

I showed my first sign of relenting from my decision never to work again when my sister, Marion, and I cut two records, *Ko Ko Mo* and *Heart Throb* for Alan Livingston's company, Capitol records. It was the first time we had sung together on a recording. Upon hearing I had cut a few records, the press was hot on my heels. I joked, "It wasn't much like work at all. I had a ball doing the numbers with Marion."

Later, I was called upon to return to Las Vegas to stand-in for Sammy Davis Jr. who had been injured in an automobile accident. I accepted the gig with mixed emotions. I was torn apart by my desire for a stable family life and my love of performing. I was slowly getting to the point where I was able to understand I couldn't have both. However, just because I could understand it, didn't mean I was ready to accept it.

On February 8th, I ended my brief retirement by announcing I was restless and bored with being a homemaker. My attempt at staying home to care for my two children was a flop. Finally, my mother said, "There's nothing wrong with you that a stage won't cure." So I decided to go back to work. I knew everybody would say, "I told you so, Betty. But to heck with them," I declared. "I can't stay out of show business. The last couple of weeks I've been a nervous wreck, blue and depressed." I signed with a new agent, MCA, and announced I was now on the hunt for new projects. As for my stage career, I was going to get my feet wet with a mid-March engagement at the *Beachcomber* nightclub in Miami.

Alan Livingston and I were married on March 8, 1955, in Las Vegas, Nevada by a District Judge. I was unable to help myself; the man was just too good looking. Our wedding was just five days after Alan obtained a divorce in Acapulco, Mexico from then wife, Elaine, and fifteen days after mine from Charles O'Curran. We honeymooned in Miami, Florida at the Beachcomber where I was scheduled to begin performing on March 17th for a three-week run.

When pressured, I admitted I finally realized I quit show business because I was terribly hurt over critical blasts against my NBC-TV show, *Satins and Spurs*, as well as having been run down and exhausted. I stated. "I suddenly ran into a streak of hard luck. Everything I touched went wrong, even my marital life, and I felt I didn't want to be in this racket."

It was a subject I was too unhappy even to think about, much less continue to discuss. Maybe I missed the glitter and glamour of show business. It could be that the sound of an audience laughing or applauding something I'd done on stage hooked me to the business like a drug addict. There is nothing normal about show business, so how can the people in it be normal? Yet, once I was hooked, I couldn't live without it. So what was I going to do? Stay in there and belt out songs was my only alternative.

"Now I'm back where I belong," I insisted "Everything's wonderful. I want to be an actress now. I'm tired of doing all those crazy roles I've always done. Nobody seems to realize I've grown up, but I have. Now I'd like to be a woman for a change, and play one on the screen as well."

For the first time, I was labeled as volatile by the press. Every article written seemed to contain that horrible word. When asked why I was making a comeback so soon after retiring, I snapped back, "Well, I just changed my mind, that's all." As I read the things I said to the press now, I understand the confusion then over my inconsistencies. I pretty much said one thing and did another. I was flying by the seat of my pants as far as the fate of my bungled career went. To tell you the truth, I didn't know what I wanted any more. I was probably too scared at the time to continue on, but at the same time too frightened to give everything up. I do know one thing, I didn't care much what the press thought; it was my life to live. That was probably a huge error in judgment on my part. The press had always been on my side. The tables were starting to turn. I never once stopped to realize, if the press is against you, your career in show business is all but doomed.

I've been asked many times if I had the chance, would I have changed any of the things I had done that I thought were mistakes concerning my career. My answer is quite simple. I don't believe I realized then that any of the things I was doing were wrong or mistakes, otherwise I wouldn't have done them.

On October 25, 1955, I returned to television with a special of my own for NBC. This time I was returning with what I knew best, a musical variety show with jokes and standard songs. I had learned the hard way from my first experience exactly what I was capable of handling on television. Although I never felt that *Satins and Spurs* was the bad show my colleagues labeled it, I did feel everyone else connected with that show escaped while I was forced to shoulder the blame. My name, having been the only big one associated with the show, had a lot to do with it. I felt more comfortable selling myself as is, a bouncy and boisterous singing comedienne, instead of in a role NBC picked for me. "This time I'm going to do it my way," I said, "and I hope they like it because I don't want to keep on retiring. This is it. If this one doesn't go, I'll just forget about television." In my upcoming hour-long show, I chose to stick to the material that made me a big hit with my nightclub audiences.

I told Aline Mosby of the United Press, "I'm very nervous. I realize I have a lot at stake. But, since I married Alan Livingston, I've regained my confidence." Alan felt I should do a show that I knew how to do, with numbers from my nightclub act and my own songs. He wanted me to feel I hadn't failed. He felt I did not have the right material before, and there was no point in my leaving TV on a bad note. "I hope people will be pulling for me and be on my side. If I stink this time, I'll be awfully sick inside. I'm not the greatest singer in the world, but I give my heart to the people."

The show was not without its problems. My dear friend, Sophie Tucker, stricken by a virus a week before show time, had to bow out. It meant having to revamp some of the numbers and to look for another big name to stand in as a co-star in addition to *Jimmy Durante*, who was already signed. Bob Hope came to my rescue, but insisted on kinescoping his monologue bit prior to the show. Kinescope is a recording of a television program or a segment of a program made by filming the picture from a video monitor. A camera was mounted in front of a video monitor, and synchronized to the monitor's scanning rate. It was an early predecessor to videotaping. I wasn't that happy with that decision, since kinescope footage was of inferior quality. It detracted from the show as a whole, but Hope did agree to appear live in the finale.

Many big-name stars were in the habit of pre-kinescoping many of their guest performances for the sake of time and convenience. Kinescopes were intended to be used for immediate rebroadcast or for an occasional repeat of a prerecorded program; thus, only a small fraction of kinescope recordings remain today. However, many episodes of programs from the 1950s and 1960s survive today thanks only to kinescoped copies. *Satins and Spurs* is still around today because a kinescope copy was filmed during the live performance of the show. The quality, as to be expected, is not all that good, but it survives, nonetheless.

In June of 1956, I accepted a comeback role in a non-singing dramatic picture, *Spring Reunion*. It was my first film in four years. Little did I know it was to be my very last. During my heyday at Paramount, I did two or three pictures a year on a flat salary of $5,000 a week. Now, co-starring with Dana Andrews in *Spring Reunion*, I received $100,000 plus twenty percent of the gross. The salary alone came to around $20,000 per week. Not too shabby for a comeback part. It wasn't due to my great demand or talent, it's just how times and salaries had changed in the past several years.

It was my husband, Alan, who convinced me to give this film a shot. He told me, "You think you've been licked, Betty? You'll never be happy until you realize you aren't. Try it again, but aim this time for the commercial success. Then, you can quit films after two or three years, contented." It seemed to be a clear-cut goal. So that was my plan. I was going to work hard for a few years, make some decent money, and then quit for good. As I think of it now, working solely for the money brings to mind a conversation I had with Judy Garland where she admitted to me, she hated performing toward the last, but continued to do so for the money. I never realized then that my career could ever come to that sort of an end.

After this movie, if all went well, I hoped to move back into television with my own series. Alan had been a Capitol Records chief when I met him, but now he was a top man with NBC. That could really work in my favor if I played my cards right.

Spring Reunion was an adaptation of a Robert Alan Arthur television play that had been seen on NBC in March of the previous year. I didn't know until much later that Alan wanted me to accept the picture because he had made a deal. If he managed to get me to sign, he was rewarded with $25,000 cash upfront. Had I known it beforehand, I wouldn't have made that dreadful picture. Once again, the script just wasn't there and I couldn't pull it off. It wasn't any one person's fault; it just never should have been made.

Filming lasted for about a month during the summer of 1956. I play a spinster who falls in love with Dana Andrews when we both get reacquainted at a reunion of their high school graduating class from Carson High. Dana Andrews was so heavily into booze at the time that it made filming very difficult. I sang only one song, a smooth and slow ballad called, *That Old Feeling*, with music by Sammy Fain and lyrics by Lew Brown.

When asked by a reporter from the United Press while on the set of Spring Reunion at Republic Studios if my subdued part might not startle some of my old fans, I responded, "I've been acting like a teenager in movies. You can't do that forever. If you can't grow up, you're not going to make it. I'm a woman in this picture instead of a kid. I'm 35 now, but in this picture, they let me be 33. Maybe they won't like this, and I'll have to go back to playing an idiot on camera. Even so, I don't care. I'm so happy at home with Alan. I no longer love work for itself. I get my kicks now out of what happens in his career! This time around I'm going for the money. Nuts to art, I've had my share of that." It seems I never could keep my mouth shut!

The New York Times commented about the film after it opened on May 4, 1957. "Although it fleetingly captures the loneliness of some of its principals, it is largely a nostalgia-ridden and unimaginative comedy-drama that makes its points haltingly and without impact. Like the members of Carson High School's class of '41, *Spring Reunion* tries desperately but fails to make its rosy dreams come alive."

If *Spring Reunion* wasn't notable for its great storyline, it was notable for being one of the first films to be made by actor Kirk Douglas' Bryna Productions. Rumor has it that the barely saleable *Spring Reunion* was deliberately designed as a tax write-off by Bryna's accountants.

The film was distributed by United Artists. It was one of only two films from my career that were not produced and released by Paramount Studios. After making this, I guess I needed to call it quits in movies. I don't know why I couldn't have just stopped when I was ahead. I suppose it isn't human nature to stop at the top. However, in the movie business, the smartest thing to do is disappear in advance of being forced to leave.

I should have called it quits for good, but with me, it was always a matter of never being able to say no. I was set to team up again with *Howard Keel* in two independent Western films ten years later, which were slated to be produced by my long-time and dear friend A.C. Lyles from Paramount, *Red Tomahawk* in 1967 and *Buckskin* in 1968. Shortly after production started on *Red Tomahawk*, I was unable to keep up with the fast-paced two-week schedule, and was replaced by the lovely actress Joan Caulfield. By that time, my heavy drug usage had depleted my energy levels and the concentration needed to perform.

After *Spring Reunion*, I had few options left. I concentrated my efforts on my stage act because it was a sure thing. I kept the idea of television in the back of my mind, sort of like you might keep five bucks in your shoe for an emergency at some later date. For now, Las Vegas was happy with me, and I was able to pull in a fairly sizable income from doing my shows there. I got in the habit of appearing in Vegas twice in the summer and twice again in the winter. I knew damned well my career was winding down, and there was little I could do to stop it. I knew I needed to take it where I could get it, since beggars can't be choosers. It was a humbling experience, but also a scary one. At thirty-five years of age, I was used to providing for myself, if not for a husband or two. The scary part was in knowing of little else but show business as a means of self-support.

In May of 1957, I was all set to do a weekly situation comedy for NBC, but backed out after making the pilot episode. Everyone was worried my refusal to continue with *That's My Mom* would be a terrible embarrassment to my husband, Alan, the West Coast chief of NBC-TV programming. I was to play the widowed mother of four children in the planned series. My fear was of being typed as the same character each week and that nothing of much interest could come from such a flat story line. *Jess Oppenheimer,* who produced the *That's My Mom* pilot, told Hal Humphrey in his syndicated column, "Betty is a perfectionist, and gets very intense about everything she does. Betty has to realize that with a series it's impossible to have a good show every week. You've got to be practical about these things." My desire to be good overshadowed my desire to be practical. I pulled out, and the television network lost a great deal of money.

I made my Vegas show into a real family affair. I felt comfortable in having everyone around. What's more, I felt responsible, as always, to care for those close to me in a financial way. I had my mother working backstage, my sister, Marion, in the chorus, and her husband, Vic Shoen, conducting the orchestra. In addition, Marion's ex-husband, Jack Douglas, had written some of the dialogue, Jay Livingston, my husband's brother, had written the songs and my husband, Alan, introduced me at the beginning of the show.

I was scheduled to do my show at the *Sahara* around the time of Christmas in 1957. After finishing up my run, Judy Garland was to take over with her show beginning on New Year's Eve. I was tired from another grueling run by the time our plane arrived home in Los Angeles. No sooner had I walked in the house, the telephone began ringing. It was the *Sahara* calling. Judy was ill, and they wanted me back to fill in. I turned to my mother and asked what I should do. "Mother," I moaned. "I'm so tired; I don't think I have the energy to make it back there." Mother piped in, "Tell them you want $100,000 for New Year's Eve, not a penny less." Thinking they would never agree to that kind of money, I felt confident they would say no, and I would be free to go to bed for some well deserved rest. When I relayed the message, they didn't flinch one bit at the request. Within the hour, we were back on the plane headed for Las Vegas.

Despite having all family around me for support, the only one who really knew what was going on inside of me was my mother. With all the pressures of my crumbling career, I turned increasingly to pills for comfort. Not only did my mother know I was using; she supplied them to me as if she were handing me a prop before going onstage. She would present me with a bottle of Jean Nate perfume for a quick spray, then a few more pills, and a drink to wash them down. That was the routine. There was never any attempt on her part to stop me, or to control my usage, in any way. Then of course, my mother was an addict in her own right. Just because her fix was alcohol, it didn't make her usage any less severe than my pill addiction. At the *Sahara* in Las Vegas, no one knew what to make of me; I had become such a bitch backstage. However, onstage I seemingly had it all together; at least I was told I did. I was terrified half the time; I couldn't remember what I had done out there. By the time the second show started, I was loaded. I guess the performer in me always managed to pull the show off. About all I remember is the applause. I often wondered why they continued to cheer me like they did. I knew one day the applause would surely end for good.

More people were heard to say during my stage show years, "I wonder how she does it?" I really struck a nerve with them, and basically that's what I wanted, to wow them enough to gain their approval. The thunderous applause that followed each seemingly successful performance in Vegas was the result of only one thing, my amphetamine use.

I don't even have the satisfaction of looking back at those years with any sense of pride or accomplishment. I know damned well I could never have done it without those pills. In the beginning, they were like a lover to me, mellowing and embracing. In the end they were devils, totally manipulating every aspect of my life. The price one pays for drug usage goes beyond the personal; it extends out to affect everyone within your reach. It's like the fallout from an atomic bomb; it continues to mushroom in all directions.

My final attempt at reaching the masses was through television. I did a string of guest appearances in the late 1950s on NBC shows such as *The Dinah Shore Chevy Show*, *The Nat King Cole Show*, and *Perry Como's Kraft Music Hall*. Being around the sets of television shows was fun; I started picking up tidbits that eventually provided me with a certain comfort level when it came to working in television. I figured, if I hung around long enough, I was bound to learn something.

Dinah Shore had a great producer on her show by the name of Bob Banner. He said, "Don't hurt the ego of an actor. That's all they have to work with." It felt good knowing someone in television understood us as performers. On the negative side, before going on camera to do a duet with Nat Cole, he warned me not to touch him. I thought to myself, what's with this guy? Being the touching sort that I am, I came right out and asked him the reason. Nat reminded me that this was television, and *all* of America was watching. If a black man was to touch a white woman, even if it was her who made physical contact with him, his show and career might well be finished. Here I thought *I* had problems! I'm happy those days are far behind us as a society.

I gained further confidence in television when on April 27, 1958, Dinah Shore allowed me to take over control of her Chevy Show for an entire episode. I was placed in complete charge, so I blatantly brought in my own writers for the occasion. I told Vernon Scott of the United Press, "I'm a perfectionist. If a show can't be done as well as possible, I'd rather skip it. I've been on TV only about five times in my life. I'm afraid of it, unless I'm in charge of what I'm going to do."

When asked about any possible connection between my husband, Alan, being a big cheese at NBC and the reason for my taking over Dinah's show, I was truly miffed. "He hasn't a thing to do with the show," I defensively maintained. "I've lined up the talent myself. George Sanders and I will do a musical sketch, and there'll be some singing and comedy bits with Miyoshi Umeki, Keely Smith, and Louis Prima. Dinah's show is the only classy show on the air. That's why I agreed to do it."

I suppose the reporter saw I was infuriated. Quite possibly that was his precise intention, to see how far I could be pushed. At the end of his column he went on to say, "Betty didn't say whether her guest stars will bring their own writers, as she would like to do on her own guest spots. From here it appears that George, Miyoshi, Keely and Louis will be at the mercy of Miss Hutton and her writers." It was clear the media were beginning to turn against me.

Shortly thereafter, in June, Alan and I announced our intention to get divorced. Our verbal disagreements, centered mainly on my wavering career, cooled considerably. Before long we were back together. Not until early April of 1959, the following year, did I eventually file for divorce from Alan Livingston. I charged him with causing me serious mental suffering. I knew full well I was the chief instigator in the majority of our arguments, but Alan manipulated me from the beginning in ways I found intolerable. At one very low point in our relationship, Alan carefully coerced me into terminating a pregnancy. He managed to always treat me in a manner that made me feel like a child. We separated until our eventual divorce.

Before our divorce, I ran into Alan at a party in the home of some mutual friends. Before I knew it, Alan had pulled me off to one side to talk. Before anyone realized it, we were pawing at each other like two teenagers. I was uncomfortable with such a public display, so we carried our tryst away from prying eyes and into a guest bedroom. Our rendezvous led to sex, after which I cried and admitted to Alan, I still loved him. I told him I was pleased, and hoped this would lead to our reconciliation. Alan turned to me and said, "Get back together? Honey, this was just sex. I'm already engaged to someone else." Our divorce was finalized on October 21, 1960.

It was around this time, I reacquainted myself with God. Without turning to religion for comfort, I wouldn't have survived the heartache. Shortly before I started work on my weekly TV series, I became a Lutheran by joining a local Los Angeles church. My pastor and my maid, Mary, came to my rescue. Mary had been with me for nineteen years and was my rock. When things got too much for me to handle, I would go off and read the Bible, if only for a few minutes. Instantly, no matter where I was, everything bad seemed to dissolve and I felt renewed.

It was announced in May of 1959 that I would be starring in my own television series starting in the fall. Our pilot film was so tempting; we sold it to a sponsor less than a week later. Because of my estrangement from Alan Livingston, my affiliations with NBC were a thing of the past. CBS said they didn't have a time slot open, but after reviewing the pilot, suddenly they found the room.

The story centers around a woman named *Goldie*, a showgirl turned manicurist who makes friends with a wealthy Wall Street customer. When he dies of a heart attack, Goldie discovers she had been made guardian of his three kids and multimillion dollar fortune. The snobbish children resent *Goldie* moving in on their lives and the family fortune. Episodes focus on Goldie's adjustments to her newfound social class, and the children to their unsophisticated and unconventional new guardian. The show went into production on July 20, 1959. It was sponsored by Post Cereals, and when it finally hit the airwaves, ran on Thursday nights opposite *Donna Reed* on ABC and *Bat Masterson* on NBC.

I had lost the mass popularity and exposure that movies had provided me with. This show was my last-ditch attempt to recapture some of the faded glory from my film career in the new medium of television. I was so sure this was the winning combination for TV, I created my own production company and I put all the necessary up-front money into the project myself, a total of $600,000. Between the start of production in July, and the premiere of the thirty-minute show on October 1, 1959, I parted company with three producers, two directors, and five writers. This was all in an effort to have things my own way. In the end, it proved to be the fatal blow, my final undoing. A reporter stated, "Betty's irrepressible style is hampered by a leaden script and tedious attention to unnecessary detail."

In many ways, Goldie's story was my own story, and the reason I found the story so perfect from the onset. Like Goldie, I was from the wrong side of the tracks, and suddenly we both found ourselves living the life of the wealthy. I put my whole heart and soul into the project, nothing new from the girl who wanted everything perfect and desired total control.

I told reporters, "I'm not going for the buck with this show. I want to be proud of it. If I'm not proud, then I want to be dead. I don't give a hoot if I don't have a dime at the end of the year." In essence, that's pretty much how things turned out. I lost my shirt.

I paid people who possessed the knowledge and experience to make correct choices for me and the show. However, since it was my show, I was never fully able to trust them. I fought so hard to make it a hit; I believe I got in the way of my own success. Nevertheless, isn't that what I had been doing my entire career? In the end, I chose to make my own decisions, based solely on my gut instincts. More often than not, my decisions were wrong or misguided. Still, I began directing some of the scenes, and rewriting others. I put lenses on cameras and dressed the sets. My actions on the set were causing me and the show to destruct in front of everyone's eyes. No one said a word; I never gave them the opportunity. At the time, I doubt I would have listened anyway.

It is difficult to imagine how I could have been so shallow, when in the beginning I told the press, I'd spent the past four years longing for a worthwhile series. Naturally, I exaggerated when I said I turned down hundreds of scripts because nobody could come up with a unique and different enough show to please me. However, with perseverance, I finally found the right one. "Nothing like it has ever been seen," I raved. "It's the cotton-pickin' end."

My statement rang true without even knowing it, because the end was closer than I could have imagined. *The Betty Hutton Show was* the cotton-pickin' end... The show ran for one season, and was canceled by the network in the spring of 1960. I had received my just reward. It was over and, for all intents and purposes, so was I and my career.

Things were never the same for me from that point on. I was totally defeated and alone, except for mother and my two children. Unfortunately, both my daughters were like strangers. They had never even been allowed the opportunity to know me, or I them. The loss of my career shook me into reality for a brief moment. I was able to see clearly for the first time how things come home to roost. My relentless obsession with my career kept me from knowing my own children. I had made terrible errors in judgment for years, and in the process had ruined my life, if not the lives of those around me. My enlightenment was snuffed out before I could change anything or help myself in any way. Instead of attempting to fix the problems, I sank deeper into them. Thanks for that I owed to my now uncontrollable pill usage.

Two months after my divorce from Alan Livingston was finalized, I jumped back into the fire by marrying jazz trumpeter, Pete Candoli. We had known each other as friends for well over a decade. I was scared to be alone. Our wedding took place at the Lutheran Church of the Reformation in Las Vegas on December 24, 1960. I was thirty-nine and Pete was thirty-seven when we married. Pete had one child, daughter Tara, from a previous marriage. We honeymooned in Europe, but by the time we reached London in April of 1961, I was already calling for an annulment of our marriage. We seemed to bicker about the littlest of things, after which an all-out war would ensue. Our mad and passionate lovemaking would calm the quarrels until the next squabble developed.

Pete came into my life when I was totally lost in drugs. The creative forces in me had been extinguished. I also slowly cut off everyone around me: my children, my agents, my friends, and even my mother. I found it difficult to understand why the one person I had always been able to turn to, my mother, was unable to help me now. Then I remembered her saying repeatedly when I was a small child, "Enjoy everything fast, it will be over in a minute." Maybe my minute was up, and since mother had witnessed my self-destruction all along, she quite possibly figured there was nothing anyone could do to help me.

I never did end up turning to my mother for any help or support at that critical time in my collapsing life and career. I suddenly remembered my youth, and how I had always been the one for *her* to turn to for help. I had been there to sort things out for years, so how in the hell could I expect her to be there for me now? Maybe she was capable of it, maybe she wasn't. It's something I have speculated about often, but will never really know the answer to. I never gave her that chance.

I was pregnant with our daughter Carrie (Carolyn) when the worst possible thing happened. It was very early New Year's Day, 1962, when I received word my mother had died from asphyxiation the night before in a fire at her Hollywood apartment. Mother managed to start a fire by falling asleep with a lit cigarette while she was in bed. My sister, Marion, came and stayed at my house in Brentwood during the funeral. That's when she told me how heavily into pills my mother had been. Sleeping pills were the cause of her falling asleep with a lit cigarette, and all the while I thought it had been from alcohol.

When they got to mama's body, they found my picture underneath her. I took it as a final gesture of her love for me. I never saw her body because I was pregnant at the time with Carrie, and they were afraid my reaction from the shock might in someway harm my unborn child. I suppose that's why to this day I never really think of my mother as gone. There was no farewell or fanfare. It is impossible for another to have loved a mother as much as I loved mine. I will forever carry with me extreme guilt for not being able to protect her from her untimely end. If I hadn't been worrying about my own life and career at the time, hadn't been strung out myself on pills, and hadn't deserted her for a string of inconsequential marriages, I think I might well have been able to save her from herself. Since childhood, I did my very best to protect her in every way I could. She had her faults and, of course, her serious sickness with alcohol, but she was mine, and I loved her more than I have ever loved myself.

Mother told me one time she knew she was going to burn to death one day. She was forever smoking up a storm. I think she managed to burn up a few upholstered chairs in her day. I protested, "If you know that mama, then why do you do it?"

Mother turned to me with a silly little grin and admitted, "The same reason I drink. I can't stop."

It had been a tremendous struggle for our family to rise from the depths of extreme poverty, all the while facing the hardship of my mother's alcohol addition. I spent the vast majority of my childhood angry over having to act as the adult in securing money to put food on our table when my mother was incapable. I made it to New York and Hollywood and had risen to the very top as an entertainer and movie star. I earned and eventually lost millions. My career was now on the verge of becoming extinct. It seemed like enough to fill several lifetimes for any individual, and yet my mother was only sixty-one years of age when she perished. A person struggles so hard sometimes just to survive in life; it seems callous that it should ever be extinguished so easily.

Our daughter, Carrie, was born on June 19, 1962. She managed to change our life for the better. She was the glue that held Pete and I together for so long. We enjoyed some really good times together as a family, despite my continued drug use. Pete had the best intentions for me and the children. It must have been difficult living with an addict who made every attempt at being as normal as possible, but never really was.

Carrie was just ten months old when a part-time nanny by the name of Margie was transporting the child in my car. The exact reason for Carrie being in the car alone with the nanny at the time totally escapes me now. What I do remember is that the police told me she had lost control of the car, and both she and Carrie were injured. I was rushed by the police to the emergency room to be with my daughter. As events unfolded, it was revealed the auto hit a tree in Brentwood with such force that the steering wheel snapped off and was thrown from the vehicle. Carrie had a severe cut on her face, but otherwise was okay. Margie suffered multiple lacerations and hip, leg, and rib fractures. Naturally, this incident hit all the papers as part of the continuing saga in the tragic life of one of Hollywood's fallen stars, me.

Within hours, Carrie was released from the hospital. We took her home where my beloved maid, Mary, the one who had been with me for decades, said she had the answer to the eventual facial scars that would show up on Carrie's beautiful face, unless we acted immediately. She was going to rub them ten times a day with cocoa butter when they were healed just enough. She told me that special remedy, along with the power of Jesus, would make those scars never appear. I gladly handed Carrie over, trusting Mary totally. Thank God she attended to my child; I hadn't the mental composure or physical strength to deal with any of the trauma. I rushed into my room to take five or six downers. I was trembling so terribly, I dug my fingernails deep into the skin in the palm of my hand until it bled. It was a trick I used often during my horrific drug days in an attempt to regain some semblance of composure. Finally, the pills took hold, and I calmed down enough to get a look at myself in the bathroom mirror. Staring back at me was a face I didn't recognize. It was the face of a woman disfigured by defeat. At a time when I should have sprung to action instinctively as a mother, the injury to my tiny daughter made me actually want to end my own life. I know what a cowardly thing that is, but the reason I took all those pills in the first place is because I truly was a coward; fearful of the world and even of myself.

My other two children, Lindsay and Candy, came into my room after hearing the news. I recall I held them in almost a death grip, I loved them so. Their mother's world was falling apart, and I didn't want them to be a part of it. I think in the past, I had always appeared to them as strong and self assured. Now I was fragile and terrified, and I knew they sensed I was in trouble. They heard the screams of anger that were exchanged between Pete and me regularly, something that obviously scared and confused them.

I waited several days until things calmed down a bit in our house to have a heart-to-heart talk with my two older daughters. The timing was bad with Carrie having just been injured, but I needed to let them know we needed to move again. What I didn't tell them was mama was unable to afford the beautiful house we were living in. If we didn't cut down on our living expenses, the financial trouble we were in would only multiply at an even faster rate.

If I had been straight at the time, free of my addiction, my love would have been sufficient to pull us all through. All children need to know is that you love them, and when they do, they will go along with just about anything. However, my abnormal behavior from the drug use was showing, and the girls began to recognize something wasn't right with mommy. They started to draw away and even began exhibiting their own unusual behavior out of fear and a break in the normal routine.

After we moved, I tried to keep my distance from the children, so they wouldn't see my erratic behavior. I spent more of my time in bed than I did on my feet. I was deeply ashamed I couldn't stop with the pills. Pete was disappointed in me because I was broke. He just didn't figure on Betty Hutton ever going broke. He refused to work, something that complicated our money situation. Pete could have made money if he had wanted to, but he told everyone in his musical world he was going to manage me. As a result, he had severed ties with pretty much everyone he had worked with before. I didn't blame Pete for hating me; after all, everything he had married me for was gone. If I still had my fame and fortune, I bet he could actually have overlooked the fact that I was now an addict.

Because of my shortcomings as wife and meal ticket, Pete took enjoyment from controlling me. He knew how sick I actually was, and took delight in making me think I was losing my mind at every opportunity. God knows it wouldn't have taken much. He would sit in the living room and take all phone calls. I was not allowed to answer my own phone. In some subtle, and even in some not so subtle ways, he conditioned Lindsay and Candy to despise me. He would tell them what a big shot I thought I was. His favorite expression was, "Look, girls, the great Betty Hutton can't even get arrested." They started to talk back to me in a way I knew they were losing all respect for me. It was the worst possible thing he could have done, using my own children against me. My heart began to break.

Finally, one day my Mary came to me and announced she could no longer stay on. "Miss Betty, I can't remain any longer and watch as you and the girls sit here being destroyed." Without my Mary, it was as if I were in a free fall from high in the sky without a parachute. I decided it was time for me to save myself from this marriage.

After losing my maid, Mary, I knew it wasn't long before the same thing would happen to my daughters. I think it was all in Pete's plan. Lindsay had been spending a lot of time with her real father, and sure enough, it came as no real surprise to me when she wanted to go live with Dad and his new wife, Colleen. They had never really been close, but since I was unable to care for myself, much less her, it was the best decision. Candy went to live with a dear woman friend by the name of Becky who owned a ranch. She had started going there to visit and stay with her nurse since she was just a baby. Deep in my heart, I was relieved. I couldn't bear for my children to remain and witness the shambles my life had become.

So now, it was just me and Carrie. I suddenly realized the two of us were prisoners. If there is a wall between you and the world, it makes little difference whether you describe yourself as locked in or locked out. Carrie and I needed to break down these walls of confinement and once more belong somewhere.

There was only one person left to turn to, my sister Marion. I had this crazy idea, in my drug induced stupor, that if we could only reach Marion in Laguna Beach, she could somehow save us. Marion belonged to *AA*, and I knew if anyone could help us, she could. After all, I had helped her many times during her life, so I felt no shame in asking for her help now.

I quickly packed one bag for us both, and we jumped into the car. Carrie was delighted to be going on a fun car trip, so I kept everything as joyful as possible. The drive was only about an hour and a half. I couldn't wait to arrive and phone my sister. We checked into a motel in Laguna and I called the local AA office for her number. When I heard her say hello on the other end of the line, I felt a huge sigh of relief, but at the same time I started crying hysterically. "Marion, it's me, it's me, Betty. I'm here in Laguna with Carrie. Please, I need to see you right away." She told me a business meeting was being held at her house, but she could come and see me right after it was over. Cold chills ran down my spine when the phone went dead. She hadn't seemed particularly happy to hear from me. I hadn't seen her since she had come up to stay in Brentwood with me when mama died in the fire. When she was with me then, she had been constantly drunk. She had behaved badly, to the point where even her husband was angry at her emotional outbursts and embarrassing behavior. I excused it because mama was dead, and I thought it had a great deal to do with her sorrow at the time. I did not know how heavily into booze she actually had been.

Marion arrived at the motel looking really great. She had always been a beautiful girl, but the drinking over the years had damned near destroyed her. She had been drinking since the age of nine. Belonging to AA, and getting her life back in order, had done wonders for her. I loved her so much and always had, but, of course, she never once believed it. It had a lot to do with the fact she never really made it into the big time, and naturally that caused friction between us. She was always under the impression I was mother's favorite, but I never saw it that way. Sure, mother lived with me all those years, and I cared for her. Someone had to. It was only natural mama and I became very close after all we went through.

When Marion was still with Glen Miller, I was in my first Broadway show and was the talk of the town. It wasn't an easy thing for her to take. On top off that, Marion had become pregnant and married a man by the name of Jack Philbin when she was at the peak of her career. He was a terrific guy, but he didn't have a job. So, I had them move into my apartment with me and I paid all the bills. She tried to pretend she was extremely happy at the time. I think if Jack had made it big then, Marion could have been truly content to remain a housewife and mother. I took care of them financially for a long while, and that is when Marion really began to hate me. She and her husband were proud people, and I think the money I offered them was misconstrued as a show of my superiority. After a time, they both became outraged. I was young and foolish, and if I in any way flaunted my newfound wealth, it was only because I had never had it before.

Jack Philbin did become a success not long after he divorced Marion. He went on to produce the *Jackie Gleason Show*. I know he held his grudge against me after I once wrote him and asked for a job, any kind of a job on the Gleason Show. His answer was colder than death. Maybe I had it coming.

All of these things ran through my head as I stood looking at my swanky new sister. From her attitude, I knew from the start she had no desire to hear my story. "Marion, please, I'm so hooked on pills. I know you belong to AA; please won't you get them to help me. In the coldest, but most straightforward voice I have ever heard her use, Marion sat me down to explain exactly how she felt. For once she was happy in her life because she had licked the booze, and so had her husband. She felt she had finally found success, and for the very first time, she felt equal to everyone else. "Betty, you have always been the star, you've had everything. When you walked into a room, you got all the attention. Well, I run AA here in Laguna, and in my own way, I'm now the star. I'm not going to ruin that for you or for anyone else. Right now it's bad for me to even be talking to you. Mine is an ongoing struggle, but it's my struggle, and I don't want you around to damage it." A long silence fell between us. I looked directly into her eyes, hoping to see a slight glimmer of love. There was none.

I had my own cross to bear. The pills had taken their toll on me big-time. All I was asking for was a helping hand, but there was none to be found. My own flesh and blood refused me. There was little love lost that day. I guess there had never been love there in the first place between us. I thought I loved Marion, but maybe money over the years had sent a wrong and hurtful message. Had I possibly been so insensitive to confuse financial support with love? Obviously, I had if Marion felt this way about me now.

Suddenly, I thought, maybe Marion was all too familiar with how addiction consumes not only you as a person, but everyone around you. Since she was on the road to recovery herself, possibly she refused to allow me to get near her out of fear that I might pull her back under with me. That reasoning I could live with. I told myself that had to be the case. If it weren't, I think I would have wanted to die. I couldn't bear any other reason for being rejected the way I had by my own sister.

I had become a monster because of the pills. It was the direct cause for the collapse of my career. People who came backstage to see me after one of my Vegas shows hardly recognized the woman in front of them. I was able to perform brilliantly onstage because I had been loaded. The pills had given me the confidence to do the impossible out there. However, by the time the show was over, the pills had worn off, and what they saw backstage was a monster. People would come to congratulate me on a great show, but I was never even sure of my own response. Often I would say, "What the hell do you know about what I did out there. Go fuck yourself!" The dressing room door was slammed in their face. Consequently, there was little love lost when my career collapsed in shambles. I had burned bridges along the way of people who were now tickled to witness my demise. Maybe my sister was one of them.

Before she left, I asked Marion if she could at least put me in touch with someone who could help find me a house. Later that day, a blonde woman walked through the door with a smile on her face and a kind word. She threw her arms around me and told me how pleased she was to meet her idol. This woman was the beginning of a whole new world for me. Her kind and patient words were enough to hold me together. It had been a long while since I had experienced kindness from anyone. Here God had sent me a complete stranger in my time of need.

This lovely lady listened to my story, but never once passed any judgment. She had been a pill addict herself, so she was able to understand where I was coming from. I told her Marion refused to allow me to go to AA. This caring woman took it upon herself to bring me the AA book and literature and to personally oversee my rehabilitation. I hadn't been happier in years. She found me the perfect house where Carrie and I lived quietly and comfortably. Carrie was enrolled in pre-school to interact with other children, and she loved it. I even bought her a scruffy little dog, we named Buffy. Things were looking up. I hoped in time to return to work; I felt that confident.

One day Pete drove up bearing gifts for us both. He was capable of being quite charming when he wanted to be. Somehow he convinced me to give him one more chance. He was working and really did seem sincere. I decided I was well enough physically and mentally, and somehow we just might be able to make our marriage work. It's strange, now that I was again truly happy inside, I felt guilt about our failed relationship, and refused to heed the warning signs that I had learned earlier to watch for with Pete. That night in bed we made beautiful, passionate love, and I fell in love with the man all over again.

Before long, the games between us started all over again. All the new friends I had made, Pete managed one way or another to turn me against. After he had me where he wanted me, back in his clutches, he rarely if ever was home. It was a frightening game he was playing. I started back with the pills in a big way. Carrie became unhappy. I started to go broke with the pill usage and mismanagement of my new life. Pete refused any type of financial support. I started selling my personal possessions in order to live. I knew I would have to leave the comfort and security of this wonderful little house soon, having to downsize an additional time to make ends meet.

Pete and I lived in separate houses after our very first separation. When we got back together, as we often did, we kept the two-house situation the same. It made perfect sense to us both. There was bound to be another split eventually anyway. I was content not having him around to argue with and happy to have my own space. He must have felt likewise: he told me would stay up until all hours playing his music or composing it. If he was involved in any extracurricular activities at the time, I was never aware. This setup was the only way we both were able to cope with our tempestuous marriage.

On November 14, 1966, I was sitting in my living room watching Rona Barrett's new Hollywood gossip segment on television. It was the year she started in TV, and she was wildly popular in Los Angeles. Everyone I knew watched to see this little pixie spew her wonderful New York accent as much as they did to hear who she was gossiping about. I casually heard her mention the name Pete Candoli. Instantly, my ears perked up. Then I heard her say, trumpeter Pete Candoli was secretly engaged to singer-actress, Edie Adams. Edie had spilled the beans to Dinah Shore. I sat for a few moments dumbfounded, unable to even move. I knew what I had heard Barrett say, but it still hadn't fully registered in the part of my brain that processes such information. When it finally did, the hurt shot from my head directly to my heart and nearly pierced it.

Although we had separated for what I figured was a final time months earlier and I had even gone as far as securing a cockamamie Mexican divorce in Ciudad Juarez in September, for all intents and purposes, we were still together. Consequently, I was completely humiliated by hearing of Pete's engagement in such a public fashion. After a few minutes of hurt, anger automatically kicked in. Pete's deception made me see red. I called his number for several hours until I finally got him on the phone. To this day, I can't remember what I said, or how I even approached the subject. Pete agreed to come down within the hour to explain and soothe my battered nerves.

He arrived at my house in Laguna Beach in an agitated state. While driving down from Burbank, his embarrassment over being revealed obviously had progressed, like mine, to the anger stage. He said he was there only to visit our four-year-old daughter, Carrie, but instead it appeared to me, he was there for the sole purpose of instigating a fight. I argued with Pete until the point where he got physical. Hitting me several times, he threw me to the floor and then threatened to kill me. I ran into the bedroom to call the police, locking the door behind me. By the time sheriff's deputies arrived, the situation between us had cooled considerably. I told the authorities we had merely argued, and I refused to carry the matter any farther.

The next thing I recollect, I woke up in South Coast Community Hospital. It took several days before I was able to piece together the sequence of events. I apparently called someone after taking an overdose of sleeping pills. I warned I was going to kill myself, but I had made that threat way too often before for my friend to take it seriously. She got worried and contacted the police after calling to check on me the following morning and I failed to answer. My friend informed police I sounded depressed and despondent when I called, but actually I was more stoned out of my head from the multiple handfuls of pills starting to take effect. The police forced entry into my house when they heard my daughter crying inside, and I failed to respond to the door.

I remember the ambulance coming, because several people were gathered around and staring down at me. I heard one of the attendants say, "How do you like this, a goddamned big movie star trying to take her life?" I could hear everything being said, of that they weren't aware. In the ambulance on the way to the hospital, they were making really nasty jokes in reference to me. I started drifting in and out. At one point, I was jarred to attention when a female voice yelled, "Oh my God, we can't let her die!"

I had been revived, and now at the hospital, they were walking me around after giving me laxatives and a host of other concoctions to cleanse my body of the toxic pills. Pete arrived to see me. He took one look at me, and with all the venom he could muster in his voice, said, "Well, look at the grand movie star, Betty Hutton, shitting all over herself." One of the two nurses helping me to walk pulled him quickly aside, but I was still able to hear what she told him. "You bastard, it's what we gave her making her do that." Pete backed off immediately, and turned to leave the room.

When I was released from the hospital after a few days, Pete came to drive me home. We had no sooner gotten into the car in the hospital parking lot, when I started in on Pete. "How could you have done that to me? I don't give a good goddamn if you decide to marry Edie, but why did I have to be humiliated by hearing it on television instead of from you? I'm *still* Betty Hutton you know. Without turning to look at me, he said, "You, are nothing..." Not another word was said until we arrived home. He put me into bed and pulled the quilt up around my shoulders and neck. He leaned down and kissed me on my forehead before saying, "It's all going to be alright."

Subsequent to my first attempted suicide, I was assigned psychiatric help. I was told a person who sincerely has the desire to kill themselves doesn't make phone calls to inform people of the intention beforehand. It is merely an attention getter in an attempt to gain sympathy. I never really wanted to do away with myself; although I got to the point many times where I felt there was nothing left for me to live for.

No one could ever understand the reason I took all those damned pills that were destroying my life. When I first started, the pills alleviated the one thing that stopped me from performing at my very best, fear. Of course, every time I took one, I remembered how they instantly transformed me into a confident and assertive person, someone I wanted to be instead of who I was. They helped me to cope with my life by supplying a force that I wanted to return and stay. But, of course, eventually they caught up with me when I couldn't function without them. The price I had to pay was way too high.

I decided an American divorce from Pete was the only truly logical way to end our marriage for good. I filed for divorce on March 23, 1967, charging Pete with causing me extreme mental and physical suffering. Then, exactly one week before our Superior Court divorce date, I filed for bankruptcy. My Beverly Hills attorney filed a petition in Federal Court stating I had debts of nearly $150,000, with practically no assets. Injudicious investments were stated as the cause for my financial difficulties.

Our divorce was granted on June 18, 1967, two days after our court appearance in which I testified, Pete had been jealous of me as a performer. I had quit my career to become a housewife because of his feelings, but financial problems arose soon thereafter. When the money problems started, so did the relentless arguments and extreme cruelty. I appealed to the court, seeking reasonable support for myself and our four-year-old daughter, Carrie, who remained in my custody. Under a property settlement, Pete was to pay $700 a month child support, and I was to receive $1 a month token alimony. I was 46 years old. I never heeded my mother's original warning when I first introduced her to Pete. "Betty, if you marry this man," she warned, "you are marrying everything you spent your young life pulling us out of."

Being married to Pete was a nightmare, but the result of that marriage saved me in the end. Carrie was my salvation. I believe God sent her to me to save my life. The road to destruction I was on had no stops or intersections. It was nonstop, straight ahead, right into hell. Only after my little miracle was born, did I take my first tentative steps back into reality. It was not any easy road back; I often stumbled and took several steps backwards before I was able to take several more in the positive direction. Of one thing I am quite sure, if it were not for Carrie at that point in my life, I wouldn't be sitting here writing these thoughts down for you to hear.

The next three years, I hardly even remember. I had Carrie with me on and off when I wasn't in a hospital for addiction or for mental evaluation and treatment. I ended up in a small apartment, but at least it was mine. My downsizing to conserve money was over, I couldn't find anything cheaper. Eventually, I ended up in a hotel in downtown Los Angeles when I wasn't able to pay a monthly rent any longer. The hotel was a place where I paid by the week. I even had Carrie with me toward the very last. Thanks be to God, Pete somehow managed to recognize the fact that without at least being able to spend some time with Carrie, I might well have ended it. She was all I had.

One morning, I packed what I had left in the way of personal belongings in a paper bag, and headed out the door of my hotel room for the final time. My room rent was already way overdue, and I had no means of raising the necessary money to pay the bill. I knew I was staying on borrowed time, and thought it best to just leave before I was asked to. I smiled halfheartedly, remembering having once said pretty much the same thing to myself about being a washed up actress; it's the smartest thing to just disappear in advance of being forced to leave. There was a church nearby where I knew I would be welcomed. There I planned to spend my afternoon hours thinking, praying, and plotting my next plan of action...

*   *   *   *   *

As I loll away the evening hours sitting here in the tranquil kitchen of Theda Bara's old Hollywood mansion, I calmly review the pages of my memoirs scattered before me. I have no fear now, nor am I in any immediate danger, except for the pain that surges through me while rereading these pages. Writing this book causes me to relive many of the agonizing events that collectively make up my sometimes tragic existence. I am unsure of my desire to continue with writing beyond this point. I have said all I can, actually I have probably said too much. I am in the here and now; I am all caught up. What is yet to come for me and my life will be as God sees fit, regardless of my personal desires. My life has been like a boat that has drifted off and on course many times. To me, it has been a respectable voyage, because it has been mine. I have no misgivings regarding my life or my actions. If I were given the opportunity, I wouldn't trade my life for the world. Someone, somewhere, might even be able to apply something of value to their own life by learning from reading what I have written. We are here to experience and to learn. I have done both to their fullest. I am contented. I have a handful of people who love and care for me deeply. More than that, any one person is not entitled to in a lifetime.

I couldn't help myself when I married Alan Livingston,
he was just too good looking. My career was already
too far gone to make my marriage with Alan work..
Photo: Betty's private collection, The Betty Hutton Estate

By the time I married my forth husband, Pete Candoli, my career
was inconsequential. It was my life that was now in jeopardy.
Photo: Betty's private collection, The Betty Hutton Estate

I had a good run when you stop to consider, nothing lasts forever...
Photo: Paramount, Betty's private collection

Part 2

Life with Betty:
Post Hollywood

Carl Bruno and Michael Mayer

340 *Life With Betty: Post Hollywood*

Chapter Seventeen

Carl Bruno's involvement with Betty Hutton began in 1970, and was an event that happened purely by chance. Gene Arnaiz Jr. was Carl's partner, and also a minister. He spent a great deal of his time attending to the needs of misfortunate souls in Los Angeles whenever he happened across one. Carl and Gene lived very comfortably in the old Theda Bara estate they had purchased on Canyon Drive in the Hollywood Hills. Bara had been one of the most popular silent film actresses of her era, and was one of cinema's earliest sex symbols. Her femme fatale roles earned her the nickname, *The Vamp*, which was short for vampire. Her catch line "Kiss me, my fool!" entered the public consciousness. Producer Buddy DeSylva expressed interest in 1949 in making a movie biography of Theda Bara's life, but the project never materialized. The star of that production was to be Betty Hutton.

It was not unlike Gene to call and leave a heads-up warning message at the Beverly Hills bank where Carl worked as its vice president to warn he was bringing someone else home who needed his help. Their estate had a large, four-bedroom main house as well as four surrounding cottages which had served as servants' quarters years before. Having an additional person at home for dinner or to stay overnight was never a problem.

Gene had been involved with church activities for several years. At the age of sixteen, he was sent from his native Stockton, California to Texas to participate in tent services in small towns throughout the state. These revivals were meant to convert new members into the church's fold, as well as to bring in needed money for the operations of their ministry. Gene was instantly charismatic in his approach to strangers. In turn, the people he met liked and trusted him immediately; they were disarmed by his gentle word and even more by his handsome good looks.

Gene was all of twenty when he met Betty Hutton at one of his neighboring Assembly of God churches in Los Angeles. After the service, the pastor made a point to introduce them; Gene was eyed as the perfect match to assist Betty with her troubled life. Gene hadn't immediately caught Betty's name, but he did hear the part when the pastor explained she had once been a famous movie star. Gene was encouraged to take the woman home and work with her; she was all strung out on drugs. Besides, she had nowhere else to go. They had evicted her from the hotel where she had been staying for nonpayment. Even if Gene had heard the pastor say her name, it wouldn't have registered; he was far too young to be familiar with the acting talents of Betty Hutton. The former star was dressed in white boots and a blue leather coat with a fur collar, all of which had seen better days. Betty had with her a solitary paper shopping bag containing a few personal belongings and some clothing.

Gene made the customary call to Carl, and said he was bringing home yet another person who needed help; this time it was a woman, and she had once been a famous movie star. Carl was outside in the yard when Gene pulled up the long drive. He made his way over to greet Gene and his newly-acquired soul as they were getting out of the car. Betty took one look at Carl and instantly broke into a rousing rendition of *There's No Business Like Show Business*. Carl believed the woman was attempting to establish her identity, but he wasn't familiar with Betty Hutton either. After she finished the song and caught her breath, she managed to stick out her hand and say, "Hi, I'm Betty Hutton." Later that evening, Gene confided in Carl; he thought the woman he had brought home from the church that day was Doris Day.

The three sat at the kitchen table in the main house for hours. While they drank coffee and ate, Betty recounted the story of her life. Carl remembers Betty was trying hard to impress them. "I guess if we were impressed enough, we would ask her to stay." That they did, but it wasn't just overnight, she ended up staying for several years. Gene worked with Betty on a daily basis. He was determined to save her soul. He would spend the nights in her bedroom, sleeping on the floor at the foot of her bed, while Betty wailed in the dark in her attempt to kick the heavy pill addition that was holding her prisoner. When she pleaded for pills or insisted she had no desire to continue living, Gene would pull her by the hand as they both fell to their knees in prayer. Gene asked the Lord to release her from her addition.

When it finally looked as if she were having a fair amount of success in controlling her habit, Gene would take her to church to be in a more formal religious surrounding. Betty really responded well to the religious structure. She even began taking an interest in light household duties, and particularly in cooking; something she really loved. In the evenings, they would sit down together as a family for dinner. Betty would slave away in the kitchen making things she had been taught by chefs she had hired to work in her own home during the height of her wealth and fame. When Gene felt she was doing well enough and emotionally stable, he decided to take a break for a few weeks to visit his family in Stockton. Carl was to remain home with Betty. In hindsight, Gene's leaving and Betty's readiness to accept it had been a miscalculation.

As the principal bread winner, Carl needed to be at the bank every day. Betty wasn't too happy with that arrangement. She had become accustomed to all of Gene's attention, and quickly became bored at home all day alone. On one particular afternoon, Betty called the bank and asked to speak with Mr. Bruno. Carl's secretary informed Betty he was in an important meeting and couldn't be disturbed. Betty responded with, "You don't seem to realize who I am, young lady, *I'm Betty Hutton.* Now connect me with Carl Bruno immediately." The secretary broke into Carl's meeting long enough to hand him a note. It said he needed to call Betty right away. Carl excused himself from the meeting to make the call. When the maid finally got Betty to the phone, she was in an agitated enough state to challenge him. She said, "Unless you come home right this minute and give me some of my pills, I'm going to kill myself by jumping off of the roof."

It had taken almost eight months of Gene's constant support and attention, but it seemed as if Betty had made some good progress prior to his leaving to visit family. Betty was still taking pills, but those were doled out carefully at night, and only then to help her to sleep. Carl returned briefly to his meeting and excused himself apologetically. He explained a family health emergency required his immediate attention. On his way home to confront Betty, Carl wasn't too happy. He had been interrupted at work, something he had repeatedly asked

Betty never to do unless there was a real emergency. Before he reached the house, Betty had already managed to climb from the master bedroom balcony onto the pitched roof of the living room. There she sat, precariously perched, when Carl arrived home. He had seen her sitting in her ridiculous position the moment he had gotten out of his car. As he approached the house, he yelled up to her, "Betty, move over to the center. That way, when you jump you will land on concrete instead of the grass. If you are trying to kill yourself, you have a better chance of doing it landing on the hard concrete. The purpose is to end up dead, not in a wheelchair for the rest of your life." Without a word, Betty began inching her way toward the bedroom balcony and returned inside the house. When Carl came in, Betty was already busying herself in the kitchen. He gave her two pills to calm herself. Not another word was spoken about the episode, but it was clear Carl had won that round with Betty. Carl never really knew if she had experienced a momentary lapse in sanity or was just testing her limits. It was never mentioned to Gene.

Betty had no source of income during this time. She was too young for Social Security or to receive her pension from the Screen Actors Guild. It was Carl and Gene who provided Betty with everything she needed to live on a daily basis. Betty had every intention of getting well enough to return to work of some sort. Carl and Gene never tried to squelch her enthusiasm when she talked of her plans to return to the entertainment world, although they listened to them with caution and concern. They were both a bit taken back when Betty announced she did, in fact, have a plan. She got in touch with her old friend, Bob Hope, and told him she was planning a show that would help her get back on her feet. Bob was encouraging, and at the end of their conversation, asked her to send Carl over to his Toluca Lake home. Carl was met by a very gracious Bob and Dolores Hope who asked him to give

Betty all their love and to wish her lots of luck. With that, Bob handed Carl a check made to the order of Betty Hutton in the sum of fifteen thousand dollars. It was doubtful if it had really been Betty's intention to do a show, but she felt respectable again by having her own money to do with as she pleased.

Betty rarely, if ever, left the house. As she progressively got better, she began asking to be taken to various places on the spur of the moment. One night she was feeling a bit anxious at home and asked if they might go out somewhere to socialize. The three of them ended up at a place called, *The Queen Mary*, on Ventura Blvd in North Hollywood. It was a gay club that had a disco as well as a cabaret room. Somehow, Betty must have gotten hold of a few of her pills, or saved up a few to take at one time; she was feeling no pain by the time they arrived. You could always tell when she had taken pills, she suddenly became rather extroverted. Under normal conditions, she was the exact opposite. The pills were her coping mechanism. It worked well for her, except for the fact she never knew when to say enough. The effects were cumulative, and after awhile she was hooked; once again becoming a pitiful mess.

Betty ended up drinking a few drinks that evening, which only enhanced the effect of her pills. Suddenly, she was sitting up on the piano in the cabaret room, belting out a tune, as the piano player played one of her better known songs. The crowd of gay men went wild; everyone knew who she was. As things started to increasingly get out of hand, Carl and Gene decided it was time she be taken home. Many people followed them into the parking lot in a long procession; it was as if they were celebrating Mardi Gras. One guy got close enough and whispered into her ear that he had some drugs, and asked if she wouldn't like to go somewhere and shoot up with him. The entire situation suddenly was way out of control. Betty naturally ate up the adoration; it was something she had done without for quite a long time. Carl and Gene literally had to pull Betty from the crowd and into the car. That was the last time they ever took the chance of allowing her into a situation without some sort of control measure they could implement at a moment's notice.

Slowly but surely, Betty began to stabilize as her drug use leveled off. She was never cured of her addition, ever, and she never stopped with the pills altogether. Her drug use was dependent upon what was going on in her life at any particular time. If she was happy, her drug usage went way down. Anxiety, frustration, or boredom meant more pills. Because of the stability offered her in Carl and Gene's home, and the work Gene was doing with her, she got fairly well. She was about as good as she could get, given the circumstances. There was no such thing as a miraculous recovery for her; that sort of thing was never even a remote possibility.

On another occasion, Betty asked Carl and Gene if they would help her to retrieve some of her costumes and sheet music that she had in storage. Naturally, they were agreeable, that is, until they found out where the storage was. Betty had walked away from her marriage to her fourth and final husband, musician Pete Candoli. Betty was sure she remembered Pete telling her he had placed many of her personal items in a metal storage shed that was in the yard at the house in which he was now living. She assured Carl and Gene it would be easy to approach the property from the hill behind the house. All they required was a hacksaw to cut off the padlock securing the shed. Betty made preparations as if she were studying a new character for a movie part. She made everyone dress in dark-colored clothing and waited patiently for the darkening evening sky. When the three arrived at the property, it wasn't as easy as Betty had made it seem. The hill behind the property was very steep. Still, all three scurried up the planted hill, as if they were on war maneuvers. The shed was located on the other side of a fence that surrounded the property. From the street, the fence appeared low and climbable, but when they got to the top of the hill, it was high and virtually impenetrable. The three bandits stood there staring at each other, waiting for some sort of revelation. Betty appeared ready and able, armed with the hacksaw like she was ready to mow down trees. Gene asked, "How did you manage to get over the studio wall in that movie, Betty?" Suddenly they broke into fits of laughter. Betty protested. "I was a lot younger then, boys." Carl suggested they abandon their efforts before they were discovered. Betty led the descent of the hill. After getting safely back into the car, the three partners in crime laughed and joked about the episode all the way home. From that time on, Betty referred to their trio as the Three Musketeers. Carl suggested they name themselves the Three Stooges.

Eventually, Betty was contacted about touring back east in a show. Carl and Gene discussed with her the wisdom of going off alone to do a show. They cautioned her by pointing out her vulnerabilities and weaknesses. Despite the hindrances standing in her way, Betty was a grown woman, and certainly wasn't being held prisoner in their home. When Betty made up her mind, nothing and no one could change it. She decided to give the show a try, but promised to return if any difficulties arose that she was unable to handle.

Betty managed well throughout most of the tour. Not until they reached a small dinner club in Framingham, Massachusetts did she experience a nervous breakdown. Literally translated, it meant she had taken too many pills. She needed to come down off of them and clean up her act. This was a constant pattern that carried well into her 80s. In 1974, the options one had to clean up from pill use were slim to none. Betty was plunked down in an alcohol rehab facility. Drinking was never Betty's problem or her addiction of choice: she was into the pills. At least, in an alcohol rehab facility, the pills were cut off and she was closely monitored. Within a few weeks, she was basically good to go.

While Betty was in rehab at the Butler Hospital in Framingham, she watched with incredible interest one day as a completely drunk woman arrived for treatment. The woman was bought into the facility by a Catholic priest. Betty observed he was patient with the woman beyond all human endurance. At one point, the woman vomited on the priest, and still he remained calm. He said to her in a low soothing voice, "That's okay, Alice. You are going to be just fine." Betty was mesmerized as she watched how the priest dealt with the woman. When he finally left, Betty went to the window and watched as he got in his car and drove away. At that moment, Betty told herself that this was the man who was going to save her life. During the remainder of her stay, Betty got close to the woman patient. She learned Alice was the cook in the rectory at the church where the priest, Father Peter Maguire, officiated in Portsmouth. When Alice was released, Betty went with her to meet Father, and to attend mass. Being the Godly man he was, Father was unable to turn Betty away. Father would never have turned anyone away. Betty stayed on at the rectory and helped with the housework and the cooking, just to be close to Father.

When Betty first came to St. Anthony's Catholic Church, she was not Catholic, and Father Maguire baptized her as such. Betty's entire life in Portsmouth centered upon Father. She loved him because he was the father she never had. Father Maguire filled that role perfectly for her, all the while providing her with love and consideration for her life experience and intellect. "Betty, you are just like a hurt little child," Father would say time and time again. Betty indeed acted like a hurt little child; she never before had the opportunity to be just Betty. What she found so wonderful about her relationship with Father was that she no longer had to pretend about the hurt she felt inside. Everyone expected so much from her, but Father knew the real Betty. He became the role model for her life. She had attempted to know God well throughout the years, but her work and career always managed to push that desire to the back burner. Betty summed it up when she said, "For me this was the answer, because, with Father, I didn't have to pretend. Father had the heart to understand me. I no longer had to belong to a studio, or any other group of people, for that matter. You see, wherever I went, God was there with me." Being in a Catholic surrounding gave Betty the structure and discipline she so desperately needed at that time in her life.

Betty lived on the third floor of the rectory. It was basically the attic, but it had been finished off mainly as an office for Father Maguire. There was a small room adjacent to the office which was Betty's. The Bishop got wind of the fact Betty was living in the rectory and he wasn't at all happy. There was a young assistant pastor living in the rectory, and it was his mother who alerted the Bishop of exactly what was happening on a weekly basis. The woman found it difficult not to put in her own two-cents worth by repeatedly denouncing the impropriety of an actress, of all the depraved sorts, living within the same walls as her sainted son. Father Maguire was called on the carpet more times than can be imagined, but in the end he did as he saw fit. After all, there was no indecency in helping one of God's children who was in need.

Alice the cook, Betty's friend, got really bombed at the rectory one night. It was Betty's birthday, and a very special dinner had been planned. The birthday girl was sitting with Father Maguire and Father Hamilton in the dining room waiting for Alice to bring out the food. A long time had passed by the time Betty became suspicious;

dinner just never seemed to materialize from the kitchen. Finally, Betty excused herself and went in to check on Alice. The lids were bobbing up and down on the pots, but no cook was anywhere in sight. Betty went upstairs and found her stone drunk on her bed. Betty comforted the woman for a brief moment, and then returned to the kitchen and salvaged the dinner. Alice never made it at the rectory: she couldn't stop the drinking. Betty said, "It is something you have to want inside, the desire to quit. My mother could never quit. Drinking has to be a disease. I knew from an early age mother had to be sick; she sure as hell wouldn't deliberately hurt me the way she had."

Betty was convinced God had placed her exactly where she was; that it was her calling. She began working with troubled people in Newport under Father's direction. Betty said of the work she did with others. "It was a joy to help a soul no one else wanted any part of, to pull them up by their boot straps and witness the improvement." Finally she went to a hospital outside of Newport where troubled nuns and priests went for help. The revelation of troubled clergy had a great impact on Betty. These were people viewed by the majority as incapable of having problems or of any wrong doing. Betty related well, she was always viewed as having the perfect movie star life. No one would ever believe someone like Betty could have problems. "That was some really heavy stuff for me to face." Betty commented. "I could really relate to those people."

Betty and Father enjoyed telling the story of Betty becoming Roman Catholic. Father had given her the instruction, and two short months after first arriving at St. Anthony's, when she was ready to receive the Eucharist for the first time, he said he was going to notify the local Catholic newspaper. Betty warned Father against doing that, given the fact the media was forever after a good Betty Hutton story. The mainstream press was sure to grab the information and run with it. Father was rather naïve to the ways of the secular world, and having never seen one of her movies, was incapable of comprehending what she had represented to the world of entertainment. Father went ahead and notified the paper, despite Betty's warning. The news traveled fast, and soon the media descended upon little Portsmouth, Rhode Island from every direction. Cameras were inside the church, out on the lawns; everywhere you might or even might not suspect. This was really big news. The photo of Betty serving coffee to the two priests in the kitchen of St. Anthony's rectory appeared on the front page of newspapers all over America on April 14, 1974, and to the rest of the world soon after. Father shook his head at the silliness of so much fuss. Betty could only laugh and say, "Father, I warned you not to tell the press!"

Betty was content, for the time being, in her new role at the Catholic rectory. She also enjoyed her new found notoriety. Betty received approximately thirty-five thousand fan letters after her story hit the papers. The story was out, and everyone wanted to speak with Betty to find out how something like that had happened to her. She played it all to the hilt, as if she were rehearsing for a new film, reporting on how she was living the simple life with Christ leading her way. In the same breath, she couldn't help but tell everyone in the press how she had squandered her almost ten million dollar fortune in movie earnings. It added even more surrealism to the entire story of her life as it was unfolding. This was fantastic fodder for newspaper columnists and talk show hosts. In the back of her mind, this fifty-three year young woman, who had been born for no other purpose than to perform, knew it.

Betty didn't remain in the rectory forever. It was a starting point to establish herself in Rhode Island. Later on, she rented a lovely old farm house in Portsmouth. There she lived comfortably, and was happy once again to call a place her own. Betty didn't really care where she was, as long as she remained close to Father.

By June of that same year, the word concerning Betty's situation had spread throughout the entertainment world. Betty needed repeated assurance and persuasion that fans and show-biz friends alike only wanted to show how much they loved her when columnist, Earl Wilson, organized a benefit for her at the *Riverboat Restaurant* and nightclub in the Empire State Building in Manhattan. The one hundred dollar a plate benefit was apparently a fund-raiser for St. Anthony's parish in Portsmouth, but all who attended were there to get a good look at the woman who had seemingly vanished from the face of the earth. The New York Times reported on the affair, "If anyone had suspicions that more was involved than an outpouring of affection for Betty, there were enough tears and gushing greetings to shame the most hardened cynics." When Betty went onstage to thank the four hundred guests in attendance, all she could say was, "I love you, I love you." It appeared as if she were enjoying every minute of it. Later, when speaking with reporters, Betty made it clear that it had been merely a one-night stand. She was returning promptly to the rectory and her duties. "I'll never leave the place," she boasted.

By December of 1974, the story was beginning to look like a different one. Betty once again suffered one of her emotional breakdowns. This time she was committed to Butler Hospital psychiatric unit in Providence by her psychiatrist. The problem obviously started when Betty had gone in for surgery on her shoulder in September. It was a recurring injury, one she originally received swinging on the bars and ropes while making *The Greatest Show On Earth*. Of course, Betty had gotten hooked once again on the pain killers they had prescribed post-operatively for her shoulder. Pain killers were among her favorite prescription drugs.

In January of 1975, an article hit the papers in which Father Maguire stated Betty would not be returning to the rectory. He told reporters, "It didn't work out. She's still a young woman and not ready to retire. She'd like to get back into show business." Everyone agreed Betty had not been the same since the *Riverboat Restaurant* benefit in New York. Friends said the old theatrical flame must have been rekindled by the experience. Father Maguire admitted Betty had been on pain killers and, "She had gotten out of control. Primary care became necessary to get her back under control." Father, the man of usually few words, must have been really taken back by Betty's relapse. He had no clue it was a habitual problem. He continued in his statement to the press, "Miss Hutton never seemed to fit into rectory life after her New York party. The routine here can get rather confining. Betty was a good cook ...when she got at it."

Father made a call to Carl and Gene in Los Angeles. He asked them if they would be willing to take Betty back for an indefinite period of time. This was the first time, but over the next twenty-five years, these back-and-forth trades happened on a somewhat regular basis. That was, of course, except for when Betty enrolled in college and, afterwards, when she taught school. Father was a Godly man, but he was mortal all the same. There were times when Betty became too much for him to handle. Because of his religious upbringing and insight, he was at times unable to relate to some of Betty's more worldly problems. In other words, if prayer couldn't handle it, Betty needed intervention from a source with which she could relate on a different level.

When Father felt it necessary, he would ship Betty back to the boys in California. There she could get her Hollywood fix, and anything else she couldn't get while living with Catholic priests. Likewise, Carl and Gene would tire of her after a time, and back she would go to her austere lifestyle in the Rhode Island rectory. As incongruous as these two lives sounded, they proved to be a good balance for her. Betty was incapable of living a cloistered life in Portsmouth full-time or a stressful one in Hollywood, for that matter. If she stayed in California, she would forever be chasing after that elusive movie role that could rush her back to the forefront of the celebrity elite. She became easily bored with everything. With boredom came her desire for pills. Going back and forth kept her busy.

Any damage that had been done to the relationship Betty had with Father was healed over night. Father was not the sort of man to hold anything against anyone. The only thing he might have been capable of is hurt; after all, he was human. Father might well have been hurt after the time and effort he spent on Betty. It was a good lesson for both of them. But for now, it was clear; Betty and Father needed a break from each other.

In Hollywood, Betty was able to spread her wings for the first time in a long while. Shortly after her return to California, she once again began writing her life story, *Back Stage You Can Have.* It gave her something to do while in Hollywood, a release of sorts for her creative talents. She felt stymied, unless she had some kind of a project or activity going. Carl was typically the one to help her with that task. They would sit together at the kitchen table, and quite often Carl would type as she spoke. It was a painful process for her to dig around so deeply in her past, but it was therapeutic for her at the same time. Often she delved deeply into the entire process of writing. Like everything else she did, she did it to the best of her ability. Then again, she could become bored and toss it aside. This is how she managed to spread the process of working on her book over the course of thirty years.

Betty never really gave up on writing her book; she would simply shelf it until she had something she deemed important to say. Then the process would start all over again. When she got back at it, often times it became an obsession. She would walk around mouthing the words until she had them just the way she wanted to write them down. On the spur of the moment, she would grab anything available to jot down her thoughts. To this day, Carl has pages and pages of notations written in Betty's own hand. She wrote on paper bags while at the store, envelopes of letters from fans, bills that needed to be paid, napkins in restaurants, and on sheet music backstage when she was performing. Whenever and wherever the urge struck, she would stop what she was doing and write her thoughts down like crazy.

Betty was superstitious about writing a book. That was the only true impediment to her writing success. For a reason that has never been made clear, Betty felt it would be the end of her life if she were to ever complete it. I suppose it goes along with theatrical superstitions like, break a leg. You never tell someone to have a good show immediately before their performance, it's deemed bad luck. So in turn, if Betty were to say to herself, I'm going to finish this book, it would have cursed it. Sound a bit too far fetched? Well, possibly, but it's as good an explanation as any.

By 1977, Betty had been back and forth between California and Rhode Island several times. While she was in California, Robert Blake called and wanted her for an episode of his popular detective television series, *Baretta,* which ran on ABC from 1975 to 1978. Betty gladly took the part. Robert Blake had been patient and kind to Betty while on the set; he must have realized she was out of her element. By this time, what she did on camera was of little consequence. Most folks tuned in just because they wanted to get a look at Betty Hutton, the woman who rose from the ashes only to fall right back down into the fire.

Several weeks later, Carl received a call from *The Mike Douglas Show* people. They requested Betty come in to tape a show as Mike's special guest. Betty was adamant, "Carl, tell them I don't play musical chairs. If he wants to see me, tell him to come up here." Carl called back and relayed Betty's message, thinking it would put an end to their interest. The following week, two enormous trucks full of sound and film equipment arrived by 7:30 in the morning at the house on Canyon Drive. Carl remembers what seemed like miles of cables running up the drive, over the grass, up the stairs, into the house, and throughout the rooms. Betty was nervous, as expected. Carl was there to calm her, but suddenly Betty turned to him and said, "I can't possibly do this with you standing there watching me." Carl ducked into the kitchen with Mike Douglas' wife, Genevieve. They could monitor the interview taking place in the living room as they sat and drank coffee at the breakfast table right around the corner. Betty appeared reasonably comfortable at the start of the interview, although she always needed time to warm up to her host. As the interview went along, her comfort level rose dramatically. By the end of the interview, Betty and Mike were singing a duet as if they were old drinking buddies. Naturally, one of Mike's first questions to Betty was, "I want to ask you what you've been through?" Betty responded by saying, "That's gonna take hours…"

Betty managed to hold back little when she actually sat down to be interviewed. If the interview with Mike Douglas had been three or four hours in length, it's a strong possibility, she could still have found something to talk about. Douglas asked her, "How does that work, you're still a star, but you've been away so long."

Betty wasn't quite sure what he meant, but she answered with, "Right, the backstage part is really tough. I have to go and see casting directors now. I almost have to literally audition for a part, and it's kind of embarrassing because the parts aren't that big yet. But, Father Maguire wanted me to get my feet wet."

It's difficult not to cringe ever so slightly; Betty had every intention of resuming her career in show business, starting from the ground up. If only she had stopped to realize, you don't turn back, you go forward. With her incredible celebrity status and a bit of assistance, she could have gone on to create new and different ways to present herself to a public who adored her. It's sad, Betty was in desperate need of a reality check, but no one would or could offer her that advice. If they had, it's doubtful she would have accepted it anyway.

The real corker of the interview comes when Betty admits, "I was trying to become a nun, but I wasn't good enough. They're all so fantastic, and it was just too tough a role for me to handle." Although Betty says things such as this in all sincerity, it is difficult for the average person listening to comprehend that a former Hollywood actress with four failed marriages under her belt is actually entertaining the idea of becoming a nun. Unfortunately, comments such as this go a long way in making Betty appear as little more than an odd curiosity from the past during this period in her life. She is caught between her love and devotion to God, and her desire to pick up the pieces of her show business career. Betty was obviously still searching for Betty.

In 1978, Betty was again called upon to be on a talk show. This time *The Phil Donahue Show* wanted to fly her to Chicago for the interview, and Betty agreed. Unlike the Mike Douglas interview, on this occasion Betty was away from familiar surroundings and in front of a live audience. Both of these circumstances put her on edge. The first question out of Donahue's mouth was, "Well, what happened to you, let's start there..." In the same breath, he leads off in a totally different direction by asking Betty what year *Annie Get Your Gun* was filmed. Betty managed to maintain her composure, despite Donahue's difficult time in establishing a meaningful conversation with her in the beginning. It was Betty who actually led the conversation where she wanted to take it. It would have been a better show if Donahue had done the slightest bit of homework by studying up on his guest before she arrived on set.

Betty was back in Rhode Island during the time she appeared on the Donahue interview. Prior to going on the talk show, she managed to land a job at the Newport Jai-alai arena as their greeting hostess. She was proud to discuss her new career on camera with Phil. Jai-alai is a sport of Basque origin where opposing players alternate hurling a leather ball against the wall and catching it. That goes on until one of them finally misses and loses the point. The state of Rhode Island permits pari-mutuel wagering on the sport, making it as exciting as betting on horse racing. In the interview, Betty says of her newfound profession, "It's amazing that God gives me a break at fifty-seven. I'm starting over in a fantastic business with the public again. Jai-alai *is* show business, with its performers, its lights, its crowds. The good part is, I'm not under fire, because I don't have to perform. Yet, I still get all the love from the people." On any particular evening at Jai-alai, Betty would stand in the main entrance and greet up to three thousand people with hugs and kisses as they entered the arena. Later, she chatted with them during dinner, and even handed out awards to the winners. It was show business to Betty, but a far cry from what she was expecting for herself when talking of a comeback in California a year earlier. Interacting with a captive audience was all that was really necessary for Betty to feel needed and loved, and in that respect, her new job at the Jai-alai fronton was perfect.

While in Rhode Island, and with the help of Father, Betty finished up her high school education. Father was an educator, and from day one he stressed the importance of an education upon Betty. She confided in Father, during the final days of her movie career, she was viewed as temperamental. "I needed to be strong in front of a producer or director, but I didn't know how to express myself. You need to be able to do it without yelling. I just didn't have the words, because I didn't have the education." Father saw to it that sort of thing would never again stand in the way of Betty's path to success.

In the following summer of 1979, Betty headed west. Carl and Gene had sold their house in the Hollywood Hills and moved to Guerneville on the Russian River in Sonoma County, northern California. There they purchased an already established resort on Armstrong Woods Road called *The Hexagon House*, a name they later changed to *The Woods Resort*. The Russian River Valley had become a popular weekend and summer destination for vacationers, particularly from San Francisco, in the late 1800s. The air was clean and the area was surrounded with giant redwood trees, a far cry from the urban sprawl of Los Angeles.

The large resort property offered not only a hotel, but also individual cottages. It all depended on how long a guest wanted to stay. Entertainers would come in on a weekly basis to perform in the beautiful hexagon-shaped main building built from massive timbers. It served as the resort's dinner club and entertainment center. Betty originally came up for the resort's grand opening celebrations in June, but she liked it so much there, she stayed for the entire summer. Father was to fly in from Rhode Island to vacation with them at the resort in August. Carl hesitated in contacting the press to announce Betty would be performing during opening week. Betty said, "I came to help you open up the place, so you better let everyone know I'm here." After the announcement was made to the press, the resort phones never stopped ringing. When society columnist, *Herb Caen*, from *The San Francisco Chronicle*, mentioned Betty was appearing in Guerneville, the resort was literally mobbed.

Newspaper reporter, Eileen Conn, from the nearby town of Santa Rosa, did a story on one of Betty's performances at the resort in August. She noted, "With each round of applause, her face appeared more vivid and her movements more lively. The voice is good and the face is pretty, but those aren't the qualities that make a star. What made Betty Hutton suddenly appear larger than life was her ability and willingness to give herself one-hundred percent to her audience."

After her final song, *There's No Business Like Show Business*, Betty introduced Father Maguire, saying, "I'm glad you get to see me not shaking to death or trying to kill myself." She went on to describe the turmoil that had taken place in her life over the past decade. After the show, people crowded around her for autographs and words of congratulations. One man who had seen the show, and whom Betty had never before met, presented her with a diamond pin.

Carl had a Rolls Royce which Betty loved driving into town. She would go from shop to shop, saying hello to locals and visitors alike, stopping often to tell anyone who was interested her story, or answer questions about her show at the resort. Everyone became accustomed to seeing Betty flash around town in her fancy car. For Betty, Guerneville was comparable to Portsmouth. They were both manageable sized towns where she could be known and recognized, but also left to do as she pleased. She liked being at the resort. She had the chance to perform without the pressures of any schedules, deadlines, or contracts.

Every summer after that, Betty looked forward to returning to Carl and Gene's resort on the Russian River to vacation and to entertain. During a few of those summer visits, she even brought Father along with her. Not to be outdone, Father would get into the act as well. On Sunday mornings during the summer in northern California, when the air is crisp and the sky is clear, Father could be found holding mass out on the lawn adjacent to the garden. His open-air services were meant for any and all who desired to worship with him.

The photograph that shot around the world. Betty serves coffee in the church rectory to Catholic Priests, Father Peter Maguire (right), and Father James Hamilton. Portsmouth, Rhode Island, 1974
Photo: United Press International

Betty at the *Woods Resort* on California's
Russian River, Summer 1979.
Photo: Betty's private collection, The Betty Hutton Estate

Chapter Eighteen

It was like the Betty Hutton audiences remembered when in 1980; she had her breakthrough comeback as Miss Hannigan in the Broadway show, *Annie*, in New York. *Annie* is a musical based upon the popular Harold Gray comic strip, *Little Orphan Annie*. Betty opened on Wednesday, September 17, for a three-week run to a packed audience at the Alvin Theater. Before rehearsals, Betty was frightened, "I can't do it, I'm not well enough." However, with Father's support and a lot of prayer, Betty managed to wow them one final time on a Broadway stage. Betty was standing-in for Dorothy Loudon as the unpleasant, whiskey-swilling orphanage matron who hated kids. In the audience to support Betty opening night were Father Maguire, Betty's two older children, Lindsay and Candy, and of course, Carl and Gene. Betty's youngest daughter, Carrie, was expected to fly in from California over the weekend. With tears of joy streaming down her face, Betty took her first bows on stage in many years, while the audience cheered her in a standing ovation.

After the show, Betty was asked to appear outside the stage door on the raised and railed platform at the top of the stairs. She was told to encourage the multitudes who had gathered to see her to disperse. The crowds on the streets surrounding the theater were packed in so tightly, the traffic had come to a complete standstill. Betty got a real charge out of Father witnessing the throngs of people who came just to see her; his eyes would never have believed it. When Father commented on the scene later, Betty reminded him, "That's the responsibility that goes along with being a star; your fans can never be disappointed."

An opening night post-performance celebration was held that evening at one of Betty's old stomping grounds, the *Copacabana*. There she partied away the night with family and her new friends from the cast, as if there had never been the slightest lull in her career. Even Annie's dog from the show, Sandy, was in attendance that evening. Betty commented to reporters about the festivities, "This is what it's all about. It's a night that is unbelievable."

Carl and Gene stayed on for another week before flying home to California. Originally from Brooklyn, Carl had the opportunity to spend time with his sister, Marie, and her husband, George, and their children. Marie wanted to have Betty over for a good home-cooked Italian meal during her stay. New York Italians take their food quite seriously, so Betty was warned to come with an empty stomach. Somehow, all of Marie's neighbors, in their tidy Italian neighborhood of Bensonhurst in the borough of Brooklyn, were aware that a famous movie star was coming to visit. When Betty and Father, along with Carl and Gene, rolled up in front of Marie's house in a limousine, the entire neighborhood was on hand to welcome Betty as one of their own.

Betty had been provided a limousine in her contract, as well as her own table at *Sardi's*, the famous restaurant on 44th Street in the heart of the theater district. *Sardi's* was a Manhattan institution that had already been the toast of Broadway for decades. Betty would meet Carl and Gene there for a light dinner after her performances, but she encouraged Carl and Gene to take full advantage of her private table and her car and driver during the remainder of their stay in New York.

For at least a time, Betty had satisfied her show business yearnings with her successful run on Broadway. It's quite possible she didn't want to press her luck, for she returned to Rhode Island. By 1981, she had completed her high school equivalency and was now ready to move on to higher learning. Father found her the perfect school nearby, and soon Betty was enrolled at *Salve Regina*, a Catholic college for women in Newport. There Betty was to pursue what she termed her favorite subject. "I majored in Psychology, what else!"

Betty became very popular at school. Her enthusiasm for learning was infectious in classrooms, and her lifelong pursuit of knowledge made her an exceptional student. She received all A's in courses ranging from philosophy to computer science. In an interview with the Newport Daily News, Betty reported, "Oh, did I work to get here. I worked more than full time, I had tutors, and sometimes I worked around the clock."

In 1983, Betty returned to the stage in New York City in a show taped for PBS called, *Jukebox Saturday Night*. Her performance in this live show was just one of several segments; the show was shared with Helen O'Connell, Margaret Whiting and Keely Smith. However, it is Betty, who clearly ruled the evening. What she managed to do in her short twenty-two minutes while on stage is extraordinary. This is considered by many to be Betty's ultimate stage performance, due to the honesty and courage she displays. She appeared lucid and totally consistent throughout the performance. Betty displays no craziness, except in her zany musical numbers where the craziness belongs. She speaks candidly of her struggles, during and after her movie career, and her rescue by Father Maguire. It is a raw and intimate portrait of the woman, with laughter from her classic comedic timing, to tears from her emotional outpourings. All the while, Betty manages to perform many of her old stand-by numbers with ease and grace. Watching this performance by Betty is to watch the woman transformed. No doubt her transformation can be credited in part to the contentment she had found in her life and within herself, but also quite possibly for the security she felt with her newfound education. Then again, part of it could simply be attributed to Betty's advancing age, something which has a way of mellowing even the most driven person. Around this time, Betty was reported saying, "I wouldn't want to go back into show business on a regular basis, it's back-breaking work." It looked as if Betty had finally abandoned her quest for a return to show business the way she had once known it. She had managed to move on to an entirely new plateau in her career. There is no pretense and no exaggeration, just Betty. In *Jukebox Saturday Night* Betty does what Betty does best, being Betty.

In 1983, Betty met a woman by the name of *Judy Rector*, someone who would become a true friend, and in many ways change the course of Betty's life. Judy had never heard any stories about Betty - good, bad, or indifferent. As far as she was concerned, Betty's friendship with her came with no prior baggage. She was simply Betty. Of course, she knew Betty was a former movie star, but she was also a good friend of Father Maguire, Judy's pastor at St. Anthony's. Judy would see Betty at morning mass on weekdays; she actually stood out. It wasn't because of whom she was, it was because she didn't hide out in the back of the church; she sat right up front like Judy did.

Betty became a devout Catholic after meeting Father Maguire. Father was the most intellectually brilliant, spiritually simple, and humanly kind man anyone could ever meet. People wanted to be near him, and Betty was no exception. After seeing a photograph or news clip of the Pope on television, Father would smile and say, "There's my boss." His philosophy of living as a Catholic priest was, "To be a fool for Christ's sake." This he told to Judy more than once in defending his reasons for standing by Betty in the face of enormous resistance from the Diocese of Providence. Betty, a fallen Hollywood harlot, was living among a handful of Catholic priests in St. Anthony's Rectory. The church's hierarchy was not at all amused.

Judy's brother, Sean, a debonair and handsome fellow with an eye for lovely women was the first to say anything at all to Betty. He would greet her after mass with an informal, "Hiya, beautiful!" Betty confessed years later that Sean's warm and casual greeting meant the world to her, because she knew he meant it.

Sean had broken the ice, but Judy and Betty continued to exchange only friendly hellos in church for several more years. Father was the one to introduce the two women when Betty was preparing to go to New York to appear in *Annie* on Broadway. Betty kindly fixed Judy and her family up with great seats for the show, and even invited them backstage after her performance. Judy recollects that particular evening with much clarity. Betty greeted her like a true movie star, all decked out in a dressing robe of silk and lace. Betty appeared truly happy that evening, glowing with a look of pride and contentment. It remains in her mind as one of her truly wonderful memories of Betty.

Their paths crossed again that same year when Judy spotted Betty in the produce section of their local

Portsmouth grocery store. Betty was attempting to select the best specimens from a new batch of zucchini. Judy approached with a friendly hello. Their conversation quickly turned to food and health, and Betty suggested Judy's family might enjoy a wonderful green vegetable soup she had been making for years. The soup was by Dr. Bieler, the prominent American physician, best known for his book *Food is Your Best Medicine*. Actress, *Gloria Swanson,* had introduced Betty to the doctor and his teachings, which advocated the treatment of disease with foods.

The following day after mass, Judy went home with Betty and learned how to make Dr. Bieler's famous green soup. That day began a friendship that lasted, on a daily basis, until Betty moved back to California for good in 1997, after Father's death the summer before.

Judy got to know the real Betty in a way few others had. During their time together, Judy got to witness for herself how Betty could size an individual up in an instant. She possessed an uncanny ability to tell you someone's life story, after seeing them for less than five minutes. It seemed to be a scary ability, and most of the time her assessment was dead accurate.

Betty also possessed hyper acute senses. Her hearing was profoundly sensitive and her sense of smell would drive you crazy. She could tell immediately if a room was dirty, even when it appeared immaculately clean. Her large hands were healing hands, although Betty thought they were her worst feature. She was meticulous throughout her life, keeping them professionally manicured, so they appeared their very best. Judy once had a fever over one hundred degrees. Betty placed her hand on Judy's forehead, prayed over her, and within a few minutes the fever had disappeared. She thought Betty knew full well her ability to heal with her hands, but chose not to use the power given her.

Betty enjoyed cleaning house, and was an outstanding cook. She sought the most complicated recipes in the most sophisticated cookbooks, and would spend the entire day creating a culinary masterpiece. She always made the dinner for someone else to enjoy. She loved to watch the happy faces enjoying her cooking. Finally, she would get everyone's attention at the table by say, "I'm waiting for the applause..."

Judy knew Betty felt a responsibility to stay as attractive as she could. After all, she had a reputation to live up to. She kept herself well groomed, her face lifted as often as necessary, and her body fit. Betty dieted whenever she felt it necessary by her own standards, well into her 80s. She refused to go out of the house unless she looked beautiful. She never wanted to disappoint anyone who might recognize her.

One day, Judy took Betty to the emergency room with a severe attack of abdominal pain and fever. A nurse came to check her and commented Betty looked terrible. When the nurse left, Betty lifted her head off the gurney and said to Judy in a voice clear and devoid of any pain, "Do you hear that, Judy, I told you so, *everyone* expects me to look perfect all the time."

Judy certainly knew Betty long enough to gain first hand knowledge of her demons. Betty loved the Lord, but she was also possessed by her demons. Although she tried over the years to rid herself of the demons that haunted her, she was never successful. Betty had been in so many hospitals and rehab centers, but nothing ever worked. Judy was with her when she received a diagnosis as manic depressive. At one point, a wonderfully astute doctor placed Betty on Prozac, and in short order, she began to get much better. That is, until she found out what the pills were, and stopped taking them. She remained unmedicated for a time, and then, as always, she decided to self-medicate. This was a problem that often led to overdoses and severe instability. The pattern continued until the end of her life.

Judy and her husband, Peter, had a family house in Newport that had been built by his father in the 1950s. Judy's mother-in-law lived at *Pen Craig Estate* until her death in the 1980s. The house was sitting empty when Judy and Peter offered the house to Betty to live in during her time in Newport at *Salve Regina*. Judy and her family were happy living in Portsmouth, and since they still had children attending school there, moving to Pen Craig was, for the time being, out of the question. Betty gladly accepted their generous offer.

Two years before Betty graduated with a master's degree in liberal studies from Salve Regina, the college bestowed her with an honorary doctorate in 1984. The college decided early on that Betty's life experience entitled her to an automatic bachelor's degree. On September 19th at an academic convocation ceremony commemorating the fiftieth anniversary of the founding of the college, Betty received her honorary doctorate along with the following citation.

Talented, dynamic, effervescent, yet equally sensitive, warm and caring...you, Betty Hutton, personify the triumph of the human spirit over adversity. A multi-gifted actress, you long held the spotlight as a star performer on stage and screen. From your classic Hollywood musicals to your recent success as Miss Hannigan in Annie, you have been consistently acclaimed in rave reviews and standing ovations.

But fame and adulation had their price, and here in affliction your strength of soul came to the fore. With indomitable courage and deep Christian faith, you surmounted personal sorrows. The fortitude and compassion gained through this struggle have been transformed into the loving kindness of a true Samaritan, who is willing to share the burdens of others in like distress.

You have come to appreciate that your genuine career is not one spangled hour of fame, but a life-long journey to permanent excellence. You came to enroll in Salve courses – not only to enrich your mind but to share your well-honed professional skills with aspiring young artists. Your searching quest for wisdom, your infectious enthusiasm, and your generous heart endeared you to the entire campus community.

Betty Hutton, as an adopted daughter of our Newport island and as a Salve associate, you are someone very special to all of us. You will always be a star – not of fleeting tinsel, but in the splendid character of a Christian woman whose enduring courage, rich talents, and unquenchable vitality are an inspiration and joy to us all. It is with heartfelt esteem that Salve Regina College confers on you the degree of Doctor of Humane Letters, honoris causa, with all attendant rights and privileges.

To say Betty was proud of this honor would be an understatement. This doctorate, coupled with the master's degree she would receive two years later, were for Betty a life altering experience. It was a turning point of sorts, a final journey to a home she had been searching for her entire life. Betty was sixty-three years of age, and more than ready to call her pursuit finished. Education for her was the ultimate life experience, and with it, she felt the world was at her very feet. It had been a selfish pursuit on her part; to absorb all the knowledge she had never been afforded. Nevertheless, once she had that knowledge, she was delighted to spread it around. When she was on stage or screen, joy radiated purely from her very being. When

Betty started teaching classes, the same thing happened. The knowledge she was so eager to impart, effortlessly sprang forth.

In May of 1986, Betty graduated from Salve Regina with her master's degree in liberal studies. In an interview where Betty was holding her diploma high above her head, she smiled and sang, "Oh no, they can't take that away from me..." That same year, Betty was named to the faculty of Salve Regina, teaching motion picture and TV classes.

After her graduation, Betty hosted a grand party at *Pen Craig*. Friends came from far and wide to help her celebrate what she had once thought an impossible achievement, the securing of a proper education. Betty had a grand piano in the living room of the estate, which sat in front of large windows looking out at the water of Newport Bay. There, she and her friends sat for hours and sang songs until way into the night. One of Betty's dearest and oldest friends from New York, Ben Carbonetto, got up and sang *It Had To Be You* to Betty. "Ben," she screamed, "I didn't know you could sing!"

Eventually, Father Maguire retired as Pastor of St. Anthoney's. He had suffered a heart attack, and knew when it was time to call it quits. He moved to his family home in Cranston, Rhode Island. There he felt useless unless he did something to help people. He got a job at the VA Hospital ministering to sick and dying veterans. On weekends, he would show up on Betty's doorstep in Newport. Father came and went, but a room was kept in the house as his very own for the occasions when he decided to visit. Betty and Father would sit out on the patio and watch the world pass by on Newport Bay. Sometimes, they sat and talked for hours. Betty would entice Father to run to the store for groceries after telling him about a new recipe she had found in *Good Housekeeping*. Later, as she cooked, Father would stand in the kitchen and entertain Betty by pretending to be a rodeo star. He would simulate swinging a lasso high about his head, and then throw it forward. "I roped another one, Betty," he would say with pride. Father was referring to roping another soul at the VA Hospital, that of a dying veteran who requested Father hear their final confession.

When Father Peter Maguire died in 1996, Betty, once again, felt abandoned. She had lost the one person in her life who truly understood her for who she was. At seventy-six, there was little opportunity to start over or to move on. What she required was someone familiar, and who could look after her in the same manner Father had. Betty decided to come back to California. Her children were all there, and she found comfort in being near them. She certainly never had the desire to live with them. That would have been out of the question for Betty and her independent spirit. The last thing she wanted to do was be a burden on anyone, particularly on her children.

Opening night in *Annie* on Broadway, September 17, 1980.
Photo: Betty's private collection, The Betty Hutton Estate

Betty celebrates Christmas at Pen Craig Estate
in Newport, Rhode Island.
Photo: Betty's private collection, The Betty Hutton Estate

Betty's hands-down favorite photograph of herself.
Graduation from Salve Regina, Newport, Rhode Island.
Photo: Betty's private collection, The Betty Hutton Estate

Chapter Nineteen

Betty had made her decision. The only sensible choice for her was going back to Carl. He was now living alone, and had moved to Palm Springs. Regrettably, his partner Gene Arnaiz, one of the first to help save Betty from drugs and herself, died an untimely death in 1993 at the young age of forty.

Palm Springs afforded Betty a much more manageable lifestyle than Los Angeles. Her only income was derived from Social Security and her Screen Actor's Guild pension. She could no longer afford to be extravagant in her lifestyle. Places like Los Angeles would be far too expensive to live for someone on a fixed income. Carl welcomed Betty with open arms. He had been miserable since Gene's death. He would arrive home from his current bank job, after picking up some carry-out, and then sit all alone and eat his dinner. Carl recollects a mirror which hung above his dining room table. Once when he was sitting in silence eating his dinner, out of the corner of his eye he accidentally caught a glimpse of himself in the mirror. "I was shocked to witness this sad looking person partaking in something as social as eating dinner all alone," he said. "It didn't hit for a few seconds that the person I had seen in the mirror was me."

Carl lived on Tamarisk Road in the famed Movie Colony of Palm Springs. The house was way too large for one person with four bedrooms, its massive beamed ceilings, and separate wine cellar. Even so, Carl didn't ask Betty to move into the main house with him. Instead, he offered her a decent-sized guest house situated on the grounds of the estate. It wasn't particularly lavish, but it was all for her. He felt it good for them to each have their own space. Carl was still grieving the death of Gene, and Betty obviously had her own emotions to confront following Father's passing. At the time, it was viewed as the best possible living arrangements. Betty, on the other hand, was dissatisfied with her new quarters. It became a sore spot for her every evening after dinner. That's when she had to exit the main house and walk a maturely-planted pathway, around the swimming pool, and over to what she referred to as "the servant's quarters." Betty could be a real snob about such things. More than that, when she had an idea about the way things were supposed to be, her mind could never be changed.

The living arrangement lasted for about a year. It wasn't where she was living, it was how, that eventually started to cause problems. Palm Springs is a laid-back resort type community. If you don't like golfing, find yourself allergic to the sun, or are not familiar with the fine art of relaxation, your existence there is all but doomed. Remembering full well Betty's need to remain active or risk the possibility of returning to her involvement with drugs was always on Carl's mind. Betty was still taking her sleeping pills at night to combat her insomnia. Those she didn't even consider drugs. They were as essential to her as breathing or eating. It was amazing, the way she could justify her usage.

As time went on, Betty became more and more despondent. It was an eventuality. Her contentment with herself and her life went in waves or cycles. As a close friend who knew her well, you could see it coming. Before you were able to do anything about it, it was too late. She would sink into one of her low periods, and remain there until something came along unexpectedly to pull her out. During these low points, drugs were more than important to her, they were everything. It is during this time Carl and Betty began to argue. She wanted more pills, and Carl refused. Father wasn't there any longer to pray for her redemption from drugs. She was more or less on her own for any sort of spiritual intervention, something that seemed to have worked quite well for her while she was in Rhode Island.

One of the major stumbling blocks that caused Betty to be discontented at home was Carl having to leave each morning for work. Betty was left home alone with the cleaning lady to figure out for herself exactly what to do all day long. One day, Carl returned home from work to find Betty had simply vanished. She had always threatened to run when things got difficult for her, but this is the first time she had actually done it. Betty left one of her often dramatic letters, explaining how her life was simply too difficult to tolerate, and how she needed a complete change. "I love you, Carl, but I must say goodbye," were her closing lines, after which, of course, the curtain came down, and the stage faded to black.

Carl soon discovered from someone, who had heard from someone else, Betty had run off to live with a new acquaintance. People were forever latching on to her when she gave them the chance. It was because of who she was, and the possibility of how she could benefit them, instead of the other way around. It was more than likely someone who offered to purchase, or had the connections to procure, all the pills she desired. Her whereabouts was unknown. Carl didn't hear from her again until it was almost too late.

In September of 2000, Carl met someone with whom he wanted to spend his life. Like Carl, Mike Mayer had lost his partner of twenty-five years less than a year before. There was an instant connection when a mutual friend introduced them. Mike said of their initial meeting, "Carl and I were both down and out from having lost our partners. It was a sad state of affairs, but in our grief, we managed to find a real connection with each other."

After Betty left, Carl sold his Movie Colony estate, and invested in a forty-nine unit residential income property in Palm Springs. The *Desert Dorado* is a series of two-bedroom, two-bath, semi-attached rental villas. Carl took two of the units nestled near one of the swimming pools and combined and renovated them into one luxury unit for himself. It took awhile to complete, but eventually Mike moved in with Carl and helped manage the property. Time goes swiftly when you have rental units to maintain. On a daily basis, something major is bound to be broken or in need of attention, and your time is filled with instructing workers and soothing aggravated tenants.

One day, and quite out of the blue, Betty called Carl. She rambled on the phone about some trouble she had been in, but the true purpose of her call was to ask if she could come back. Carl jotted down her phone number and promised he would call back the next day with an answer. That evening, Carl explained to Mike everything he knew about Betty and her background, before suggesting the one available unit that was directly across from their back patio would be a perfect one for Betty. Carl asked Mike if this arrangement was something he thought wouldn't interfere with their new relationship. Mike said it really didn't matter to him, one way or the other. There were many tenants in the complex, and one more or one less was not a problem, even if this one happened to be a famous movie star.

At least Mike knew who Betty Hutton was. He remembered picking up a newspaper on the airplane the day it was discovered Betty was living with Catholic priests in Rhode Island. At the time, he had been a flight attendant for *Delta Airlines*, and it occurred after a flight from Chicago to New Orleans. All the passengers had finally deplaned, and morning newspapers were scattered throughout the aircraft. While waiting for cabin service to come aboard to clean the cabin, Mike plunked himself down in a comfortable first class seat and read the dramatic headline story of the fallen star.

"No, you really don't understand, Mike. This is *Betty Hutton*. The woman has a history of screwing things up big-time, and it's just not that simple." Carl sounded a bit more tentative about making a decision.

"Carl, are you asking me or are you telling me? I have no problem with it. I'm not sure right now if you are trying to convince me we should take her in, or if I'm supposed to be convincing you. Carl, I'm in. If you care about this woman at all, particularly if she needs help, then by all means, yes."

Carl was still unsure. Mike had no idea what having her around would entail. However, that difficulty was all speculative anyway; maybe she had changed, and it would be different this time. Carl said he would call her the following morning and say okay. "Please, Mike, if this ever gets out of hand, and it very well might, *please* don't say I didn't warn you. Okay?" Carl's final words on the subject were rather disturbing. Mike suddenly wondered if he had said yes with too much haste.

The next day, Carl called Betty and told her they were willing to set her up in an apartment. There was, however, one stipulation; Carl was to control her medications. If that were unacceptable, she would need to go elsewhere. Of course, Betty agreed. She was out on a limb with nowhere else to turn.

It took a week of constant preparations to get the apartment ready for a movie star. Mike was vehement that everything needed to be perfect for their special new tenant. The place was painted head to toe, new carpeting was installed, and, finally, the entire unit was furnished. Mike had come from his own house before moving in with Carl, so there were plenty of furnishings to pull the place together. The only thing that was missing was a sofa. After eyeing the one in their living room, it was deemed perfect, and that too made its way over to Betty's new apartment. Even potted trees were arranged on the outdoor patio off of the kitchen, so Betty could have a park-like setting in which to sit and reflect.

The day Betty arrived, she looked dazed and confused. Carl helped her from the car and continued to hold her by the arm to steady her as she walked up the pathway to her new place. Inside, she cried uncontrollably to see the beautiful apartment that had been appointed especially for her. Oil paintings hung on the walls, pink roses adorned the living room coffee table, and even photographs of Betty's children and mother were framed and arranged on end tables and dressers scattered throughout the apartment. An 8x10 photo of Father Maguire hung on the wall next to her bed, and a mosaic cross purchased for Betty at the Vatican in Rome, hung directly over her bed. Her clothes were arranged in the closet, as if they had always hung there.

The major portion of Betty's personal items had been picked up days earlier so that everything would be in place upon her arrival. It was all in an attempt to make her feel instantly at home. After walking through several times, Betty had to admit she felt as if she had lived there for years. Both Carl and Mike were content their hard work had paid off. Even the refrigerator was pre-stocked. Betty opened it and grabbed a pear to eat, as if she knew it had been there all along. The boys smiled and excused themselves. Betty settled in by taking a long and restful nap. She must have needed it; she didn't wake up until the afternoon of the following day.

It wasn't until the second day, and after her long nap, that Betty began describing in detail all she had been through since walking out on Carl almost a year earlier. Shortly after leaving, she fell and broke her arm. Carl knew it was probably a drug induced accident, but said nothing. She was laid up to the point where the person who had taken her in had to do everything. Desiring to pay restitution, Betty gave this person her bank ATM card to withdraw funds from her account at the bank. Whether or not this person abused the privilege is unknown, but the bank contacted officials and before Betty knew it, the State Of California had taken her into temporary conservatorship. It all happened so fast and without her knowledge. It was for her protection, but to Betty it didn't quite feel that way. She was removed from where she was living, and because her arm was broken, she was placed in a nursing facility. There she was forced to share a room with three other elderly women. To a woman as private as Betty, that came as a real shock.

Betty went back to court for a routine hearing. She told the court she had the ability to earn money and to care for herself. She was told that if she could produce some written evidence of her ability to earn money, the conservatorship would be lifted. Earning money would show the court she had the ability necessary to control her own affairs.

Betty knew she had this in the bag. *Turner Classic Movies* had contacted her shortly before and wanted her for a new interview show they were doing called, *Private Screenings*. Betty already knew the man who hosted the show, *Robert Osborne*. Betty and Bob had met at an informal get-together in California with musical team Jay Livingston and Ray Evans, and they had managed to become friends. If she could only figure out the logistics, she just might be able to pull this off.

First, she called Ben Carbonetto in New York and asked for his help. Ben agreed to fly to Atlanta and be there for her moral support. Next, she called *Turner* and asked if anyone could help her with the plans to get her there and back. Turner was more than happy to accommodate her in any way they could. They made all the necessary arrangements in Atlanta, including air, hotel, meals, make-up, hairdresser, and one tanning session for Betty at a salon the afternoon before she filmed the show. A bit of color always made her feel better. For years, it had been her substitute for makeup. In addition, a woman was hired specifically to travel with Betty, to make sure everything went smoothly. Betty received a packet of materials which spelled her itinerary out to the very last detail. A production schedule gave an hour by hour rundown of everything that would take place. It started with a car and driver arriving to pick up Betty at her door at 10:00am on Tuesday, April 25, 2000, in Palm Springs, and ended with her being delivered back to the same place she started on Friday, April 28. The best part of all, Betty's contract provided her with the sum of ten thousand dollars for her appearance. This is exactly what she needed to win her freedom.

Betty was now determined this was going to work. Immediately, her attitude and self-assurance changed for the positive, she was on a mission. Suddenly, it was like old times again. Only one additional detail needed to be addressed. Never being one interested too much in money, Betty somehow managed to get a hold of a rather large sum of it and went to Saks to purchase a new wardrobe for the interview. It's possible she requested an advance from her court-appointed public guardian. With Betty, money had always been easy come, easy go. She often said, "If it could buy you happiness, then it would mean something." Wherever it came from, Betty managed to spend $5,000 on everything she needed to make sure she looked her best for her four-day trip.

In Atlanta, it is doubtful Betty would have gone through with doing the show if Ben hadn't been there for support. She was frightened to death before coming out of her dressing room, and for a short while actually refused to do so. When she did come out, the cameras were already running. Osborne knew they had to get whatever they could. Bob and Betty just casually started talking. One thing led to another, and Betty was off and running. It was hard to stop her once she got started. In fact, Betty became so animated in what she was saying; several times technicians had to come in to readjust the position of her clip-on microphone. Betty kept beating her chest to make a point, and in the process, gave the mike some good whacks which released some terrible sounds on camera. Those parts of the interview had to be edited out.

Before they started in earnest, and after the first mike adjustment, Betty asked for her lipstick and the lucky hand mirror she had bought along with her from home. "You know, you have to have good-luck everything." Betty commented. Osborne laughed at her superstitious nature. After rummaging through her purse several times, Betty let out, "I can't find the damned lipstick." Betty was instantly happy someone arrived with her lucky tube of pink. She took one last look in the mirror and said to herself, "Betty, do it right."

After two hours of conversation and everything was covered that Osborne had wanted to talk about, Betty held up the rosary beads she held the entire time and said, "See, this is what got me through this. It's also why I don't miss entertaining; I figure I'm entertaining Him." Her eyes glanced upward as if to thank the Lord for seeing her through this present ordeal.

The final thing they wanted to do is show Betty a sequence of her film clips and let her comment. They were going to put a small ear-phone in her ear so she could hear the picture. She was then to say out loud anything that came to mind. "How much am I supposed to say, Bob?" She seemed unsure of the process.

"As much or as little..." Bob piped in.

"I'm sorry, Bob. I really don't want to watch it. I'm honest with you; it would kill me to have to do that. I don't want to go back. I'm here with you, now."

Back in Palm Springs, Betty was released from her temporary conservatorship. She was free to do as she pleased for the first time in a long while. That's when she decided to call Carl and ask if she could come back. The Turner interview had been the thing she needed to raise her from the low period she had been in for well over a year. It was amazing to see how Betty could rebound at almost eighty years of age. Now she had only one additional problem to deal with. Betty had not filed tax returns for several years, and, by this time, the government was after her for back taxes. Before coming back to Carl, someone Betty thought had been a friend in Los Angeles, told her they had a family member who would gladly handle the matter for her. When she received a bill for thousands of dollars just to begin working on the problem, Betty withdrew her request for assistance. She didn't have the money to pay her taxes, much less the thousands requested just to deal with the matter. She turned it all over to Carl. He got his own tax person involved and after many months of negotiations with the government, a reasonable compromise was reached with a pay-off schedule that was easy to accommodate.

Shortly after Betty moved in, someone on the phone from back east mentioned to her how items relating to her career were being sold on the computer. At first, Betty was very upset because she didn't understand. She headed out the door and made her way over to see the boys. Mike sat down with her and patiently explained the workings of internet auctions. After their conversation, Betty was really excited at the prospects and asked if they might do the same. "Why shouldn't I?" she asked. "After all, it's my name."

The videotape of *Annie Get Your Gun* had just been released. (This was before DVDs were even introduced to the market.) That video, along with whatever other videos of Betty's movies were available at the time, were purchased in quantity with the intention of reselling them online. Betty signed the jacket inserts from the videos or the video boxes themselves, and Mike put them up for auction. Their small start-up company was an instant success. Suddenly, Betty had a drawer full of twenty dollar bills to fall back on for her essentials. It was the place where she turned for such things as grocery money and to pay her manicurist. It was no longer necessary for Carl to be running to the bank so often and thereby depleting her rather modest account.

Finally, Betty suggested making phone calls to the winning bidder. Mike proceeded with caution so as to insure her privacy and to make sure they could provide exactly what they offered. A five-minute phone call from Betty was added to the auction listing, and the bidders were told they would receive instructions after the close of auction. Immediately, people were bidding in excess of $150 for a video signed by Betty, just to receive the personal phone call. An e-mail was sent to the winning bidder coordinating a time for the call to take place and a request for their number. The end result was amazing. Mike or Carl would call the person on their cell phone and hand it over to Betty. Typically, the first five minutes of the supposed five-minute call were spent with Betty attempting to calm the person down just enough to talk. Often tears of joy went on for several additional minutes. It was suspected early on that Betty might get bored with the entire process, but instead, she relished the occasions. She managed to have some meaningful conversations with some adoring fans. The most productive result was in Betty gaining first hand knowledge of just how many people were still out there who loved her.

One such video sale was to a very special woman in Los Angeles. Sondra Locke, the youthful and beautiful blonde actress and Academy Award nominee for best supporting actress in the 1968 film, *The Heart Is A Lonely Hunter*, was an enormous Betty Hutton fan. Shortly before their contact, Sondra released her own book, *The Good, The Bad & The Very Ugly*, on her successful, but sometimes stormy career journey in Hollywood, and relationship with *Clint Eastwood*.

Both Sondra and her husband, Gordon Anderson, felt a very strong and special connection to Betty Hutton that went back years. When they were both growing up in Shelbyville, Tennessee, Sondra and Gordon became enchanted with Betty's performance in *The Greatest Show On Earth*. Since there were no VCRs back then, Gordon took a huge reel-to-reel audio tape recorder to the drive-in theatre so that he could record the entire soundtrack to *The Greatest Show On Earth*. He accomplished that by putting the microphone from the tape player in front of the audio box that you hook onto your car window. Sondra and Gordon even set up a circus in their yard, as if they were both actors appearing in their favorite Betty movie.

Years later, Sondra would end up starring in her own circus movie with Clint Eastwood, *Bronco Billy*. Ever since becoming a Hollywood star in her own right, both Sondra and Gordon had been searching for Betty. Gordon recounts, "Every star-studded party we were invited to in Hollywood, we always appeared at; just on the chance that someday we would get to meet Betty Hutton." Once they both attended a party at Charlton Heston's house, Betty's co-star in *The Greatest Show On Earth*, but sadly, no appearance by Betty Hutton. During the party, Gordon managed to slip away at one point into Mr. Heston's library. After a brief search, there on a shelf in a rich leather cover was Charlton Heston's copy of the original script to *The Greatest Show On Earth*. Gordon was instantly in heaven, and admitted it had been very difficult for him to return the script to its rightful spot on the shelf.

On Thanksgiving Day in 2001, Carl and Mike hosted a festive Thanksgiving dinner at their house in Palm Springs. Betty was looking forward to the occasion because she had never met Sondra and Gordon in person, although they had corresponded often. When they arrived in Palm Springs, they presented Betty with a dozen of her favorite pink roses, a bottle of her favorite white wine, and lots of Betty memorabilia to share with everyone that they have been collecting for years - all from their favorite movie, *The Greatest Show On Earth*.

As fate would have it, Gordon managed to track down another leather-bound copy of the original script from *The Greatest Show On Earth*, just like the one he had seen in Charlton Heston's library. Gordon received word via phone that the deal had been made and the copy would indeed be his. That phone call came on Thanksgiving Day, the same day Sondra and Gordon finally met Betty Hutton for the very first time in Palm Springs.

Betty had enjoyed the day and the dinner, but she excused herself early. She had tried her best, but became uncomfortable with the crowd of people. These days, she preferred more one-on-one interaction; it was a calmer and more manageable way for her to relate with people. In addition, Betty never forgot who she was, and what she thought people expected from her. She never liked standing out in a group of people since her Hollywood days. If she could have blended into the background, and become as unassuming as any stranger on the street, she would have been perfectly happy to do so.

Chapter Twenty

A joyful Christmas came and went, and on New Year's Eve, Betty toasted in 2002 with champagne and by watching the festivities happening in Times Square on television. Carl and Mike attempted to make the evening special with streamers and party hats, but it was already way past Betty's bedtime. She was more in the habit of getting into bed early in the evening after taking her sleeping pills. She would watch television until the pills took effect, normally around 7:00. Then by 4:30 in the morning, she was scurrying about the kitchen for her strong coffee and donuts.

Betty appeared happy to have someone to share meals with. The boys made a point of having at least one meal a day with her, typically dinner. They would usually whip something up over at their place and then transfer everything piping hot on large trays over to Betty's apartment. After dinner, stories of the day's events were shared as someone did dishes and another would pack up leftovers for Betty to enjoy the following day. She responded well to living where someone could interact with her as often as she found necessary, as long as that person kept a close eye on monitoring the pills she used for sleep.

Someone came in weekly to give Betty a manicure and take her wigs to be cleaned and styled. She loved keeping her hands just so. Her collection of wigs had gotten old and tired, and Betty finally decided she wanted a shorter and more modern hair style. Someone delivered an entire collection for Betty to keep for several weeks so she could try them all and have the time to make up her mind. When she finally selected her favorite style, it was her intention to order a half dozen of them, that way she would always have spares on hand when the others were off being styled.

While the wigs she had not selected were still lying around, Betty would don one or two of the silliest ones each day and wander over to the boy's house as a gag to entertain them. On one memorable occasion, Betty was putting on a particularly humorous show with a long red wig she was wearing. As she was leaving, the hair accidentally covered one of her eyes just as she was stepping out onto the boy's back porch. The hair momentarily blocked her view, and simultaneously caused Betty to miss the first step. As she tumbled head-over-heels down into a planted area, her wig took flight and landed on a bush while her glasses crashed to the pavement and broke. Carl and Mike ran to the door to assist her, but Betty waved them off before they could even make it outside. She immediately rose to her feet, gathered up her belongings, and she simply continued on her way. Naturally, the boys felt terrible for the embarrassment the incident had caused her, not to mention how concerned they were that she might have hurt herself terribly during the tumble.

Several months went by in the New Year before Betty started taking a plunge into another low period. This time, Carl and Mike didn't see it coming. Betty contacted a local friend she had made during the time she had been away from Carl. He was a friendly and likeable younger man who would have done anything for her, but that was not always the proper approach with Betty. She knew the people she could talk into doing things for her that Carl and Mike wouldn't do, especially like helping her to procure pills. Betty talked this good-natured friend into driving her all the way down to one of Mexico's border towns. There she visited a doctor and told him about her ailments. The doctor prescribed valium at her request. Before leaving Mexico, Betty went to several pharmacies and stocked up. She came home with two bags full of valium in bottles, something Carl and Mike never knew. Within a few days, the boys began noticing a real change in Betty's behavior. At first she said she wasn't feeling well and just needed rest. Finally, she lost interest in eating. By the time they became concerned, she was spending most of her days in bed. The boys thought she may have come down with a bug, so they waited a few more days before really getting suspicious. Betty only got worse. Slowly, they started to piece the story together.

They made a call to the friend who had taken Betty to Mexico and inquired if she had purchased anything there that would make her sleep all day. He revealed Betty had seen a doctor there, but was unsure what she had in the two large bags she returned home with. Mike and Carl had a key to Betty's apartment in case of emergency, so quietly they entered and made their way through her apartment to her bedroom. Betty was in bed and appeared to be sleeping. Carl told Mike to check the night stands next to her bed for any pills while he checked her closet and purses for any evidence. As Mike slowly pulled open the nightstand drawer, Betty turned to him and faintly mumbled. "Leave those alone..." The drawer was approximately eight inches deep, and it was packed full with bottles of 10mg. valium. Mike was counting the bottles in the drawer just as Carl rushed from the closet into the room.

"Betty!" Carl shouted. "How many pills have you taken today?" She didn't respond to his question. Carl shook her. This time she half-opened her eyes, but still said nothing. "Betty, how many pills have you taken?" Carl opened another drawer in the nightstand on the opposite side of Betty's bed. It was there he found the answer to his own question. The drawer contained five identical empty valium bottles, and each had contained thirty tablets. Only then did the boys realize the grand old time Betty had treated herself to over the past six days.

Repeated attempts were made to bring Betty around, but to no avail. It was then the boys called 911 and had her rushed to the *Desert Regional Medical Center* in Palm Springs. Naturally, the hospital staff knew who Betty was, but it was decided she would be registered under the name of Betty Bruno to protect her identity all the same. Betty remained in an unresponsive state for a total of eight days. Carl and Mike were extremely worried, but also felt responsible at the same time. If they had watched Betty closer, they felt they could have been able to avert the unfortunate episode all together.

As it turned out, some unknown person reported the event to the *National Enquirer*. The report they had was sketchy, so they somehow found Carl's number and called him to see if he wished to plump up the story for their readers. Carl decided to give them the information he wanted them to have in order to squelch the story. He told them Betty was in for tests after having suffered what might have been a mild stroke, but that she was resting comfortably and in no immediate danger.

At one point, Carl and Mike actually went in to say their goodbyes to Betty. She just wasn't showing any signs of improvement. When they called Betty's dear friend, Judy Rector, in Rhode Island to report the seriousness of the problem, Judy said she had seen it all before, and she figured after the toxic pills had a chance to make their way out of her system, Betty would come around. Sure enough, the next day the boys went in to see Betty, and she was awake and asking when she could come home. "The food is terrible here, Carl. I need a big steak and a baked potato!"

The boys had suffered a real scare, and because of it, had other plans for Betty. Carl called A.C. Lyles at Paramount to ask if he could arrange admission for Betty at the Motion Picture Country Hospital in Woodland Hills. The boys thought it necessary for her health to be reevaluated, and if necessary, to have her remain permanently at the in-home care facility of the Motion Picture Country Home. They just weren't ready to allow her to return home and risk the same thing happening again. Betty wasn't even told where she was going. Lyles had an ambulance drive in from Los Angeles to pick her up at the Palm Springs hospital and transport her back to Woodland Hills. Carl and Mike said goodbye to a dazed Betty as the ambulance drivers wheeled her onto the hospital elevator. She was still talking to the boys when the elevator doors slid shut, separating them from her. As Betty made her way to the waiting ambulance, the boys were left behind inside the hospital wondering if they had made the right decision.

A.C. Lyles was in Woodland Hills awaiting Betty's arrival. She was admitted to the hospital unit, and over the next ten days was put through a series of medical tests to assess her current health. In the interim, A. C. came to visit and announced to Betty that he had managed to secure her a beautiful private bungalow at the care facility on a permanent basis. Betty reacted by telling A.C. she had only one problem with staying. "I know you have a lot of pull around here, A.C. So if you could just get them to change the name from Motion Picture Country Home to Motion Picture Country Club, I just might consider it." She had no intention of staying. After her ten days were finished, Betty insisted on returning to Palm Springs, and the only home she wanted to know.

The boys were happy to have her back, as long as they could be assured this sort of thing would never happen again. Carl put listings in the want-ad section of the local newspaper, *The Desert Sun*, in an attempt to find a suitable woman to come in on a daily basis to take care of Betty. They wanted someone to arrive in the late morning and stay on until after the dinner hour. The woman needed to cook, clean, and most importantly, be there as a friend to make Betty's days at home more enjoyable. Betty liked the idea. That was, of course, until the actual prospective women arrived for duty. More than once, Betty sent a crying woman packing within hours of her arrival. One woman came with a thick novel and proceeded to curl up on Betty's sofa for a day's worth of reading. Betty was particularly incensed that this woman somehow thought she was there to play babysitter to an elderly invalid. Betty was so mad she took to her bed for the entire day, just so she didn't have to look at or speak with the woman. After she left, Betty called in her complaint to Carl and Mike. Carl had to call the woman at home and tell her not to bother coming the following day.

One day, Charlene Helm walked into everyone's life. Carl and Mike had found her, and they were sure Betty would like her. The boys never once told Betty they were just about at the end of their rope, and had exhausted virtually every qualified person in the Palm Springs area. Somehow Betty and Charlene hit it off perfectly. They became more friends than they did anything else. Betty even took up cooking dinners for the boys. That is, Charlene did most of the work, as Betty directed and choreographed the event from start to finish.

Betty would have Charlene stop at *Jensen's Market,* the local gourmet grocery store, before arriving at her apartment in the morning. Charlene had specific instructions on all the necessary ingredients for her upcoming dinner creation. If she messed up by substituting an inferior ingredient, Charlene was sent back to the store.

Sword fish was one of Betty's favorites, and she insisted that all fish, along with all other meats, never be purchased anywhere else. Often she would spend $150 on a nightly dinner. Carl was pleased that she had something she enjoyed to occupy her days, but cringed at the amount of money she spent for the food. *Jensen's* naturally had the finest quality, but the price was prohibitive for Betty's budget, and an unnecessary amount for her to spend on a normal evening meal. Carl began purchasing lesser cuts of meat at regular big-chain supermarkets and would wrap them in saved Jensen's butcher paper so Betty wouldn't complain. The trick worked, and Betty never failed to comment about the delicious meat. "You see Carl and Mike; you get what you pay for. I would never eat anything but the best." Carl and Mike would smile and shake their heads in agreement as Betty gave her same food lecture night after night.

Things went along really well for quite a long period of time after Charlene came on the scene. Having someone around to spend the entire day with, as well as being motivated to keep busy around the house, made all the difference for Betty. During this period, even her daughter, Carrie, made a weekend visit to her mother from Burbank. Although Betty had a spare room for guests, Carrie stayed with Carl and Mike at their place. Betty was much too set in her ways to have someone stay overnight. Just knowing someone else was in the apartment while she was trying to sleep would have been sufficient cause to prevent it. Anyway, Betty had wanted a tanning bed, and the one the boys bought for her took up a major portion of the already small guest room.

Mike's sister, Trish, came from Milwaukee for a visit, and Betty was very responsive to meeting her. Actually, the two hit it off famously right from the start. After that, they would talk on the phone often when Trish went back to Wisconsin. Betty was generally intimidated by most women, but she picked up immediately on Trish's natural Midwestern sense of values and genuine kindness. One evening the boys took Betty and Mike's sister to the Palm Springs Follies. It is a grand vaudevillian affair in which all the cast members are over the age of fifty-five. The audience is accordingly mostly up in age themselves.

The boys had called in advance to secure house seats for their group in Betty's name. The show's organizers were always kind in accommodating Betty's desire for tickets at the last minute, if and when someone she knew was coming into town and wished to attend. The man who originated the show always enjoyed introducing celebrities when they happened to be in his audience. It made the entire evening all the more spectacular when someone famous stood to take a bow. At the beginning of the second act, Betty was introduced and graciously rose to her feet to give a friendly wave to the audience. The crowd went wild with applause.

Shortly after the show had ended, Betty was bombarded at the front of the theatre with people wishing to get near her to talk and for autographs. She later commented she felt trapped surrounded by people with nowhere to go. Carl took one look at Betty's face, and as he moved closer, he sensed she was beginning to panic. When he turned to ask if she was alright, Betty replied, "Carl, get me the hell out of here, fast." With Trish's assistance on one side, Carl managed to shift the entire mob in the direction of a side door. When they reached it, Carl ushered Betty out quickly. She was visibly shaken. Mike had already gone for the car, and was just coming up the side street when he saw Carl flagging him down. Betty, Trish, and Carl piled in, and told Mike to pull away fast. Fans had followed immediately behind, and were still pawing at Betty as she got into the car. Under normal circumstances, the situation would have been considered typical for a well known celebrity. But for a woman who had been out of the public eye for years, the out-of-control adoration shown by the crowd was very alarming. Betty wanted little more from life than to eat good food, watch television, and get to bed early. Her days as a public figure were long gone, and something she chose to avoid at all costs from that moment on.

By 2003, Carl and Mike were ready to sell the large rental property and move into something that required less of their time. Real estate was starting to boom, and they saw it as the ideal time to make the move financially. Betty panicked when she first heard the news, but the boys promised to take her along when they found the perfect replacement property. She was warned it might take several months to get settled and get a suitable unit ready for her. She was assured they would see her daily, and Charlene was there to see her through the transition period.

Carl and Mike found the perfect building on South Camino Real in Palm Springs. The eleven-unit property had a great owners unit and several large tenant apartments, one of which they sensed would be perfect for Betty. It just so happened, a single woman who lived in an apartment which the boys saw as the most desirable for Betty's needs, was being transferred out of town. After she moved, the boys readied the unit for Betty with new appliances, carpeting, tile floors, and paint. Betty was moved over to the new place in a way that caused her the least amount of stress and discomfort. The day the boys brought Betty over for good was the first time she was to see it. Everything that had made her feel at home in her old apartment was there, ready and waiting. All she needed to do was sit down and call the place home. Once again, Betty cried with joy. It had been an easy transition, and the move actually ended up being good for her. The new scenery was, for a time, a welcomed change.

One day, Carl received a call from someone seeking the beneficiaries of Betty's estate. It was never made clear how they got Carl's name and phone. After asking who they were and what their business was, Carl immediately said there were no recipients to Betty's estate because she was still alive. The people on the other end of the call said they represented a music conglomerate whose job it was to process residuals for musicians and singers. They mentioned they had a rather sizeable sum of money that had just accumulated over the years since they had been unable to locate Betty. Carl arranged to have Betty call the company at a later time to identify herself and to fill in any missing information. After returning completed and notarized paperwork that had been issued by mail, Betty received a check by mail several weeks later.

When the funds arrived, the first thing Betty asked Carl and Mike to do with a portion of the money was to go and purchase a cemetery plot for her. They chose the Desert Memorial Park in Cathedral City, the same place where many notable celebrities like Frank Sinatra, Busby Berkley, and Sonny Bono are buried. It hadn't been a particularly pleasant task, but the boys had done as Betty requested. The one and only time she asked about the plot, the boys told her it was a beautiful spot under a tree. Betty immediately seemed relieved in the knowledge her final resting spot was no longer a worry.

Carl and Mike were in the process of making extensive renovations to their own apartment, and consequently, were kept very busy. At one point, it became necessary to take out a wall to enlarge their dining area, and after they had done so, discovered the elevations of the two floors that came together were a mismatch. On the day a worker had to break up the floor and remove it in order to pour a new level surface, the boys went looking for floor tile at a local store. It was then that Betty decided to call the boys at home for a few additional pills. She was now in the habit of taking the sleeping pill, Ambien, simply to calm herself during the day. She could take four or five during the course of a day, and they did little more than relax her. Those, along with a host of other prescribed medications, were kept in a kitchen cabinet at the boy's house. In the mornings, Charlene would stop over and pick up Betty's pills in a small paper cup.

Charlene must have been grocery shopping when Betty couldn't get the boys on the phone. She took it upon herself to wander over to their apartment, thinking they just hadn't heard the phone. If they were gone, she would go in and look for the pills herself. Instead of using the front door, she decided to come through the dining area French doors. They had probably been left ajar since workers were there working on the floor. However, at the time she came over, the workers had knocked off for lunch. Betty opened the door and fell right into the area where the floor had been removed. It was basically a dirt surface, approximately five or six inches below level. Betty fell and broke her arm. The workers were out in the back of the apartment eating their lunches and did manage to hear her cries for help. They called 911, and Betty was rushed by ambulance to the local hospital.

When Carl and Mike arrived home, they were informed of what had happened. They flew over to the hospital's emergency room where Betty was being treated. The hospital staff had given her morphine for the pain. That, combined with the other pills in her system, gave her a violent reaction which caused Betty to throw up several times. When Carl and Mike finally got her in the car for the ride home, Betty said, "I don't want to take that stuff ever again. Boy, it really made me sick."

Betty now had a broken right arm, and was unable to care for herself. The boys were beside themselves trying to arrive at an alternative living arrangement. It was finally decided Betty was to go to an assisted living facility in Palm Springs where she could get the necessary care. The boys were incapable of doing it, and Charlene was unable to stay with Betty on a full time basis.

Carl and Mike attempted to downplay the facility as little more than a period of rehabilitation. It was suspected that Betty knew all along where she was going, but she had little choice, and said nothing. She realized she was failing, and needed help. At least in assisted living, she didn't need to worry about anything but getting well. She had a large private unit with separate living and bedroom areas. Betty never once went to the communal dining room to take her meals. She stayed pretty much to herself, relaying on daily visits from the boys to brighten her days.

Having registered nurses controlling her medications proved to be a huge success. Betty knew they were unsympathetic to any requests for additional pills. The nurses had no personal relationship with Betty, and didn't really care if she wanted more pills or not. What was prescribed was all she received.

It may seem as if Carl and Mike were unable to fully control Betty's pill usage. However, it is extremely difficult to control any person who relies so heavily on drugs. Betty was in the habit of doing or saying anything necessary to get what she wanted. Anyone who has been there knows how hard it is to deny someone you love something they desire badly that will make them immediately contented.

Oftentimes, she would repeatedly call the boy's apartment and leave messages of anguish, pleading for additional pills. At least one of the boys was home most of the time, but didn't always answer the phone. It was done quite simply to avoid an altercation. It became an absolute and total mind game with Betty over the pill situation. Having Betty in the assisted living facility gave them all a much needed break from each other.

It became necessary during her stay in assisted living to have a health directive drawn up. Carl never had power of attorney to make any health decisions for Betty, something which might become necessary in the future. The health facility insisted upon someone having that power. Carl and Betty found an attorney who came right out to see her and drew up the necessary papers. She allowed Carl to make any and all health decisions for her in the event she was unable, and Betty also decided to make Carl the executor of her estate and sole beneficiary. Carl only found out that information after the fact. He had been asked to leave the room while she and the attorney worked on fulfilling her wishes.

Eventually, Betty wanted to return to the boys. Her health was in decline, and she had mellowed considerably. Her yearning for pills became less and less. Due to a host of medical problems, she just couldn't tolerate as much usage as she had once been accustomed. Carl and Mike decided she needed a lot more in-home care if she wanted to remain on her own. Betty was moved to a different apartment the boys set up for her. This one had a spare bedroom they outfitted as a den and television room for Betty. In the back of their minds, they knew someday the room would be needed for a live-in and around-the-clock care.

Some good times were still to follow. Betty's health and well-being went in waves. You never knew until the morning if Betty was going to have a good or bad day. The good days were exceptional. After everything that happened in her life, when she was feeling well, Betty had a burning desire to be just Betty. She would sit on her back porch and talk with the boys. They soon realized she received a great deal of satisfaction from reminiscing, so Mike rushed out and purchased her three rocking chairs for the patio. One, of course, was for Betty, and one each for Carl and Mike. They wanted their informal daily chats to be comfortable ones. Betty never initiated the conversations about her past. All that was necessary to get her started was to ask her one simple question, such as, "Did you really carry Eddie Bracken up that huge flight of stairs?" and they were off to the races. One thing led to another, and two hours later after telling us how *Dwight D. Eisenhower* took her to an important luncheon in Washington which eventually led to a little known peace treaty with *Liechtenstein*, Betty would say, "Carl, what time is it? You know I don't like missing my Oprah show on TV at 3:00."

The bad days were terrible. On those days, everything seemed to be wrong with her. She was suffering from macular degeneration in both eyes, and found it difficult to read or even watch her beloved TV. The boys bought her a big-screen television for her birthday, temporarily solving the problem.

Carl and Mike made sure someone was there on a daily basis to help her. The only time she was alone was at night. She was tucked into bed before the final person left, and someone was there in the morning when she arose. She was becoming weaker, and her girls even needed to help her to bathe so she wouldn't fall.

In August of 2006, Betty was having a difficult time eating. She was losing weight and feeling generally poor. Her doctor put her into the hospital for a series of tests, some of which never got done. Betty insisted on her morning coffee and donuts. When Betty was insistent, no one would dare say no! The doctor was extremely upset when he arrived because she wasn't supposed to eat prior to several of the scheduled tests. He dismissed her by telling Carl several tests indicated higher than normal levels, revealing cancer somewhere. Where exactly it was located was unknown. The doctor said that as long as she remained comfortable, the boys might as well take her home. He did warn that at some point, it was more than likely some problem would arise, but when that would happen was anyone's guess.

In February 2007, Betty stopped eating for eight days. She became so weak, she was bedridden. She developed a severe pain in her right leg that became almost unbearable. Her doctor came to visit, and after several tests, it was decided that hospice was the best alternative, especially since Betty wanted to remain at home. On March 1st, hospice came in and took over Betty's care. The pain in her leg had gotten so extreme, morphine was administered for her relief. The boys were there when the first three drops of the drug were placed under her tongue. Within minutes, Betty had her painful leg pointing toward the ceiling. She screamed out in delight, "WOW, look at this Carl and Mike, I can move it again!" Suddenly, a worried look came over her face. "Carl, what happens to my other pills?" She didn't want to be cheated out of anything to which she was entitled.

"Don't worry, honey, you can have those too; anything that makes you happy." A wide grin came across Betty's face. For the first time in a long time, she was content.

Carl had hired a woman by the name of Velma months before to help with Betty's care. The woman was a saint. There was nothing she wouldn't do to help Betty. She would make food and attempt to get her to eat. If Betty said no, Velma would make something else and give that a try. She stayed all day until a night woman arrived to take over the night shift. In the morning, Velma was back to care for Miss Betty. The boys also hired a weekend woman, and, of course, Charlene was there along with everyone else helping out.

The second day of hospice care, a hospital bed was delivered to be put in Betty's bedroom. It would make caring for her that much easier. Carl told hospice they might use an additional trained hand in helping to transfer Betty temporarily to a wheelchair while the bed was being assembled. Instead of one person, four arrived on scene. Carl and Mike were taken back by the flood of people in Betty's apartment walking aimlessly back and forth. Mike took Betty in her wheelchair into the spare bedroom in an attempt to shield her from any unnecessary prying eyes. Betty was fairly out of it from the morphine. The man who was setting up the hospital bed was way off in Betty's bedroom, but his loud voice managed to carry throughout the entire apartment. Mike was sitting on a chair directly in front of Betty when she raised her head and said, "Boy, he sure likes to hear himself talk." She was referring to the loud bed assembler. Mike laughed that Betty was aware enough of what was happening in the apartment to make a typical Betty Hutton comment. He couldn't wait until everyone who didn't belong there had left; it felt like such an invasion. The boys appreciated the efforts of those from hospice, but never could understand or justify sending four additional people to complicate an already bad situation.

Before Betty got too bad, even Judy Rector came from Rhode Island to see her. Betty didn't really care to have additional people around, but Judy was an exception. She told the boys afterwards how much the visit had meant to her. Whether or not Betty realized it would be their last visit is still unclear. She refused to talk in final terms. Toward the very end, however, she did make Carl promise that upon her death, he would not announce it until after she was in the ground. Betty had a terrible fear that somehow reporters would hound her even at the very end. She wished for no strangers to see her after her death.

Within a few days, Betty was all but unresponsive. Her breathing was labored. A nurse came in several times a day to check her vitals. No one ever said it, but it was only a matter of time before the inevitable happened. Everyone around her was preparing for it.

At 10:30 on Sunday evening, March 11, Betty slipped quietly away. Velma had been on her watch, and immediately called Carl and Mike. The boys rushed over and called the hospice nurse. She told them she would come and pronounce Betty dead, but she was on the other end of the valley attending to patients. They were told to just wait; that she would arrive as soon as possible. After her arrival and the necessary paperwork had been completed, the boys would need to have a funeral home come to pick up Betty's remains.

While waiting for the hospice nurse to arrive, Carl reached Forest Lawn on the telephone. They said to call back after the nurse had finished; that they could be there within an hour. Carl called Judy Rector in Newport and Ben Carbonetto in New York, informing them both of Betty's death. He also called Robert Osborne in New York and left a message. Betty had so admired the man, and Carl thought it would be a nice gesture.

The hospice nurse arrived and Betty's official time of death was listed as fifteen minutes after midnight, the 12th of March. After the nurse had completed her duties, Forest Lawn arrived. The two soft-spoken and respectful gentlemen asked Mike's assistance in carrying Betty's body out into the living room where they had been forced to leave their gurney. The hallway into Betty's bedroom was too narrow to navigate the turn. Carl and Mike put a small turban on Betty's head before she was taken from the apartment, as if to protect her from the night chill.

The following morning was a busy one. Robert Osborne called back and expressed his sincere sympathy. The boys had to run to the funeral home to finalize the arrangements and to make payment. They were told if they came back at 4:00pm, Betty's body would be ready for their private viewing and goodbyes. Then it was over to the cemetery to inform them they needed the plot opened. All they needed was a death certificate for the burial to go ahead. The funeral home was working on that, and as it turned out, someone at the county seat in Riverside actually stayed late that evening to make sure the certificate was finished for the following morning. The doctor also needed to be contacted so that a cause of death could be listed in order to complete the certificate. Everything depended upon several people doing their job, and in the end, it all happened. It is unsure where or how it was revealed that Betty died from colon cancer. The cause of death listed by her physician on her death certificate is from metastatic breast cancer. Nevertheless, the doctor was never really sure of Betty's complete diagnosis, because she had been uncooperative with the tests. There is really no telling how the cause was actually determined in the end.

After taking care of all the necessary business, the boys stopped home to clean up before going to the funeral home. When they arrived home, there was something like forty messages on their answering machine. Somehow, *Turner Classic Movies* had rearranged the main page of their website, and posted a notice which announced that Thursday would be a schedule change, with a full evening of programming to honor the late Betty Hutton. The press had picked up on the story, and Carl and Mike's phone had begun to ring off the wall. In the short time they were home, ten other calls came in, all wanting a story. Carl said he could not confirm reports that Betty had passed away. It was the promise both boys had made to Betty before her passing.

Carl and Mike called close friends, as well as Betty's care-givers, to invite them to her grave-side services at 11:00am on Tuesday morning. They were running late when they arrived at the funeral home in Cathedral City. One of the girls at the front desk told them that a floral arrangement had been delivered for Miss Hutton earlier in the day, but they had refused it. Carl had asked for their cooperation in remaining silent to the press. The girl on duty at the time stated to the delivery person that no one by the name of Betty Hutton was at that funeral home. She had noted on a slip of paper who the flowers had been from, and the girl presently on duty, now handed it to Carl. The one any only floral arrangement that anyone had attempted to deliver was from Elizabeth Taylor.

Carl and Mike went into a private chapel to see Betty. Carl had with him her favorite rosary, and he draped it over her hands. A photograph of Father Maguire was slipped into the side cushion of her casket, just in case Betty needed help in recognizing him when they met up in heaven. For a few minutes, they talked to her, as if she were there to understand. The boys did not stay long; there was nothing more that could be done.

The following morning, the twenty-five invited mourners met Carl and Mike at the cemetery. A Catholic priest was there to say kind words to those in attendance. The boys had picked up Betty's favorite pink roses from the Palm Springs Florist, and each person graveside placed one atop Betty's pink and silver metal casket before it was lowered into the ground. The boys sweetly kissed the closed casket and said their final farewell.

After the noon hour, the phones once again started ringing. Carl was inundated with calls from everywhere in the world asking if it were indeed true, that Betty Hutton had passed away. He was now able to tell the story; he had fulfilled his promise to Betty. Within hours, the news spread throughout the world. The woman who had bought so much happiness to so many was gone.

On March 23, 2007 at 11:00 in the morning, a memorial service planned by the boys was held at St. Theresa Church in Palm Springs by Father Robert Guerrero. Carl got up and read several letters Betty had received before her death from World War II servicemen. They were a touching and poignant tribute to the woman from the same generation who had climbed into the fox holes to be with the boys who fought for America. A. C. Lyles, Betty's long-time friend from Paramount Studios, eulogized the life of a true Hollywood movie star. Local musical celebrity, Rudy De La Mor, played piano and sang some of Betty's famous songs. The service culminated when the crowd, who came to pay tribute to Betty, sang in unison a rousing rendition of, *There's No Business, Like Show Business*. Betty was given one final round of applause and a standing ovation.

*   *   *   *   *

Betty Hutton left the world a rich legacy with her talent, a gift to be enjoyed and treasured by many for countless years to come. Those lucky enough to know Betty the woman, separate from the Hutton, are the truly fortunate. She had so much more to offer than her talent. She was a human being who possessed a wealth of knowledge and humor. When Betty knew you, she took pleasure in showering you with her knowledge and humor; it was love she was offering up in the way she knew best. We will always appreciate, Betty Hutton, the performer, but we will love for all eternity, Betty, the woman.

One of the very last photographs taken of Betty,
along with Carl Bruno in early 2007.
Photo: The Betty Hutton Estate

Betty's funeral at Desert Memorial Park
in Cathedral City, California.
Photo: The Betty Hutton Estate

Betty's headstone adorned with pennies from heaven,
left by adoring fans.
Photo: The Betty Hutton Estate

Betty's star on Hollywood's Walk of Fame, after her death.

Photo: The Betty Hutton Estate

Betty Hutton (1921-2007)